East Asia's Re-emergence

East Asia's Re-emergence

Philip S. Golub

polity

The right of Philip S. Golub to be identified as Author of this Work has been asserted in accordance with the UK Copyright, Designs and Patents Act 1988.

First published in 2016 by Polity Press

Polity Press
65 Bridge Street
Cambridge CB2 1UR, UK

Polity Press
350 Main Street
Malden, MA 02148, USA

ISBN-13: 978-0-7456-6465-1
ISBN-13: 978-0-7456-6466-8(pb)

A catalogue record for this book is available from the British Library.

Library of Congress Cataloging-in-Publication Data

Names: Golub, Philip S., author.
Title: East Asia's reemergence / Philip Golub.
Description: Malden, MA : Polity, 2016. | Includes bibliographical references
  and index.
Identifiers: LCCN 2015025877| ISBN 9780745664651 (hardback) | ISBN
  9780745664668 (paperback)
Subjects: LCSH: East Asia--Economic conditions. | East Asia--Foreign economic
  relations. | East Asia--Economic policy. | Capitalism--East Asia.
Classification: LCC HC460.5 .G69 2016 | DDC 330.95--dc23 LC record available at
http://lccn.loc.gov/2015025877

Typeset in 10.5/12 Sabon by
Servis Filmsetting Limited, Stockport, Cheshire
Printed and bound in Great Britain by CPI Group (UK) Ltd, Croydon

The publisher has used its best endeavours to ensure that the URLs for external websites referred to in this book are correct and active at the time of going to press. However, the publisher has no responsibility for the websites and can make no guarantee that a site will remain live or that the content is or will remain appropriate.

Every effort has been made to trace all copyright holders, but if any have been inadvertently overlooked the publisher will be pleased to include any necessary credits in any subsequent reprint or edition.

For further information on Polity, visit our website:
politybooks.com

CONTENTS

PREFACE

The guiding theme of this book is that East Asia's re-emergence in the late twentieth and early twenty-first centuries as a semiautonomous core of the world economy constitutes one of the most significant world-systemic transformations since the Industrial Revolution and Eurocentric globalization in the nineteenth century. Thanks to a coherent developmental dynamic of remarkable intensity, duration, and spatial scope, the most populous region of the world is gradually regaining the position in the world economy that it enjoyed prior to the great East–West and North–South divergence, commensurate with its demographic weight. In the wake of Japan, which played a precursor role and served as a development model, countries that not so very long ago appeared caged in subordinate positions in the world capitalist economy, or, like the People's Republic of China (PRC), stood outside it, have been climbing the development ladder, becoming determining actors of the movement of East–West and North–South rebalancing that is one of the main features of our global present. Over the past four decades, East Asia's share of world Gross Domestic Product (GDP), in purchasing power parity (PPP), has thus risen from less than 10 percent to 30 percent, a ratio that should rise by 2030 to just over 40 percent. China, long a marginal actor in the world economy, has become the world's second-largest economy in current exchange rates (the largest in PPP), and the gravitational core of increasingly thick South–South linkages that are altering the vertical structure of North–South relations constructed during the age of Western empire and industry. The politics of re-emergence has lagged behind economics, but a gradual reordering of world politics is evidenced in the growing voice of the global South in international public organizations such as the International Monetary Fund and

World Trade Organization (IMF, WTO) and clubs (G20), their activism in various issue areas of world politics, and institution-building efforts bypassing traditional centers of authority (IBSA, Shanghai Cooperation Organisation, the New Development Bank, and the Asian International Infrastructure Bank). In short, a repatterning of international relations is underway that is closing the historical chapter opened by the rise and globalization of the West.

The amplitude of the rebalancing movement has become apparent only quite recently. Aside from a few authors, such as Janet Abu-Lughod, who perceptively foresaw a "return to the relative balance of multiple centers" (Abu-Lughod, 1991: 370–71) that characterized the world in the early-modern period, most observers in the 1980s and 1990s thought the possibility of North–South and East–West rebalancing remote. Surveying the world political economy in the mid-1980s, Stephen Krasner wrote: "Southern states are subject to external pressures that they cannot influence. . . . They are exposed to vacillations of an international system from which they cannot extricate themselves but over which they have limited control." Noting the "important exceptions" of South Korea, Taiwan, Hong Kong, and Singapore, as well as of China and India, special cases due to their size and isolation from the world economy, he nonetheless came to this general conclusion: "The gap between Northern and Southern capabilities is already so great that even if the countries of the South grew very quickly and those of the North stagnated (and unlikely pair of assumptions in any event), only a handful of developing countries would significantly close the power gap within the next one hundred years" (Krasner, 1985: 4). Notwithstanding growing evidence of a general albeit uneven movement of East Asian economic ascent (World Bank, 1993), there were still serious doubts in the 1990s over the breadth and significance of the phenomenon. In a well-known article in *Foreign Affairs*, Paul Krugman (1994) dismissed "Asia's miracle" as a myth: "current projections of Asian supremacy extrapolated from recent trends may well look almost as silly as 1960s vintage forecasts of Soviet industrial supremacy did from the perspective of the Brezhnev years." East Asian growth, in his view, was being driven by "perspiration rather than inspiration," with few signs of productivity increases, technological upgrading, and other qualitative improvements. The Japanese financial crisis of the early 1990s, which ushered in a long period of economic stagnation, and the sharp regional financial crisis of the late 1990s, lent weight to the argument by calling into question the depth and sustainability of the East Asian model of state-led or state-governed economic development. By the end of the decade, at the high point of neoliberal intellectual hegemony (the Washington Consensus), the "miracle" was widely and blithely recast as a "mirage."

Too closely bound to the moments in which they were formulated— a general problem of social scientific observation but one that is particularly salient in international analysis—sometimes reflecting Orientalist biases, these and like judgments missed the structural character of the East Asian developmental dynamic. Fundamental social changes unfold gradually, resulting from cumulative processes whose inner logic becomes perceptible, hence theorizable, only when they impose themselves as social facts. The Industrial Revolution "was a general and slow phenomenon, with distant and deep origins" (Braudel, 1985: 111–12) that was not discernible to Adam Smith and other contemporaries who were living through its initial phases. It was only toward the mid-nineteenth century, when Great Britain became the heart of a world-encompassing system of production, trade, and credit and the primary force behind the globalization of the West, that the properly revolutionary implications of industrialization became clear to observers such as Marx. In like manner, the United States' emergence as the world's leading industrial power in the latter part of the nineteenth century resulted from a long process of eco- nomic, demographic, and territorial expansion, the significance of which became fully evident only in the mid-twentieth century, when the United States superseded Europe at the center and apex of a reno- vated world capitalist system and a new international economic and political hierarchy. Though current global rebalancing is still in an early stage, and East Asia's re-emergence remains far from complete, the evidence clearly points to a restructuring of the world economy comparable to these earlier instances of systemic change in terms of its transformative effects.

This book delves into the deep and distant sources of the trans- formation and interrogates its implications for understandings of globalization and capitalist development. Like the author's earlier work on United States and Atlantic imperial history (Golub, 2010), it mobilizes a historical sociological approach to world politics that pays careful attention to historical structures and seeks explanation, or at least deeper understanding, of the present in the ontogenesis of social phenomena rather than the abstract theorizing that character- izes synchronic analysis (Hobson, 2010). It thus weaves together social theory and historical narrative to analyze the structural and contingent factors that gave rise, during distinct but interconnected moments of world history, to what might be called the East Asian economic revolution. Moving from present to past and past to present it successively examines the early modern European-Asian encounter, the imperial collisions of the nineteenth century, Pax Americana and the postwar constitution of authoritarian capitalist developmental states, and China's state-capitalist turn in the late twentieth century. The focus is on the ways in which imperialism, war, and revolution shaped modern nation- and state-building efforts—the international interactions that led to the rise of specific developmental state forms in the nineteenth and twentieth centuries which, to varying degrees, proved able to harness transnational forces to national institutions and purposes, and to successfully alter national positions in the global economic hierarchy. Major emphasis is put on the regional character of the post-1945 capitalist dynamic: like the Industrial Revolution, which spread unevenly and at different rhythms in different parts of Europe but obeyed an overall developmental logic, East Asia's re-emergence should be seen as a general movement that spread sequentially if unevenly from its original Japanese epicenter to the rest of the region. The chapters of this book, whose structure is detailed in Chapter 1, unfold these arguments and points.

The conclusions drawn diverge from the set of ideas and assumptions regarding global integration and the nation-state that lie at the core of liberal globalization theory: the conjecture of an epochal change from modern to post-Westphalian or post-international politics (Rosenau, 1989), in which transnational flows would have obliterated territory, sovereignty would have been fundamentally reconfigured, and power tamed by global forces and transnational networks transcending and submerging the historic nation-state (Habermas, 2001; Held and McGrew, 2000; Castells, 1996). As I, as well as other authors (Rosenberg, 2005) have argued, real-world events over the past decade and a half have undermined the strong globalization hypothesis. The conclusions also contrast with those neo-Marxist interpretations that, from different theoretical starting points and different normative perspectives, have postulated the constitution of a postnational condition structured by global capital and characterized by the domination of a transnational capitalist class (Hardt and Negri, 2000; Robinson, 2004). This study points instead to new concentrations of national power and assertions of national purpose, reflecting the fluid and historically contingent character of state–market relations, and the variable impacts of transnational forces on different societies and states. If late-twentieth-century globalization has generated systemic pressures affecting all states, transnational flows produce differential effects according to the uneven distribution of state capacity and effective sovereignty. Some states have indeed been submerged and seen their development pathways conditioned by global forces and transnational networks outside their control. But the incorporation of the global South in the world capitalist economy has not produced uniform effects. In East Asia, in most cases, notably but not only China, internationalization has led to upward international mobility and, despite new world market dependencies, an increase of the relative international autonomy of the state (the way China has obliged global firms to defer to state preferences is discussed in some detail in Chapter 5).

It should be said that the book does not foresee the constitution of an Asian-centric or Sino-centric world system (Frank, 1998; Arrighi, 2007). In his grand fresco of historical capitalism, Braudel (1985, 1992) came to the conclusion that the world economy seemed to require a single center of gravity. Basing himself on the European record, he notes the way in which successive centers emerged as the "capitalist dynamic" unfolded, from the merchant city-states of the early Renaissance and the early modern period to the industrial capitalist nation-states of late modernity. Thus, in the case of Europe, the center would have shifted from Venice (1380) to Antwerp (1500), Antwerp to Genoa (1550–1560), and Genoa to Amsterdam (1590–1610) in the prenational era, and thence to Great Britain and the United States in the nineteenth and twentieth centuries. Each center, in his reading, finds itself possessing decisive comparative advantages for a time—the knowledge and technical know-how, the market and state institutions, the most profitable industries and long-distance trades, and often the military power that together give it the means to direct if not always to command the way a large part of the world works. For a time only, since these advantages gradually wane, and new more vigorous and brighter stars appear during "struggles, clashes . . . prolonged economic crises," and the recurrent violent divvying up of the world. The movement of history, the mechanism of systemic change, is thus given by the rare, irregular, but decisive shifts from one center to another. The picture, on which world systems theorists drew to derive their own more deterministic reading of capitalist hegemonic cycles, is of successive systemic restructurings and expansions leading to capitalist formations of ever-greater power and ever-wider spatial scope. There are, however, no Newtonian laws of historic motion. The end of the long cycle of Western world economic predominance is not coterminous with absolute Western "decline": global rebalancing is ushering in a plural world that will revolve around relatively equal and deeply interdependent centers of gravity. For observers concerned with the problem of international inequality, such as the author, this is normatively desirable a priori. But the transition constitutes a major challenge and is unlikely to be frictionless.

A note on the terminology used throughout the book: Along with the waning of colonial/imperial modernity, the categories that previously organized knowledge of world social space have become problematic. North, South, Third World, and so on, traditionally used to denote the sociospatial positioning of societies in the world political economy, no longer fit present realities. In terms of living standards, increasingly important population segments of the global South can no longer be considered part of the Third World. And there are significant population segments in the historic North that, in similar terms, can be considered part of the South (indeed, relative poverty in the most advanced Western industrialized countries is generally concentrated in minorities stemming from the global South). Insofar as they continue to structure actor self-understandings and point to the unfinished character of global rebalancing, these categories nonetheless remain useful. "East" and "West" are used in the book to denote historically constructed understandings, not fixed and essentialized cultural identities. The reader will, I expect, find her way around this problem.

This book owes a great deal to the work of authors whose specialized fields it trespasses into, to borrow Weber's expression regarding comparative studies. I have drawn on a vast historical literature to found my arguments about globalization and the state. As the reader will surely notice, I owe a particular intellectual debt to Bruce Cumings's work. Thanks are due to the colleagues and friends who in various ways encouraged this project: Raffaele Laudani, who gave me the opportunity some years ago to present a first sketch of the work at the Department of Historical Studies of the University of Bologna, as well as many others who generously offered their support, expertise, and critical comments: Richard Beardsworth, Noelle Burgi, James Cohen, Stephen Golub, Jean-Paul Maréchal, Susan Perry, and my research assistant Anna Wiersma, whose competence and critical eye made this a better book. I also would like to thank Pansak Vinyaratn for having invited me to explore East Asia in the 1990s, when the seeds for the book were first planted, leading to a long-term intellectual engagement. The editors of Polity Press must be warmly thanked for their encouragement and support during the long gestation of the book.

— 1 —

GLOBALIZATION, EAST ASIA, AND THE DYNAMICS OF CAPITALIST DEVELOPMENT

The unequal division of the modern world into North and South and East and West has always been one of the core problems of social theory and one of the main lines of fracture of world politics. In the course of the long Industrial Revolution and Europe's synchronous movement of formal and informal imperial expansion in the nineteenth century, an increasingly interdependent but stratified world system came into being that was centered in the Atlantic and ordered by the West. If European overseas expansion and conquest began in the early modern period with the colonization of the Americas and the commercial penetration of Asia by the various East Indian companies, it was only in the late-modern period that imperialism took world-encompassing scope. Drawing on the energies of modern capitalism and made possible by technical evolutions (steamships, the telegraph, railways, and of course guns) that transformed the spatial and temporal conditions of transnational relations, Europe's late-modern "conquest of the universe" put an end to the "multi-secular era" in which various relatively equal and relatively autonomous *économies-mondes* (world economies) had coexisted and interacted in a plural and polycentric world without a dominant center of economic or political gravity (Braudel, 1992).

As imperial globalization unfolded over space and time, European guns and commodities battering down "all Chinese walls," the long-standing parity between East and West was supplanted by a new and durable hierarchical world order characterized by structural North–South and East–West asymmetries. Asia, for centuries the locus of advanced societies and sophisticated commercial cultures, became enmeshed in the webs of European empire and the Atlantic-centered world market. Great Britain, the first industrializer and most

1

expansive European colonizer, was the primary, though not the sole, agent of this tectonic shift. Britain, Hobsbawm writes, became the systemic center of a new international division of labor characterized by "a set of economies dependent on and complementary to the British, each exchanging the primary products for which its geographical situation fitted it for the manufactures of the world's workshop" (Hobsbawm, 1990: 136). At the height of British economic predominance in the 1860s, when Britain accounted for 20 percent of world manufacturing, more than half of global coal, iron and cotton cloth production, and over a third of world steampower, observers noted that the "several quarters of the world," from the Americas through the Mediterranean to the Far East and Australia, had become Britain's "tributaries" (Jevons, 1865: 16.2). At the time, approximately 300 million people had been incorporated into European overseas empires—86 percent in British Crown colonies, and many millions more in the magnetic fields of the vast informal empire instituted by the "imperialism of free trade" (Gallagher and Robinson, 1953). By the end of the century, at the apogee of late-modern globalization and the nearly complete internationalization of economic life (Keynes, 1920), the population in the formal empires producing the sugar, tea, spice, cereals, cotton and other raw materials and commodities destined to the world market had reached 553 million, of which 393.8 million were under direct British rule (Bairoch, 1997, Vol. 2: 608–9). When semi-sovereign partially colonized states such as China and the nominally autonomous but economically subordinate societies of Latin America are included, nearly half the world population had been enmeshed in the regimes and controls of empire. Aside a few important exceptions, notably Meiji Japan, which managed to preserve its political autonomy and avoid economic entrapment through its own industrial revolution and the building of a modern state, and which went on to play a major role in interimperialist competition in Asia, the overall outcome of late-modern globalization was the great divergence (Pomeranz, 2000) between East and West and the division of the world into dominant cores and dependent peripheries.

Rather than spreading outside of Europe and leading to convergence, the Industrial Revolution generated asymmetric interdependence. Because of the patterns of specialization instituted by colonial regimes, industrialization and economic expansion in the northern Atlantic world conditioned other world regions, warping or arresting development in the newly constituted peripheries (Parthasarathi, 2001), whose living standards stagnated and whose share of world income declined sharply throughout the nineteenth century. According

2

to Paul Bairoch's thorough if necessarily approximate estimates, peripheral living standards, measured by average per capita output, were only marginally higher in 1900 than they had been in 1750, whereas they had more than tripled on average in the newly industrialized economies of Europe and the neo-European settler colonies. The disparity was even greater with the most industrialized countries, where average per capita output was four (Britain) to five (United States) times higher (Bairoch, 1997). The limited industrialization that did occur in colonial or semi-colonial areas in the late nineteenth century—for instance the construction of railroads and infrastructure to facilitate commodity transport to ports that shipped goods to Northern markets, or the creation of new textile manufacturing facilities in India—did not produce the cumulative results of self-sustaining growth, integration of national markets, and rising overall living standards observable in Europe. Rather, it elicited new patterns of spatial unevenness: the structure of international production and trade generated demographic inflation and unbalanced urbanization in coastal trading centers that became warehouses for the primary products and staples destined for the world market. If there were some pockets of quantitative development in India or Qing China, due to local entrepreneurship, capitalist modernity in colonial or semi-colonial Asia became coterminous with unevenness and durable international inequality. Europe's "machine revolution," Braudel aptly writes, was "not merely an instrument of development" but "a weapon of domination and destruction of competition" (Braudel, 1992: 535).

This outcome was not quite the one envisioned by Marx in his brilliant albeit Eurocentric depiction and analysis of late modern globalization and capitalist development. Writing from within the systemic transformation, he observed that the development and internationalization of "colossal productive forces" had "given a cosmopolitan character to production and consumption" and generated "universal inter-dependence" in a world economy integrated through transnational flows (Marx and Engels, 1978). Thanks to the "rapid improvement of all instruments of production [and] the immensely facilitated means of communication," Europe was incorporating the rest of the world into its developmental movement, making "barbarian and semi-barbarian countries dependent on the civilized ones, nations of peasants on nations of bourgeois, the East on the West." Just as the emergence of capitalism in England flowed from a process of progressive historical change, he envisioned Europe's worldwide economic and spatial expansion as part of a necessary movement of the world toward industrial and urban civilization, hence human liberation from natural constraints and the "idiocy of rural life." By drawing Asia into the developmental logic of capitalism and enmeshing her in the "net of the world market," European imperialism would hasten the transition from "oriental despotism" and the "village system" to industrial capitalism. Europe's intrusion in India and China would destroy stagnant socioeconomic systems and revolutionize the "social state in Asia," thereby "fulfilling mankind's destiny" to be the "sovereign of nature" (Marx, 1963: 35-41).

Marx was well aware of the great violence of the incorporation process, devoting many eloquent pages to the "atrocious exploitation" of India and to "English ferocity in China." He showed acute interest in contemporary national uprisings in China and India that, he believed, would help to spark revolution in Europe.[1] But he detached analytical and normative judgments in his theory of history and his analysis of capitalist development. Violence was foundational to the revolutionary rise and expansion of the world capitalist system: "The discovery of gold and silver in America, the extirpation, enslavement and entombment in mines of the aboriginal population, the beginning of the conquest and looting of the East Indies, the turning of Africa into a warren for the commercial hunting of black-skins, signalised the rosy dawn of the era of capitalist production" (Marx, 1977: 751). As the Industrial Revolution matured, thanks to this first or "primitive" phase of capital accumulation, England became the midwife of modernity in Asia: "Whatever may have been the aims of England, she was the unconscious tool of history in bringing about the revolution . . . England has to fulfil a double mission in India: one destructive, the other regenerating—the annihilation of the old Asiatic society, and the laying of the material foundation of Western society in Asia" (1963: 37). Following the "natural laws of capitalist production," industrialization would spread to the rest of the world. Precapitalist systems of social reproduction based on subsistence agriculture and household manufactures would be supplanted by modern capitalist development. In that sense, the more economically and technologically advanced countries "simply [presented] others with a picture of their future."

For most of the non-European world, that future never fully materialized. The breakdown of the European world order after the Second World War due to the combined effects of anticolonial resistance and metropolitan exhaustion gave the postcolonial South de jure equality but not effective autonomy. With some major East Asian exceptions—Japan and the People's Republic of China (PRC), whose

4

modernization and state-building efforts are central concerns of this book—the structural disparities brought about in the late nineteenth century widened considerably. Notwithstanding the promise of self-determination, universal "well being," "equal rights," and "economic and social progress and development" contained in the United Nations Charter, average living standards in the postcolonial South were only marginally higher at the time of the Bandung Conference (1955) than they had been in the mid-eighteenth century. Nor did independence lead to an improvement of the relative economic position of most postcolonial Southern states. With three quarters of the world's population, the global South's share of world income (around 25 percent) was nearly three times lower than it had been in 1750 (Nayyar, 2013) and its share of world manufacturing output had fallen from over 70 to 6.5 percent. Relative decline was most pronounced in Asia (outside Japan), whose share of world manufacturing (craft and industrial) had fallen from more than 60 percent to less than 5 percent. Per-capita levels of industrialization reveal deep decline: per-capita industrial output in China in 1953 was half what it had been in 1750. In India it was 3.5 times lower. In contrast, per capita industrial production in Japan had been multiplied 5.7 times (Bairoch, 1982).

By the early 1970s the South's relative position in the world economy had not significantly improved. While its share of world manufacturing output had increased to 9 percent in a much expanded world economy, it nonetheless remained inferior to 1900 levels. The most important gains were concentrated in a handful of industrializing states: in 1970 South Korea, Taiwan, Singapore, Hong Kong, Brazil and Mexico accounted for nearly one third of industrial production, outside of China, in the South. In 1971, the United Nations (UNO) launched the Second Development Decade on a sombre note: "Countless millions of people in the developing world ... are often still undernourished, undereducated, unemployed and wanting in the many other basic amenities of life. While a part of the world lives in great comfort and even affluence, most of the larger part suffers from abject poverty, and in fact the disparity is continuing to widen" (UN, 1970). Critical observers of international relations and international development specialists were thus well founded when they argued that the "obscene inequalities that disfigure the world" constituted the main theoretical and normative challenge for the social sciences and the fundamental problem of world politics (Seers, 1969). Ambitious efforts by a constellation of postcolonial leaders, international public servants (UNCTAD), theorists and activists in the early 1970s to alter the post-1945 world economic order and institutionalize a global redistributive order (the New International Economic Order), founded on new binding multilateral regimes, failed (Golub, 2013).[2] Having little world market power and no voice in decisions taken by the most powerful Northern states, the position of many Southern world regions substantially deteriorated in the late 1970s and early 1980s. This was notably the case of Africa and Latin America, which were confronted with exogenously driven debt crises that ushered in economic stagnation and social regression.

In Latin America, parts of which had experienced significant economic gains in the first two decades of the postwar period due to import substitution industrialization (ISI), this led to the end of "peripheral Fordism" and the "asphyxiation of industrialization" (Lipietz, 1984). At the time, the few and rather small industrializing countries of Northeast and Southeast Asia (South Korea, Taiwan, Singapore, Hong Kong) that accounted for the lion's share of Southern manufactured exports did not appear systemically significant. Despite the beginnings of industrialization and strong growth in the 1970s and early 1980s, the developing capitalist countries of Southeast Asia were still peripheral actors in the world economy. China was contemporaneously swept up in the turbulence of the Cultural Revolution that dislocated the economy and nearly caused a general breakdown. In the early 1980s, the economy was just beginning to recover, thanks to the gradualist market reforms of the post-Mao leadership, and a capitalist transition, the tensions of which erupted into the open during the 1989 mass protests in Tiananmen Square in Beijing. Overall, downward mobility and/or crisis rather than convergence appeared the general trend for much, though not all, of the historic South. At the end of the 1970s the developmental impasse seemed so intractable and the disparities so great that Braudel pessimistically concluded that the South would somehow have to "break down the existing international order" (Braudel, 1992: 535) to gain upward economic mobility and achieve de facto rather than de jure equality.

A historical turn

Fundamental changes in the world economy over the past thirty years have overturned this assessment: due to the economic revolution that has unfolded in East Asia, the vertical world economic structure that came into being in the nineteenth century is being gradually altered from within. As publications of the United Nations Development

Program (UNDP) and the World Bank (WB) have recently noted, we are experiencing a historic rebalancing that is leading to the dissolution of the hierarchies that became coterminous with Eurocentric modernity. "Throughout the course of history," notes the Bank report,

> paradigms of economic power have been drawn and redrawn according the rise and fall of states with the greatest capabilities to drive global growth. . . . In the first half of the second millennium China and India were the world's predominant growth poles. The Industrial Revolution brought West European economies to the forefront. In the post-World War II era, the United States was the predominant force in the global economy. . . . In more recent years the global economy has begun another major transition. . . . The rise of emerging economies will inevitably have major implications for the global economic and political hierarchy. (World Bank, 2011:1)

Announcing the 2013 *Human Development Report*, the UNDP likewise emphasized: "The World is witnessing an epochal global rebalancing. The rise of the South reverses the huge shift that saw Europe and North America eclipse the rest of the world, beginning with the industrial revolution, through the colonial era to two World Wars in the twentieth century. Now another tectonic shift has put developing countries on an upward curve" (UNDP, 2013). There is ample evidence supporting these claims. Over the past thirty years, the world GDP share of developing countries in purchasing power parity (PPP) has more than tripled, from approximately 15 percent in 1980 to 50 percent; their share of manufacturing value-added has risen from 8.8 to nearly 30 percent; and their share of world merchandise trade from 25 to 47 percent. New regional and transcontinental South–South economic linkages have concurrently come into being that are repatterning the geography of world trade and investment flows. South–South trade has expanded over the past two decades more rapidly than global trade and currently accounts for 25 percent of the total, 21 percent of world manufactures exports, and a quarter of exports of manufactures with medium and high technological intensity. Trade between developed countries fell during the same period from 46 to less than 30 percent (UNCTAD, 2012; UNDP, 2013).

Global rebalancing has been driven by East Asia, which has experienced a process of economic expansion and ascent whose amplitude, spatial scope, and duration have been remarkable by historic standards. Starting with Japan's revival soon after the Second World War,

Table 1.1. Per Capita GDP (PPP, current international dollars) 1980–2013

East Asia	1980	1990	2000	2013
China	253	799	2,382	9,844
Indonesia	735	1,549	2,432	5,214
Japan	9,307	19,111	25,520	34,295
Korea	2,322	7,858	16,578	33,189
Malaysia	2,351	4,817	9,173	17,747
Philippines	1,345	1,879	2,445	4,682
Singapore	7,121	17,962	33,195	64,583
Taiwan	3,601	9,895	20,320	37,763
Thailand	1,099	2,921	5,014	9,874

Source: *World Economic Outlook Database*, April 2014, IMF.

industrialization and technological upgrading spread sequentially to the newly industrialized countries of Northeast Asia (South Korea, Taiwan), the industrializing countries of Southeast Asia (ASEAN 4) and most consequentially, over the past three decades, to China. East Asia's aggregate share of constantly growing world GDP in purchasing power parity (PPP) has increased from around 10 percent in the 1970s, more than half of which was attributable to Japan, to 28.8 percent in 2014, with China's share growing from less than 2 percent to over 15 percent against Japan's current 5.4 percent (IMF, 2014). By 2020 the region's share will reach 32 percent and by the end of the following decade it should rise to 40 percent. Per capita GDP (PPP), a finer quantitative measure of development, has grown since 1980 by a factor of 14 in South Korea, 10 in Taiwan, 9 in Singapore and Thailand, 7.5 in Malaysia, 7 in Indonesia, and nearly 40 in China—a spectacular increase reflecting the intensity of growth over long periods and its cumulative impacts (Table 1.1). The mature industrial economies of the region have achieved quantitative and qualitative development levels comparable or higher than Europe's ($35,000 per capita on average), while many developing economies have experienced significant absolute gains. Though China's growth rates have declined in recent years due to the global slowdown following the 2008 world economic crisis, average per capita GDP (PPP) is expected to reach $16,000 in a few years. Longer-range projections that assume a growth trajectory similar to Japan's in the late twentieth century suggest that per capita GDP will reach current Japanese or European levels by the mid twenty-first century. After a long historical caesura, China is thus gradually regaining a position in the world economy commensurate with its demographic weight.

8

While varying initial conditions, state capacities, and social structures have led to differentiated national outcomes, a general movement has been at work, as seen in deepening regional economic integration. Regionalization was initially driven by successive Japanese industrial relocations in the 1970s and 1980s to the Newly Industrialized Countries (NIC) and then to developing Southeast Asia that led to a concatenated Japan-centered regional division of labor. Since the 1990s it has derived its impulse from China, which has become the hub of a constantly expanding and increasingly complex regional and transcontinental trade network. Intraregional trade as a share of total trade has thus risen steadily over the past four decades: from 20 percent in 1970 to 32 percent in the early 1980s, 47 percent in the early 1990s, 54.8 percent in 2000, and 60 percent in 2010 (ADB, 2007). China has supplanted the United States as the leading trade partner of nearly all East Asian countries, Japan included (WTO, IMF 2014). While these ratios overstate the degree of regional integration, since a significant share of the value of final exports that are destined to world markets is captured by transnational firms through horizontal production and commodity chains, regionalization has unquestionably gone much further than in other Southern world regions, and led to industrial upgrading along various steps of the value chain (Pottier, 2003; Gereffi, 2014). Trade integration has been complemented by closer monetary coordination among central banks, a trend that reflects the will of leaders since the 1997–1998 regional financial crisis to shield their countries from exogenously driven shocks, as well as to reduce their reliance on the dollar as a currency of settlement (Golub 2010). This monetary dimension of regionalization is not the least significant: since the late 1990s, the Chinese renminbi has been increasingly used in intraregional trade settlements as part of the state's exploratory moves toward the internationalization of the currency. Today, around one-eighth of China's trade is settled in renminbi (RMB), a ratio that is set to rise rapidly and significantly. Crossborder investments in the currency are growing: from RMB 10 billion in 2007 to RMB 276 billion in 2012. While still distant, the prospect of a tripolar world monetary system underpinning global exchanges has become a realistic possibility (Subramanian and Kessler, 2012).

Over the past two decades the region has also become the gravitational center of new transcontinental South–South linkages that are repatterning the geography of world trade and investment flows. While the largest economies of Latin America, Africa and South Asia account for a small fraction of East Asian total trade, the region

9

is playing an increasingly important and sometimes pivotal role in their international commerce. East Asia has become a major source and destination of exchanges for countries such as Brazil, Argentina, Chile, South Africa, Nigeria and India. East Asia is Brazil's main trading partner, ahead of the United States and Europe, accounting for 27 percent of the country's total trade (China, 17 percent; ASEAN, 4 percent; Japan, 3.37 percent; South Korea, 2.92 percent). The rate of increase should be emphasized: merchandise exports to China have grown from 0.9 percent of total trade to over 17 percent today. Similar trends are observable for Argentina, Chile, and the smaller South American economies. China is Chile's main export destination, well ahead of the United States, and the second largest source of its imports (22.8 and 16.9 percent respectively). As far as Argentina is concerned, exports to China, as a share of the total, have risen from 1.1 percent twenty years ago to 9.7 percent today. South Africa's export share to China has risen from 1.8 percent in 1998 to over 12 percent, while imports rose from 3 to 15 percent; Nigeria's trade with East Asia is less important but has nonetheless risen substantially, from 0.5 to 6.9 percent. In South Asia, the share of Indian exports to China has risen from 2.9 to over 10 percent, and imports from 2 to 12 percent. The constitution of an East Asian-centered South–South trading system, with China at the core, has lessened the single-market dependencies of Latin American and Sub-Saharan African countries on the United States and Europe. It has, in other words, begun to shift the vertical North–South patterns that previously structured Southern international trade.

Spatial and social unevenness

The developmental trajectory sketched above tells only one part of a complex, multidimensional story of social change. Like the European Industrial Revolution, East Asia's re-emergence has not been a seamless process of progressive ascent. Gains have been uneven, with significant international human development differentials, intranational economic and social disparities, and environmental damage. Aggregate figures and averages are far from meaningless, but they are mute on distributional outcomes among social groups and on the violence of the mutation. Capitalist development has rested on the ability of authoritarian and semi-authoritarian states to mobilize labor and suppress dissent. Time-compressed modernization and insertion into the world market has generated spatial and social unevenness. Outside of the already highly industrialized countries of

Northeast Asia, whose growth and modernization occurred under historical conditions that required relative social fairness, new sharp social stratifications have appeared. This is evidenced in China and most of Southeast Asia by the sharp divergence of conditions of the new middle and upper classes, on the one hand, and the urban underclasses on the other. These latter are composed of unprotected migrants uprooted from the countryside and working in export processing zones or urban infrastructure projects, as well as pauperized segments of the peasantry in rural areas. Moreover, as Bair and other critical authors rightly emphasize, the exploitation of labor in East Asian capitalist development is a gendered process (Bair, 2014). The social geography of the megalopolises of China and most of Southeast Asia is characterized by the spatial proximity but radical social distance between these population segments. This observation applies more broadly to all postcolonial urban spaces, as do the sociospatial asymmetries between the metropolitan centers and rural hinterlands. The persistence of authoritarian and semi-authoritarian political regimes containing and silencing movements of protest and revolt has meant that social polarization has yet to translate into effective collective political or trade union action. Since the legitimacy of these regimes is inextricably bound to continuous economic expansion, there are serious questions regarding the social and hence political sustainability of a transformation that will undoubtedly be punctuated, as in 1997–1998, by economic downturns and crises. Industrialization and urbanization has simultaneously generated major problems of environmental sustainability, notably in China. If these are not corrected, they could compromise the region's ascent.

Nevertheless, while capitalist development raises crucial normative issues of social justice and urgent issues of ecological sustainability, these problems should not obscure the transformational power of the region's developmental movement or its world-systemic effects. Just as there was an essential unity in the European Industrial Revolution, in the sense that variations in national trajectories occurred in the context of a general mutation, there is an essential unity and historical continuity to the East Asian transformation (Cumings, 1984). The social unevenness and country-to-country variations in growth rates, living standards, and levels of technological maturity evidenced in East Asia today are comparable to national variations in Europe in the nineteenth century, where industrialization diffused, unevenly and in different temporal sequences, to much though not all of the continent. As Paul Bairoch and Kozul-Wright point out, in the second half of the nineteenth century advanced industrial development was confined to a very few countries that concentrated most of the West's advanced manufacturing output (Great Britain, Germany, and the United States): "Industrial development in much of Southern and Eastern Europe was weak and erratic in comparison to the successful catch-up economies. This was the case for France, Italy, Russia, and Austro-Hungary, each of which had pockets of advanced industrial development by 1913 but were unable to reach and sustain the very rapid rates of growth of the other newly industrializing economies" (Bairoch and Kozul-Wright, 1996: 15). European and U.S. modernization in the nineteenth century was also punctuated by periodic national or systemic crises of greater or lesser intensity, the long trans-atlantic depression of 1873–1896 being an instance of systemwide crisis. Industrialization was characterized, again with national variations, by harsh rural-urban transitions, unbalanced urbanization, and universally by the exploitation of labor at domestic and international levels: children's and women's labor in Europe, colonial labor overseas, slave and cheap immigrant labor in the Americas. Thomas Piketty has recently reminded us that Jane Austen and Balzac, among others (Zola, Dickens, Upton Sinclair, etc.), offer carefully drawn pictures of the appalling working and health conditions of wage laborers in Europe and the United States during industrialization (2014). Periodic crises, the exploitation of labor and the suppression of working-class dissent were defining features of European modernization, which was far from being spatially uniform and was built as much on "perspiration" as on "inspiration." Social and spatial unevenness and recurrent crises are inherent features of capitalist development, or what Braudel (1985) aptly calls the "capitalist dynamic."

Comparison with the "European miracle," to which we return in various sections of the book, draws out structural analogies but also the distinctiveness of the East Asian economic revolution that is reshaping the global economic landscape. Though "revolution" has always been a somewhat problematic concept to describe the cumulative effects of technological, economic, and social change, it is used here not only to denote the relatively sudden, considerable, and sustained increases in the rate of growth (Gerschenkron, 1962) that the region has experienced, but also and more broadly its systemically transformative effects. The East Asian economic revolution, like the European revolution before it, is slowly changing the order of the world. Seen in long historical perspective, East Asia's re-emergence marks the end of a long sequence of world history in which power and wealth were durably concentrated in the hands of a few Northern societies and states, and the beginning of a new sequence in which the world will revolve around plural if interdependent centers of gravity.

Capital, hegemonies, and states

This structural change undermines teleological readings of world history that long equated modernity with a supposed singularity of the Occident (Max Weber's term), and that stressed the weight of cultural factors inhibiting the diffusion of capitalism outside of northern Europe and its settler-colonial offshoots. The overriding question that presided over the rise of the social sciences was "Why the West?" Today the main analytical challenge is to account for the end of the "extraordinary historical continuity" (Halliday, 2002) of North–South and East–West hierarchy. How are we to explain the waning of a durable historical structure and the rebalancing process? At the most general level, one can argue that in *longue durée* no society or group of societies can maintain advantages placing them permanently at the center and the apex: "societies that are in the vanguard (modernizing) at one point give way to others at another; the pendulum swings" (Goody, 1996: 41). The modern historical record suggests that this is indeed the case. But the apparent regularity of the phenomenon does not explain why or how the swings, or in the current case rebalancing, occur. (To be clear, Goody's careful exploration of early modern world history and his trenchant critique of Eurocentrism are not designed to accomplish that. Rather, he aims to deconstruct the Western metanarrative of modernity and does so compellingly.) The "why" and "how" raise issues of interpretation regarding globalization and capitalist development, notably the problem of dependency and dependent development, and the issue of the relative autonomy of capital and the state. Both are discussed throughout the book but a restatement of core theoretical issues helps to frame the debate.

Global rebalancing means that major parts, though not all, of the historic South are breaking out of the structural constraints that until recently inhibited international upward mobility and convergence with the advanced economies of the North. In the 1960s and 1970s dependency theorists developed a cogent theoretical framework to account for the development impasse that emphasized global pressures, and focused on the mechanisms of production and reproduction of international inequality. The core argument of the various strands of dependency theory (DT) was that historically constructed relations of subordination and dependency continued to operate

13

through world-level mechanisms holding back the development possibilities of Southern postcolonial societies. Patterns of specialization established in the nineteenth century—an international division of labor confining the Third World to the production of primary goods or low value-added manufactured products—led to unequal terms of trade between the highly industrialized countries producing capital-intensive goods and the producers of primary products. As a result, rather than leading to convergence, international trade cumulatively tended "to cause ever greater international inequalities between countries as to their level of economic development and average national income per capita" (Myrdal, cited in Arndt, 1987: 74). In a world political economy in which power, capital, and knowledge are concentrated, and in which trade and financial regimes are set in the North, the postcolonial South was subject to world market forces and decisions taken by the most powerful states over which they had no voice and which conditioned their development paths. Technology diffusion and appropriation was inhibited by monopolistic ownership, the accumulation of domestic capital by foreign control of productive facilities and the outflow of surplus, economic differentiation by the rudimentary character of domestic markets. Single market dependencies (Latin America and East Asia on the United States, Africa on Europe), and reliance on capital inflows and debt for domestic industrial investment generated structural vulnerabilities: crises originating in or decisions taken by dominant capitalist states exposed the South to exogenously driven changes to their growth and development paths. Dependency was thus theorized as a "historical condition which shapes a certain structure of the world economy such that it favors some countries to the detriment of others . . . a situation in which the economy of a certain group of countries is conditioned by the development and expansion of another economy, to which their own is subjected" (Dos Santos, 1971: 226).

The resulting persistent metropolitan-satellite or core-periphery polarity reflected the "structure and development of the capitalist system as a whole" (Frank, 1966). For neo-Marxists, the implication of this line of analysis was that autonomous development could only be achieved outside of the world capitalist system through exit (a solution that seemed more plausible in the 1960s, when the Soviet Union or the People's Republic of China offered a plausible alternative to the capitalist system, than in later decades when the Soviet Union began to decline and China broke from autarky and initiated its economic internationalization). World systems theorists offered a similarly deterministic picture, allowing for little or no fluidity in international hierarchy. Wallerstein's introduction of an intermediate category of semi-peripheral states, corresponding to partially industrialized or industrializing countries, did not open the possibility of change within the capitalist system. As Schwartz rightly points out, semi-peripheral states were never really distinguished from the periphery (Schwartz, 1989: 11) and the tripartite framework never specified how upward mobility could be achieved in a world system whose general logic is over-determined by an axial division of labor that establishes relations of domination and inequality between different parts of the world capitalist economy. To the contrary, Wallerstein argued that the "semi-periphery is needed to make a capitalist world-economy run smoothly...(it is a normal condition) to have a three-layered structure" (Wallerstein, 2000: 89–90). Global capitalism requires states with variable capacity to maintain systemic stability: like peripheral states, semi-peripheral countries are described as having a prescribed role in system reproduction. This functionalist approach makes the semiperiphery an ad hoc category of analysis mobilized to take into account irregularities that, differently interpreted, would otherwise not fit into his general theory of systemic change.

Starting from the assumption that the world capitalist system, as a historical construction, is characterized by recurrent patterns of hegemonic ascent, supremacy, decline, and succession, reflecting the cyclical rhythms of capitalist expansion, change derives from general crises: one hegemony leads to another, and the center of world capitalism shifts as one relatively stable historical configuration tends toward entropy and another takes its place. In Arrighi's formulation: in transitional moments of "systemic chaos ... whichever state or group of states is in a position to satisfy the system-wide demand for order is presented with the opportunity of becoming world hegemonic" (Arrighi, 1994: 30). Following this scheme, the rebalancing toward East Asia would reflect the decay of the United States' hegemonic order instituted in 1945. U.S. hegemony would have entered a long phase of "terminal decline" in the late 1960s, punctuated by intensifying economic crises and a loss of political control (Wallerstein, 2000; Arrighi, 1994; 2005). China's re-emergence would thus be the latest in a series of successive restructurings and recenterings since the emergence of the modern world system in the sixteenth century, the end phase of the long decline of U.S. hegemony (Arrighi, 2007). The model bears some formal kinship to the geopolitical transitions scheme of structural realist international relations theory (Gilpin, 1981). They differ, however, on an essential point: the latter envisions

15

global power transition as a timeless attribute of world politics under conditions of anarchy, whereas world systems theory envisions the demise of capitalism as a historical social system. As capitalism reaches its spatial, social, and ecological limits, a "process of world government formation" will impose itself, leading to the "withering away of the modern system of territorial states" (Arrighi, 1994: 351).

Once the functionalist and teleological problems of world systems theory are set aside, along with other variants of dependency theory, world systems theory offers important insights and investigative tools to grasp the mechanisms of uneven development. The literature on the new international division of labor of the 1980s refined dependency perspectives by investigating transnationalized production and commodity chains and showing how these were dominated by core capital and shaped by core markets. In most but not all cases, the worldwide redeployment of manufacturing led to shallow industrialization in Southern countries incorporated in multinational firms' networks. Critiquing neoclassical assumptions regarding the optimizing character of markets, Fröbel et al. argued that export-oriented industrialization (EOI) based on "world market factories" generated industrial enclaves isolated from the local economy: "Even in the very few developing countries where ... centers of partial industrialization have been established there are no signs that they are being supplemented by a wider industrial complex which would enable them to free themselves eventually from their dependency on the already industrialized countries for imports of capital and other goods, and for the maintenance of their industrial installations" (Fröbel et al., 1980: 6). The growing weight, reach, and autonomy of transnational companies (TNC) and finance made global production and commodity chains key units of analysis of globalization and development (Gereffi, 1989).

The globalization of production and finance gave capital the greatest degree of autonomy since the late nineteenth century. It appeared to lock Southern countries into new and highly constraining dependency as low value-added producers and assemblers of products whose value is unequally captured along the value chain. Since production has become largely denationalized and fractioned into different steps—design, raw materials sourcing, components production, final assembly, marketing, and retailing—absolute and relative national gains depend on the position of countries in value chains and their ability to upgrade, that is, move up the knowledge-technology ladder into higher valued-added activities.

16

In buyer-driven chains, global firms without factories, for instance in the textile and shoe industries, subcontract production of labor-intensive goods in peripheral or semi-peripheral countries, generating cost competition among suppliers who stand at the very bottom of the value chain. This is also the case in the electronics industry: TNCs holding proprietary designs and patents capture most of the value in global production chains. The classic example is the distribution of value in the production of the Apple iPod (Linden et al., 2009), where the final assembler in China (a Taiwanese company) captures a small fraction of total profit while the owner-designer captures approximately one third. Mainland Chinese gains from activities in this sector are minute, confined to labor inputs (see Chapter 5). Levels of value-realization vary in different industrial sectors: they are significantly higher in production-driven chains where greater skills and more sophisticated local inputs are required for the manufacturing process. But upward mobility in these sectors (aeronautics, machinery, and so on) is hindered by the intellectual property rights regimes that became an essential component of the legal architecture of international trade in the 1990s, limiting or inhibiting the diffusion and appropriation of knowledge and technology. The mobility of capital in liberalized and fully globalized financial markets compounds the problem by accentuating interstate competition for TNC investment.

These are powerful insights that make dependency theory still relevant. Yet they fail to account for how the transnational processes associated with world capitalist expansion have produced a differentiated geography of development in which some parts of the former South have experienced major and mostly unexpected absolute and relative gains. As Gereffi argues, a good deal of the literature was too broad-brush, not sensitive enough to historical or institutional factors: "The developmental consequences of these different types of dependency turn, in large degree, on the ability of the state to convert these external linkages to national advantage. Successful 'dependency management' depends on the historical timing of these efforts as well as institutional factors" (Gereffi, 1989: 510). This book builds on that and argues that the explanatory gap reflects a set of assumptions about the retreat—or indeed the vanishing—of the state, and an economistic a priori that leaves little or no room for history and politics.

The hypothesis of a shift from the modern to a postmodern or postinternational configuration of world politics, in which the nation-state becomes subsumed in or submerged by global mechanisms outside its control, remains one of the core assumptions of liberal globalization theory (Rosenau, 1989; Held and McGrew; 2000) and some neo-Marxist perspectives on transnational empire, transnational class formation, and the competition state. The former points to the ways in which the compression of time and space induced by transnational interactions and the ICT revolution have altered the basic nature of social relations by erasing the boundaries between the "inside" and the "outside," and transcending the segmentations of modernity. The latter points to various phenomena associated with the reconstitution of capitalist world space after the end of communism: the reconfiguration of states into agents of the internationalization of capital (Gill, 1995; Amin, 1997), or competition states (Cerny, 1997); the rise and rule of a new transnational order of domination and resistance (Hardt and Negri, 2000); and the constitution of a new global or transnational ruling class (Robinson, 2004).

While there is no question that the redeployment of world capitalism in the late twentieth century has affected state–market relations and the balance between capital and labor in South and North, these readings of globalization tend to lack historical depth. In the history of modern capitalism (as distinct from the merchant capitalism of the early modern era), the relative autonomy of capital and the state has varied from moment to moment. At times the state has relaxed control, leaving capital to freely roam the world, while at others it has tamed capital and reclaimed control. Capital at times works at cross-purposes with the geopolitical aims of the territorial state, while at others there is a coincidence of their respective wealth and power maximizing logics. Marx's elliptical description of the state as the executive committee of the capitalist class has tended to obscure this question: If there was a symbiosis of purpose at the height of the internationalization of British capital flows in the late nineteenth century (Feis, 1973), the breakdown of the "liberal" nineteenth-century international order in 1914 decisively shifted the balance between capital and the state. As Polanyi shows in his historical sociological analysis of the "double movement" (Polanyi, 1972 [1944]), the respective autonomy of the state and capital vary according to historical flux and sociopolitical circumstances at domestic and international levels. His argument, which remains relevant today, is that market expansion and generalized commodification at the expense of other social needs reached its limits, provoking a contrary protective movement that led to the constitution of different types of strong states (fascism, Stalinism, and the New Deal state in the United States) that reclaimed control over markets. Moreover, and more important for the purposes of our argument, there is great variability in state capacity to mediate and act on world market forces. As in the nineteenth century, the current cycle of globalization is characterized by a complex mix of power relations and state–market interreactions in which *some* states continue to play a major role in shaping the course of capitalist development, and in which new territorialized concentrations of wealth and power have manifestly occurred.

Harnessing transnational flows

Transnational flows produce differential effects as capital deploys across national spaces and interacts with societies with distinct institutional systems, weakening some but not all states. The constraints induced by power asymmetries and world market mechanisms are not uniform, and can be reduced through appropriate political or state action. Cardoso and Faletto rightly argued as much in the early 1970s when they noted that the purposeful constitution of national industrial sectors could create the conditions for dependent development, leading to a lessening of the grip of MNCs on Latin American economies. State-led capitalist development would create bargaining power with MNCs and institutionalize more equal patterns of North–South relations. (Hirschman had made a similar point much earlier when discussing the manoeuvring room of dependent East European countries that were able to transform asymmetric trade relations with Germany by gaining greater bargaining power through political action, leading to "considerably reduced asymmetry" (Hirschman, 1945). To the extent that relatively autonomous national capital comes into being, transnational linkages and incorporation into the world market do not mechanically translate into underdevelopment. The world capitalist economy allows "room for some kind of associated capitalistic development" (Cardoso and Faletto, 1979: 188). The crucial variable is the role played by the state: "The lack of private investment potential, the political need to prevent multinational corporations from single-handedly appropriating the most strategic sectors of the economy and their most dynamic branches . . . has led local states [in Latin America] to expand their functions and thereby to create a national basis from which to bargain with the multinationals" (206). The interaction between the state and transnational capital involves conflicts and compromises, the balance between the two fluctuating according to international and domestic circumstances (the strength of the state and of the productive sectors controlled or nurtured by it).

This argument, which has since been refined by students of historical political economy and of the developmental state (Evans,

1995; Amsden, 2001; Woo-Cumings, 1999), is clearly relevant to the current cycle of globalization, which has not generated homogenizing outcomes but rather led to differentiation. East Asia has benefited from the concentration of investment flows by harnessing them to historically specific institutional systems (Boyer, 2001). This endogenizing process cannot be understood in the absence of state action, which constitutes the key explanatory variable for failure or success (Evans, 1985; Weiss, 2007; Woo-Cumings, 1999). Given the differential distribution of effective sovereignty and state capacity resulting from distinct historical pathways, some states are better positioned than others to deal with global pressures, bargain with transnational private actors, and shape developmental outcomes. As East Asia's re-emergence shows, rather than representing the triumph of world capitalism over the nation-state, or of liberal economics over statism, late twentieth-century globalization has contributed to the expansion of the power and relative international autonomy of those states with the capacity to harness and channel transnational flows to endogenous developmental purposes (China is particularly representative of this trend).

This is not a new phenomenon: while transnational capital flows from Europe in the nineteenth century enmeshed Latin American countries in debt dependencies, they contributed significantly to the economic growth and development, and hence the national power, of the United States (Golub, 2010) and Japan. According to Cull and Davis's detailed research (Davis and Cull, 1994), capital flows "played a critical role in shaping American development," accounting for 22 percent of new capital formation between 1816 and 1840, 16 percent between 1861 and 1870, and 9 percent between 1880 and 1890. The first period "saw the rapid development of the nation's first man-made inter-regional transportation system; the second encompasses the years of the Civil War and reconstruction and the completion of the first inter-continental railroad; and the third captures the development of the American West and its integration into the national economy" (111). Transnational investment helped to finance national and local government, and to build the infrastructure (roads, canals and railroads) that was essential to economic expansion and modern industrial development. (Of course, they also contributed to financial bubbles, accentuating booms and busts.) Together with successful import substitution policies—between 1866 and 1883 the average tariff on imported manufactured goods was 45 percent (Bairoch and Kozul-Wright, 1996)—transnational capital supported the emergence of an industrial system that overtook Britain's in the

20

1890s. By then, the U.S. had become a world power. Transnational capital flows were also important in the consolidation of the modernization efforts of the Meiji state through the financing of its "armaments, its wars and its economic development" (Feis, 1974: 429). If U.S. industrialization occurred under high tariff protection after the Civil War (1861–1865), the Meiji state's modernization is perhaps more remarkable in that it succeeded despite Japan's lack of tariff autonomy resulting from the Ansei Treaties of 1858 that remained partially in force until 1911 (Chapter 2). Like Japan during that period, China and other late twentieth-century East Asian developers have demonstrated that there are many nontariff protective measures that developmental states can quite effectively employ to govern the market, limit foreign penetration and competition, and channel investment flows to national purposes (Amsden, 2001; Wade, 1990).

Regional continuities

In a 2014 review of global value chains (GVCs), Gereffi notes a shift of world patterns of dependency and development due to the "end of the Washington Consensus and the rise of contending centers of economic and political power," and the "geographic consolidation and value chain concentration in the global supply base which [in some cases] is shifting bargaining power from lead firms in GVCs to large suppliers in developing economies." He emphasizes: "The most dynamic growth poles in the global economy are constituted by an expanded number of rising powers that combine relatively large domestic markets, skilled workforces, capable producers and a push towards indigenous innovation." These rising powers have moved up the value chain and they are moving from industrialization based on externally driven demand (export-oriented industrialization) to "inward approaches focussing on domestic and regional markets" (Gereffi, 2014: 29). Though there is a hint about the way in which contingent world political evolutions might have made this possible—the weakening grip of the United States and the demise of the Washington Consensus—history, politics, and power are largely absent from the analysis. The question remains how the rising powers in fact managed to rise or re-emerge in the first place, and then to shift the balance.

This book seeks answers to the question by focussing the analytical gaze on state- and nation-building in East Asia during different sequences of globalization: the efforts to build modern states in Japan and China during imperial globalization in the nineteenth century, the constitution or re-constitution of capitalist and communist authoritarian developmental states in the aftermath of the Second World War, and the state capitalist turn in China in the 1980s. The exploration of these sequences, the first two of which involved considerable violence, highlights strands of continuity in state- and nation-building efforts over long periods and accounts not only for the emergence of authoritarian developmental states but also for the creation of a regional political economy in which capitalist development could flourish.

The chapters of this book retrace these sequences. Chapter 2 explores the passage from the plural and polycentric early modern world system to the hierarchical late modern Atlantic-centered system. The way in which the East–West encounter evolved into a series of broadening and sharpening collisions in the nineteenth and early twentieth centuries, setting the stage for the constitution of the modern Japanese and Chinese states, is also concerned in this. The European globalizers that incorporated Asia into formal and informal empires challenged the integrity of long-established unitary polities that more or less successfully fought to secure national autonomy and unity in the face of an existential foreign threat. Building on the economic foundations laid by the *ancien régime*, the modern Japanese state arose out of an acute sense of national crisis provoked by intrusion: the Meiji reformers who overthrew the Tokugawa dynasty in 1868 founded a centralized bureaucratic state and organized an economic revolution from on top to avoid political subordination and economic entrapment. Forced industrialization was a response to the forced internationalization of the unequal treaties—China in 1842 and 1858, Siam in 1855, Japan in 1858—that eroded East Asian sovereignty. The Meijis proved catastrophically successful in their state- and nation-building efforts: by the end of the nineteenth century Japan had been transformed into a modern industrial and military power, but anticolonial nationalism morphed into imperialism and ultranationalism, leading to conquest in China (1931–1937) in the early Shōwa era, and ultimately to disastrous military defeat (1945). The late-imperial Chinese Qing state, which became the prey of the imperialist powers and which was confronted with massive concurrent internal threats, haltingly engaged in Meiji-styled "self-strengthening" efforts in the latter part of the nineteenth century, but eventually collapsed (1911). Chinese nationalism in its revolutionary and conservative variants, and the modern Chinese state, came into being out of this cauldron. Twin authoritarian developmental regimes emerged out of the ashes of world war and civil war in the mainland

22

THE DYNAMICS OF CAPITALIST DEVELOPMENT

and Taiwan, both of which were rooted in the self-strengthening movement and early Republican modernization efforts.

The continuities of these state-building efforts after 1945 are analyzed in the subsequent parts of the book. Chapters 3 and 4 look into the factors, exogenous and endogenous, accounting for the re-creation (Japan) or creation (South Korea, Taiwan, and parts of Southeast Asia) of capitalist developmental states. Chapter 3 points to the role of war-making in state-making, and the way U.S. interventions shaped the regional political economy. In sharp contrast to Europe, whose division into rival blocs led to a stable strategic balance and a prolonged period of cold peace, East Asia became the main battlefield of the post-1945 competition between the United States, the Soviet Union, the declining European colonial powers, and the People's Republic of China. East Asia was nearly constantly at war between 1945 and 1979: when the casualties of the Chinese Civil War are included, over 17 million people died during the wars and civil wars of an era that is quite improperly called the Cold War. Regional war-making proved crucial to the rise and consolidation of conservative bureaucratic authoritarian developmental regimes that became platforms for the United States in its global anticommunist containment effort. For Japan, the Korean War was a "gift of the gods," in the oft-cited words of then-Prime Minister Shigeru Yoshida. It fuelled Japan's economic revival in the 1950s, with U.S. demand, aid, and infrastructure investment creating favorable conditions for the mobilization of preexisting human and material capacities that the war had not erased. From the Korean War onward Japan experienced intense and sustained growth under the guidance and governance of the reconstituted prewar bureaucratic state. Developmental nationalism (Chapter 4) became the means not only to rally the population behind official objectives and legitimate the de facto one-party state, but also a way to restore continuity with the country's prewar history. In like manner, the U.S. Vietnam War (1963–1973) stimulated the South Korean economy's rapid growth and industrialization in the sixties and seventies. Third-wave industrializers in Southeast Asia, likewise conservative authoritarian regimes, were favored to a lesser degree, but they too benefited from U.S. war-related demand and became platforms for U.S. infrastructure investment.

Unlike the nineteenth century European imperial system, the post-1945 U.S.-centered regional political economy did not generate underdevelopment even if it led to deep strategic and trade dependencies. For reasons related to U.S. strategic objectives during the 1950s and 1960s, the U.S. political economy in Northeast Asia authorized upward economic mobility for key allied states that were integrated in subordinate positions in the internationalized U.S. security apparatus and that, like Western Europe, became recipients of strategically driven U.S. aid and investment. Facing broad and deep regional revolutionary ferment, the United States required a belt of secure and relatively prosperous states in Northeast Asia to curb revolution and contain the Soviet Union and the People's Republic of China (until the definitive late 1960s Sino-Soviet split). Unlike other postcolonial world regions where the U.S. encouraged authoritarianism without much (Latin America) or any development (Africa, the Mideast), in Northeast Asia and a few Southeast Asian countries the United States helped to erect and sustain states with strong despotic and infrastructural power or state capacity (Mann, 1984) that were able to mobilize large parts of society behind overriding developmental objectives while suppressing labor and silencing political dissent. Neomercantilist industrialization strategies—a mix of import substitution industrialization and export-oriented industrialization—were tolerated, indeed often promoted, so long as allied states deferred to U.S. strategic preferences. For a few decades they were given essentially unrestricted access to the U.S. market, while maintaining the closure of their own markets to transnational investment. As Bruce Cumings emphasizes, the understanding on the U.S. side was that "Japan's sun was to rise high but not too high; high enough to cause trade problems for the allies in declining industries" but certainly not so high as to become a competing center of the world capitalist economy (Cumings, 1999). The same reasoning applied *a fortiori* to the smaller capitalist developmental states of Northeast and Southeast Asia.

During the late 1960s and early 1970s Japan became an increasingly important regional economic actor, accounting for a significant share of development aid and foreign direct investment (FDI). While the U.S. was spending lives and a vast amount of capital in a failed and extraordinarily destructive effort to subdue revolutionary nationalism in Vietnam, Japan seized the opportunity to reinvest the region and reconstitute the "Asian international economy" of the late nineteenth century (Sugihara, 1990), this time as a trading state rather than as an empire. In 1970, one-fifth of total Japanese foreign investment was directed toward East Asia. Between 1969 and 1981 nearly half of total aid going to the ASEAN countries stemmed from Japan, supplanting the United States, which had begun to retrench its commitments. Chapter 4 examines this economic redeployment in East Asia and how it spurred regional economic integration in the 1980s. Japanese overseas development assistance tripled from $703 million in 1980 to $2.18 billion in 1989 and a new and large wave of investments occurred as a result of the coordinated response of Japanese multinational companies and of government to the 60 percent appreciation of the yen after the 1985 Plaza Accords. The Accords pushed multinational Japanese firms to relocate activities worldwide to restore their price competitiveness, with a significant transfer of manufacturing capacity to the rest of East Asia. By the end of the 1980s, a concatenated regional division of labor had come into being and single-market dependence on the U.S. had begun to decline. The result was a noteworthy, if uneven, upgrading of the industrial fabric of the Southeast Asian countries that became incorporated into the Japanese productive system.

Following the state-capitalist turn in the 1980s under Deng Xiaoping, China was in turn integrated in this regional dynamic (Chapter 5). Seeking a third way between Western capitalism and the failed imperative planning system of the late Maoist period, the post-Mao leadership looked to the East rather than the West for modernization models that would pull the country out of economic crisis while preserving the Party-state's power and authority. The example of the Japanese and other East Asian developers that had successfully modernized under the guidance and control of strong or authoritarian bureaucratic states influenced this transition. Gradual and controlled internationalization led to investment flows from Japan as well as from East Asia-based transnational Chinese business networks. While investment was initially concentrated in low-value-added manufacturing, this first phase of internationalization allowed China to "[benefit] tremendously from the capital, market networks, and management as well as the technical know-how that capitalists from Japan and the Four Tigers brought with their investments" (Ho-Fung Hung, 2009: 12). Chapter 5 takes a close look at China's subsequent integration into the world capitalist economy, which resulted in a hybrid developmental system. This system combined key features of the state–market relations of precursor Northeast Asian developmental regimes—a highly autonomous interventionist state, a large state sector, administrative guidance, industrial policy, neomercantilist trade promotion, and managed currency policies—with two characteristics that distinguish the Chinese experience from Japan, South Korea, and Taiwan during their initial developmental ascent: a higher degree of penetration by transnational capital and dependence on continuing inflows to maintain the country's extraverted growth momentum, as well as sharp social and spatial unevenness.

Engineered from the top by the authoritarian state, capitalist transformation has led to spatial polarization, large-scale continental mass migrations, sharp new social stratifications, and major problems of environmental sustainability linked to energy consumption and urbanization. The scale of urbanization in China is historically unprecedented: nearly half of the population lives in urban areas today, against 10 percent in 1900 and less than 35 percent in the early years of the capitalist transformation. By 2030, the United Nations expects that 70 percent of China's population, around 950 million people, will be living in urban agglomerations. Sustained growth has been made possible by the mobilization and exploitation of a vast subordinate labor force, notably women concentrated in low-value-added activities such as textile manufacturing and electronics assembly, raising major issues of gender and class. Chinese critics have warned that the country has in fact become caught in a dependent development path that will not allow convergence with the most advanced countries. Global constraints coupled with neoliberal domestic policies would severely limit China's development potential (Jianyong Yue, 2010). While these problems highlight the need for vigorous corrective measures, without which the country's further development is likely to be compromised, they should not obscure the fact that the strategy followed since 1978 has been broadly successful. This is not meant to justify disciplinary Chinese labor policies, much less the authoritarian regime that is piloting and profiting from capitalist transformation. Rather, it points to the fact that China's modernization is incomplete. Like Japan's nineteenth-century experience, it is contradictory, tension-filled, and remains to be fulfilled.

The book's final chapter is devoted to the implications of rebalancing, the questions of meaning and purpose raised by postcolonial re-emergence. Late twentieth and early twenty-first century globalization is characterized by contradictory but intertwined processes of transnationalization and nationalization, integration and fragmentation, power diffusion and power re-concentrations. Deepening interdependence has given a truly cosmopolitan character to production and consumption, far more so than in Marx's epoch. Yet national segmentation remains a stubborn social fact: the imagined communities constructed with the rise of the modern nation-state are based on ontological assumptions about identity and belonging that resist dissolution in the global market. For reasons relating to historical experiences of subjugation or subordination, postcolonial Southern states tend quite understandably to adhere to modern conceptions of power and sovereignty. So too, of course, do most Western states,

26

notably the most powerful, the United States. Rebalancing and the end of hierarchy, while normatively desirable a priori, accentuates rather than diminishes inter-state competition and therefore carries risks. For the historically dominant countries, the intellectual challenge going forward will be to accommodate a decentered world in which power is shared. For the re-emerging nations that are restructuring world capitalism from within, the challenge is just as great: if rebalancing conforms to the historic aim of generations of anti-colonial leaders and thinkers to gain upward mobility and achieve sovereign equality, the way in which it is occurring represents a sharp break with the past. Anticolonialism still constitutes a component of the identity and discourse of the re-emerging "South," including in conservative nationalist circles that read the current transformation in oppositional cultural terms. But unlike the first generation of postcolonial leaders who aimed for revolution or sought to invent a "Third Way" between capitalism and communism, the actors of the current shift of global power relations are claiming a central competitive place in the world capitalist system that their predecessors had attempted to either reform or supplant. The success of that claim has dampened, and in some cases entirely submerged, the broader emancipatory or universalistic dimensions of the long struggle for independence, equality, and social justice.

— 2 —

EARLY-MODERN ENCOUNTERS, LATE-MODERN COLLISIONS

The ontogenesis of the East Asian economic revolution can be traced back to the collisions caused by the general movement of late-modern Euro-Atlantic expansion that engulfed the Orient. A new historical structure emerged, supplanting the plural and polycentric interactions of the early modern world with novel world-level structures of hierarchy. Arrighi, Hamashita, and Selden have proposed a useful historical scheme situating East Asia's current re-emergence in three temporal frameworks defining "successive stages in the formation of the East Asian regional political economy" and the latter's interaction with the globalizing European interstate system: long, intermediate, and short perspectives covering the early modern, late modern, and post-1945 periods. Their focus is primarily on the role of transnational Chinese business networks and Chinese capital that, in their account, constitute the invisible threads of continuity in the East Asian historical experience from the sixteenth century to the present (Arrighi, Hamashita, Selden, 1997; 2003). This chapter retains the tripartite temporal scheme but addresses the problem of continuity/ discontinuity by focussing on Chinese and Japanese state- and nation-building in the late modern period when ever-larger parts of Asia were forcibly incorporated into the globalizing Atlantic-centered political economy. While transnational private trading and business networks have certainly been important actors in the promotion and diffusion of the region's recent capitalist dynamic, the East Asian economic revolution derives first and foremost from the determining role of developmental states whose foundations were erected in the nineteenth century in the face of intensifying external pressures that threatened the territorial integrity and historical identities of long-established polities.

28

Imperial globalization flowed from the maturation of the Industrial Revolution in the nineteenth century and the concomitant competitive drive of Euro-Atlantic nation-states to expand their power and reach. The overall outcome, as noted in Chapter 1, was the fracture of the world into dominant cores and dependent peripheries: by the end of the nineteenth century one-third of the world population had been incorporated into formal empire, with another third into informal systems of long-distance control. Power and wealth became extraordinarily concentrated in the north Atlantic. The incorporation of extra-European world regions was, however, an uneven process. It occurred at varying rhythms and had differential impacts depending on local state institutions, capacities of adaptation, and resistance. In East Asia, the globalizers challenged and came into collision with advanced societies and unitary states that resisted intrusion and were compelled into modern nation-state building as a condition of survival. The threat of submersion left no alternative but to build or try to build modern armies and strong states, and to appropriate Western technologies of power and adapt them to national institutions. The modern Chinese and Japanese states emerged out of nineteenth-century efforts to maintain national autonomy and unity in the face of exogenous threats. Although the late imperial Qing state ultimately collapsed in the face of combined external and internal pressures, the "inexorable progression" (Philip Kuhn, 1999) of the republican state in the twentieth century—from the 1911 revolution through Mao to Deng Xiaoping—derives from the violent struggles of the late nineteenth century that awoke Chinese nationalism and stimulated the state's "self-strengthening" efforts (Kuhn, 1999; Feuerwerker, 1992). The modern Japanese state likewise arose out of the need to curb "barbarian" intrusion, proving catastrophically successful in its quest for wealth and power and its nation-building efforts. Anti-imperialist nationalism morphed at the end of the nineteenth century into ultra-nationalism and imperialism, and into militarism in the decade that led to world war in 1941. One dimension of the state-building program survived the disasters of war: the postwar developmental state reproduced and perfected the industrial system of the late nineteenth and early twentieth centuries. In Korea and Taiwan, authoritarian anticommunist states supported by the United States inherited and nationalized Japanese developmental institutions and practices; in Indochina and Indonesia, anticolonial liberation wars, led by movements whose roots dug deep, forged modern nation-states. Nationalism, as Prasenjit Duara perceptively notes, "became more strongly rooted in this region in the twentieth

29

century than in most other parts of the non-Western world" (2009: 223).

This chapter discusses the passage from the polycentric structure of the early modern world to the hierarchical late modern Western-centered system, and the way in which the East–West encounter evolved into a series of broadening collisions in the nineteenth and early twentieth centuries which set the stage for the rise of the modern East Asian developmental state.

From polycentrism to hierarchy

Since Braudel's pathbreaking *The Perspective of the World* (1984), the French edition of which appeared in 1979, a growing body of world historical scholarship has drawn a new and compelling picture of the early modern world and of historical globalization that has under-mined Eurocentric accounts of modernity in essential ways. Weber's influential account of the supposedly singular cultural sources of the Occident's successful and problematic quest to master nature and dominate the world—disenchantment and rationalization—still casts a lingering shadow on discussions of the "rise of the West" and the "decline" of the Orient, spawning vulgar variations that contaminate political discourses. Very few scholars, however, still countenance the long-held but fundamentally flawed orthodoxy that "for the last thousand years, Europe (the West) has been the prime movement of development and modernity" (Landes, 1998: xxi). As the excavation and interpretation of historical evidence from early modern Asia has broadened and deepened,[1] the periodization of the "great divergence" between East and West has been pushed forward to the maturing of the Industrial Revolution and Euro-Atlantic imperial globalization in the nineteenth century. While parts of Atlantic Europe and some of its settler colonial offshoots were certainly expanding economically and territorially prior to 1800, their early modern encounter with Asia had little in common with Europe's intrusion in the Americas, the impact of which overwhelmed and depopulated indigenous Amerindian societies. Far from being the dominant center of world production, finance, and trade that she later became, until the early nineteenth century Europe was merely one among many "world economies" (*économies-mondes*)[2] in a polycentric universe in which there were plural polities, relatively equal and autonomous if com-mercially interconnected (the Ottoman Empire, the Mughal Empire, Persia, China, Japan, and so on).

The compelling picture of the early-modern world that has emerged is not one of longstanding Western advantage founded on superior scientific-technical capabilities and more advanced market institutions and market activities. Nor does it present a stationary Orient (much less a declining one) fatefully locked in precapitalist modes of production and religious cosmologies inhibiting economic and technical improvement. Rather, it depicts a world of "surprising similarities in agricultural or commercial development and proto-industrial activities" (Pomeranz, 2000: 8) between major world regions moving more or less synchronously along parallel "Smithian" developmental lines,[3] engaged in industrious revolutions involving the move from subsistence to market economies with widening proto-industrial activities, the commercialization of handicraft manufactures, the development of market institutions, and the expansion of sophisticated intra- and interregional trade networks. From the sixteenth to the late eighteenth centuries, the Indian subcontinent, China, Japan and Southeast Asia saw the emergence of structured and increasingly integrated national and regional markets for grain, textiles and other goods, and experienced deepening specialization in which rural communities engaged in both agricultural and craft production were linked to urban centers and overseas markets through networks of production, credit and trade, mediated and organized by growing and dynamic merchant classes. Locational specialization generated development poles, technical improvements and in many cases rising productivity. Peasant households producing silks and cottons as well as other manufactures for the market, and who also engaged in seasonal agricultural employment, were not simple subalterns to feudal landlords but actors engaged in evolving and expanding markets. The "cluster of similar dynamics of economic change in Europe and late-imperial China" that R. B. Wong discusses (Wong, 1997: 6) also applies to Tokugawa Japan, South Asia, the trading centers of Southeast Asia, and parts of the Ottoman Near and Middle East.

The symmetry with European proto-industrial and commercial development implies that there were few if any qualitative economic differences between the western and eastern parts of Eurasia prior to the early nineteenth century. "There is little to suggest," writes Pomeranz, "that Western Europe enjoyed decisive advantages" in terms of physical capital, market institutions, agricultural productivity, or proto-industrial output. While they are inevitably approximate given the lack of systematic data from the period, general estimates of per-capita output show that average living standards, based on real consumption measured in grain rather than monetary earnings,

31

were comparable in Europe and Asia until the end of the century (Parthasarathi, 1998; Bairoch, 1997). Life expectancies were on the whole analogous: "Except in the most prosperous regions of Europe, life expectancies did not surpass the Chinese level until the end of the nineteenth century" (Wong, 1997: 27). The case made for East–West socioeconomic convergence prior to the age of European empire and industry becomes even stronger when the unit of analysis is changed, and comparison is made not between individual European nations and China or the Indian subcontinent but with provinces within these vast differentiated ensembles (Pomeranz's innovative and important methodological move). Data retrieved at the local level on life expectancies and per-capita calorific intake (the rice or wheat available to people) confirm that circa 1750 living conditions in the most commercially vibrant and wealthiest regions of China and India (the Yangzi delta, South India, or Gujarat), or in Japan, were comparable to those of Great Britain, by far Europe's most economically advanced country. Parthasarathi's estimates suggest that the annual real earnings of weavers (in grain) were in fact higher in South India than in Britain (Parthasarathi, 1998). Estimated average life expectancy oscillated between 35 and 38 years in eighteenth-century Britain, reaching 40 in the early decades of the nineteenth century. These are levels similar to those that prevailed in Japan (41) and the most prosperous provinces of China (between 34 and 39) (Pomeranz, 2000). In France, western Europe's most populous country at the time, average life expectancy in the first half of the eighteenth century was significantly lower: 25 years, rising to only 30 at the end of the century and to 37 in the first decade of the nineteenth century (INED, 2006).

Variations within the *économies-mondes* were more significant than variations among them. By the eighteenth century, Great Britain was well ahead of continental European countries in terms of industrialization levels, manufacturing output, and other basic measures of economic modernization such as urbanization and energy use. In 1800, per capita output in France, the German states, Switzerland, or Sweden was approximately four-fifths Britain's, reflecting the latter's more precocious and broader industrialization. Twenty percent of the British population was urbanized at the turn of the century, when most continental countries had urbanization rates only slightly above 10 percent. Notwithstanding the diffusion of the Industrial Revolution in continental Europe, the gap between Britain and other newly industrializing countries widened considerably in following decades, narrowing only at the end of the nineteenth century with the catch-up of late-industrializing countries (Germany, Switzerland,

Belgium, and, on the other shore of the Atlantic, the postbellum United States). In 1830, the per-capita rate of industrialization—the ratio of industrial output to population—in Britain was twice that of France, nearly three times that of the German states, and almost twice of the United States (Bairoch, 1982). Similar sociospatial differentiation was manifest in China, the coastal regions being far more prosperous than the landlocked spaces of the continental interior.

European technological advantages were neither longstanding nor pronounced. If anything, the Asian "super world economies", to borrow Braudel's expression, in the sixteenth, seventeenth, and early eighteenth centuries were producing manufactured goods, notably textiles and porcelain, of a higher quality than Europe's and in much vaster quantities. Early modern South Asia produced iron and weapons and her naval shipyards, the "wonder of wonders," manufactured large seagoing ships in Bombay and Bengal that sailed throughout Asia. And, as has been abundantly documented, "all of India processed silk and cotton, sending an incredible quantity of fabrics from the most ordinary to the most luxurious all over the world" (Braudel, 1984: 509), which Europe's East India companies paid for with silver extracted by slave labor from South American mines (there was little or no Asian demand for European products). South Asia quite literally "clothed the world," accounting at the end of the eighteenth century for "a quarter of the world's textile output and almost certainly a larger percentage of the world's seaborne trade in textiles" (Riello and Roy, 2009: 6). In contrast, until the late 1760s, the British cotton industry was "backward, small and unable to compete with Indian calicoes or muslins in either quantity or price unless protected" (Phyllis Deane, 1979: 88). Indeed, in *The Wealth of Nations* (1776) Smith remarks: "In the (British) clothing manufacture, the division of labor is nearly the same now as it was a century ago, and the machinery employed is not very different. There may, however, have been some small improvements in both" (Smith, 2005: 208). As intercontinental trade expanded in the eighteenth century, competitive pressures pushed European textile interests to lobby their governments to take protective measures against the import of Indian cloth.

Thanks to Needham's work we have an authoritative picture of China's premodern scientific and technical achievements under the Ming dynasty, and her relative advance until at least the European Renaissance in domains such as textile production, metallurgy, mechanical clocks, the compass, printing, gunpowder, and of course crucial irrigation techniques. Chinese ships long surpassed those of Europe in number and quality (Needham, 1954). China did not subsequently stagnate or become trapped in Malthusian constraints, but experienced slow but sustained expansion under the Qing. Writing on the eve of the long Industrial Revolution, the fundamental effect of which—self-sustaining growth through rises in productivity due to the socialization of innovation—only became apparent in the course of the nineteenth century, Adam Smith cautiously surmised from travellers' accounts that China had become "stationary" but remained in relative terms quite rich: "Long one of the richest, most fertile . . . best cultivated, most industrious and most populous countries in the world," China "may perhaps stand still (but) does not seem to go backwards. Its towns are nowhere deserted by their inhabitants. The lands which had once been cultivated are nowhere neglected" (Smith, 2005: 64–5). In fact, increases of agricultural output kept up with population growth; markets expanded, household production of proto-industrial goods in rural areas became generalized, weaving a widespread industry. Evolving commercial networks linked peasants to local, regional, and world markets. The coastal provinces were particularly dynamic: synthesizing research on Jiangnan in southern Jiangsu under the Qing, Peter Nolan notes "an extremely high level of commercialisation and urbanisation (and) enormous quantitative advance," notably in cotton and silk production, the volume of which tripled during the eighteen century (Nolan, 1993: 13). Pierre-Etienne Will makes the case that there were sprouts of "qualitative development," not simply quantitative expansion, in some provinces from the sixteenth to the eighteen centuries:

> In spite of serious recessions during the dynastic transition between the Ming and the Qing, the general growth of the economy in China (production and exchanges) since the sixteenth century is a massive and irreversible phenomenon. . . . The eighteenth century is generally considered as brilliant and prosperous. . . . Here and there, and not necessarily synchronously, one can identify local or regional development 'pockets' [evidenced in] per capita growth, the global enrichment of society, the aptitude to invest in infrastructure, urbanisation, and the transformation of social relations through growing commercialisation. Moreover, one observes that the State and its representatives sometimes played a decisive role or actively tried to play such a role in these episodes (without always succeeding). (Will, 1994: 863–66).

The late imperial state, whose role we come back to in our discussion of Asian responses to imperialist intrusion, was far more competent and better organized than most contemporary states, demonstrating a "quite remarkable level of efficiency" (866) in fulfilling its Confucian mandate: securing the welfare of the people and maintaining socioeconomic stability in a vast sovereign space. It "provided unusually favourable conditions for commercial development" allowing for the development of "huge internal trading areas within which (and between which) commerce could develop largely unhindered" (Nolan, 1993: 18). The Qing state implemented large-scale hydraulic works and other infrastructural projects. It reformed state monopolies (salt, for instance), encouraged agricultural development, and created a sophisticated food supply management system— a network of provincial granaries that stored millions of tons of grain and that "represented (a commitment) to material welfare beyond anything imaginable, let alone achieved, in Europe" (Wong, 2002: 98). Will emphasizes that the imperial state succeeded in its eighteenth-century "agricultural improvement programme," an enormous achievement given the spatial and demographic scale of the country.

Similar developmental patterns were manifest in Tokugawa Japan, which experienced "a century of extraordinary economic expansion" between 1600 and 1700, "in which arable land had greatly increased, castle-towns in all parts of the country grown rapidly, and national population more than doubled" (Smith, 1988: 3). Thomas Smith and other historians (Nakamura, 1981; Saito, 2005) have documented a diversification of the economic activity of rural households, the urbanization of rural Japan, rising crop yields due to seed selection and an advancement of agricultural technology, rising GDP per capita and rising real wages, a spread of literacy through schools for commoners, and a "spectacular growth of manufacturers catering to mass consumption" of textiles (Smith: 16). Unlike China, population growth stagnated in the course of the eighteenth century due to population control measures in a country with high demographic density (100 persons per square kilometre, against 14 in China). This had modernization effects: "The modernization of rural villages ... was vastly reinforced by the effective population control during the Tokugawa period" (Nakamura: 273). Output gains consequently led to rises in real per capita income. The state—the Shogunate (Bafuku) in Edo and the local rulers of the domains (Daimyo)—encouraged development through "projects to reclaim undeveloped land, to convert upland fields to paddy fields, and to increase the availability of water for irrigation" with a stress on rice production (Nakamura: 270). Relative economic isolation after the 1635 edict to close the country to most international trade stimulated the local production of handicrafts. This early modern experience of rural development and import-substitution provided the basis for industrialization in the late nineteenth century.

Table 2.1. World Population by Region 1750–1900 (millions)

	1750	1800	1850	1900
World	791	978	1262	1650
Europe	163	203	276	408
Asia	502	635	809	947
Africa	106	107	111	133
Latin America	16	24	38	74
North America	2	7	26	82

Source: U.N. Department of Economic and Social Affairs, www.un.org/esa/population/publications/sixbillion/sixbillion.htm

At the intersection of the great Indian Ocean trading system that stretched "from the Near East to the coast of Vietnam down to Indonesia and into the China Seas towards the Philippines" (Goody, 1996: 89) and the Chinese world economy, Southeast Asia experienced similar economic evolutions from the late fifteenth to the late eighteenth century: deepening specialization of the division of labor and peasant engagement in production and commercialization of handicrafts for local and long-distance markets. Malacca was one of the world's great commercial hubs; the maritime trading states in pre-colonial Java and Sumatra in the Indonesia archipelago were prosperous and rather cosmopolitan commercial centers, as was the inland Kingdom of Ayutthaya in Siam. Based on criteria such as estimated rice consumption, living standards are thought to have been the "equal of those prevailing in Western Europe," possibly with slightly higher average life expectancies (Dixon, 1991: 52). In sum, until the end of the eighteenth century

> In many areas, various non-European societies remained ahead. Irrigation was perhaps the most obvious; and in many other agricultural technologies, too, Europe lagged behind China, India, Japan and parts of the Southeast Asia. . . . In many areas of textile weaving and dyeing, western Europeans were still working on imitating Indian and Chinese processes; the same was true of manufacturing porcelain. As late as 1827 and 1842, two separate British observers claimed that Indian bar iron was as good or better than English iron. . . . various parts of Africa also produced large amounts of iron and steel that were of a quality at least as good as anything available in early modern Europe. . . . Medicine was probably not terribly effective anywhere in the world, but east (and probably southeast) Asian cities were far ahead in crucial matters of public health, such as sanitation and the provision of clean water. (Pomeranz, 2000: 45–46)

36

Table 2.2. Share of World Manufacturing 1750–1900 (percent)

	1750	1800	1830	1860	1880	1900
Europe	23.2	28.1	34.2	53.2	61.3	62.0
GB	1.9	4.3	9.5	19.9	22.9	18.5
USA	0.1	0.8	2.4	7.2	14.7	23.6
China	32.8	33.3	29.8	19.7	12.5	6.2
India	24.5	19.7	17.6	8.6	2.8	1.7
Japan	3.8	3.5	2.8	2.4	2.4	2.4
Orient*	73.0	67.7	60.5	36.6	20.9	11.0

Source: Bairoch [1982] *Orient is this author's term for what Bairoch calls the Third World.

These quantitative and qualitative findings do not imply that East or South Asia were at the threshold of an industrial revolution that would have spontaneously evolved out of Smithian growth (the idea that the British Industrial Revolution itself constituted a spontaneous or "natural" evolution is highly problematic). Nor do they substantiate sinocentric accounts of decisive Chinese or Asian competitive advantage and dominance in the early modern world economy (Frank, 1998). But they indisputably show a world in balance circa 1750, one in which parts of Asia seem to have had a slight competitive edge in some productive sectors. In 1800, with 64 percent of the world population, Asia (West Asia included) still accounted for over 60 percent of world proto-industrial manufacturing output. Braudel is quite definitive on this point: "It can hardly be questioned that until the nineteenth century the rest of the world outweighed Europe both in population and, while the economic *ancien régime* lasted, in wealth" (Braudel, 1984: 534–35).

The equilibrium between eastern and western Eurasia was reflected in global and regional trade patterns. The early modern Asian world was interconnected through transcontinental land and maritime crossroads linking West Asia, India, Southeast Asia, and Northeast Asia, in which Europe played a growing though not a dominant role. The European traders who came into early contact with Asia found highly advanced societies, many with long constituted bureaucratic states, with which they were forced to deal on terms of equality. Sixteenth- and seventeenth-century European commercial expansion in the Indian Ocean and the South and East China Seas did not overwhelm the secular intra-Asian networks of exchange. Rather, European commercial penetration initially complemented existing networks and even favored the expansion of regional and long-distance Asian commerce. The Portuguese, principally involved in the spice trade, sought to monopolize regional trade, but they "settled within the structure and were, in a way, swallowed by it" (Dasgupta, cited by Bose, 2006: 19). In sinocentric Asia, European trade was subsumed in the "tributary system (that) came to constitute a multilateral trading network capable of absorbing commodities from outside itself" (Hamashita, 2008: 22).

The shift from the Portuguese to the Dutch East India Company (VOC) as the preponderant European actor in Asian trade did not fundamentally alter the balance. Though it succeeded in territorializing its power through violence in parts of the Indonesian archipelago, and proved even more successful in forcibly supplanting the Portuguese, the VOC suffered military defeats in China, Vietnam, and Cambodia in the first half of the seventeenth century and again in China in 1662, obliging the Company to ply much of its regional trade through overseas Chinese or Indian merchants. It established a strong commercial presence in Siam, a regional trade hub, cooperating with rather than dominating the royal court of Ayutthaya. In the crucial Japanese market, the VOC, which became the sole company authorized to trade in the archipelago after the Tokugawa "closed country" edict of 1635 and the expulsion of the proselytizing Portuguese, "came to the conclusion that the total subservience by its personnel to the local rules and customs was the only option if the Company wished to continue to trade in that proud empire" (Blussé, 2008: 21). The VOC became a major actor in the intra-Asian network, but it too was incorporated into the larger Asian production and trade systems. Having never established political control over the mainland polities of Asia despite growing military commitments, it was not in a position to supplant local producers and merchants, on whom it depended for the supply and flow of spices and textiles, or to dominate regional markets. In the latter part of the seventeenth century, the Company experienced a sustained decline in profitability in its intra-Asian trade stemming from trade restrictions imposed by China and Japan, as well as intensifying competition from other European companies, notably the English East India Company (EEIC) after the 1670s (de Vries and van der Woulde, 1997). In the early eighteenth century, Indian textile suppliers had real bargaining power over supply and price, and the VOC had to come to terms with the fact that the "weavers can no longer be coerced" (Prakash, 2009: 224).

The EEIC proved a far more successful monopolist. It gradually supplanted all other actors in trade to Europe, taking over Bengali trade after the battle of Plessey (1757) and hindering Dutch market access. But it established effective hegemony over trade in Asia only in the 1830s after the first Opium War (1839–1842). In India itself the Company faced armed resistance to its further expansion after the conquest of Bengal, and its control of the important textile industry of western India remained contested until 1818 when the EEIC asserted direct political control through the annexation of Gujarat. "The subordination of the merchants and manufacturers in Surat (was) a protracted and prolonged process which was essentially determined by the EEIC's political authority in western India. . . . This enabled local commercial and weaving groups to retain their autonomy and demonstrate greater bargaining power in the negotiations with the Company. Even after 1800 when EEIC hegemony was no longer in doubt," weavers continued to resist the Company's monopolistic practices (Subramanian, 1998: 75). In Blussé's general assessment: "The East India Companies sometimes were able to impose monopolies on indigenous populations, but it also happened—and this was most often the case—that Company servants simply had to follow the rules that Asian rulers imposed on foreign trade" in the seventeenth and eighteenth centuries (Blussé, 2008: 36). While the early modern East–West encounter was hardly frictionless—monopoly-seeking European mercantilists came with god and guns, not only goods—it occurred under overall conditions of relative economic and political equality.

Forced production and trade regimes

Like the Industrial Revolution itself, the East–West divergence unfolded gradually, accelerating and deepening in the latter part of the nineteenth century. A new international hierarchy was constructed as the Euro-Atlantic states enmeshed ever-larger parts of Asia in formal systems of domination or the force fields of informal empire, challenging the autonomy of her early modern states. The visible and invisible hands of empire combined to warp developmental paths and to create new dependencies, opening the way for the collisions of the late nineteenth and early twentieth centuries. If the aggregate rate of growth of the British economy was relatively low during the "classic phase" of the First Industrial Revolution (1770s–1830s)—less than 2 percent per annum (Crafts, 1985 and 2014)—it was higher than in Asia or in continental Europe. More important, there were some industrial sectors, notably textiles, which became a globalized industry, where growth was more intense and where productivity was much higher than in the rest of the world, and which gave British manufacturers a major advantage over Asian and European competitors. In 1830, South Asia, China, and Japan still accounted for a significant share of world manufacturing output (Table 2.2), but East–West disparities became increasingly marked thereafter due to the mechanics of comparative advantage under asymmetric conditions of power and sovereignty.

Between 1815 and 1840 the British textile industry grew at a much faster pace than the overall economy—6 to 7 percent on average. By 1860, cotton cloth accounted for 50 percent of the total value of British exports and nearly half of total world textile output (Hobsbawm, 1990). The global production chain underpinning this ascendancy rested on peculiar nineteenth century institutions: slavery, indentured labor, and colonies. Most of cotton spun in Manchester (by women and children) was sourced in the southern slave states of the United States. This region became the world's main producer in the 1820s and accounted for over two-thirds of world output in the mid-nineteenth century.[4] On the Asian end of the chain "forced free trade" (Sugihara, 2009) became the rule. In South Asia, the East Indies, and Indochina the colonial powers imposed unilateral manufacturing and trade restrictions ruling out competitive manufacturing, making these territories into forced exporters of primary goods and importers of European manufactured products. In countries that avoided direct rule (China, Siam, and Japan) unequal trade treaties imposed by force or the threat of the use of force led to limited sovereignty and varying levels of incorporation and subordination in the emerging Atlantic-centered international division of labor.

Britain imported ever-larger volumes of colonial staples from the New World (sugar, cotton, tobacco, etc.), produced by slaves or indentured workers, many of whom were "coolies" from India or China, and financed its rising Atlantic trade deficits through the surpluses generated by the production in India under "highly coercive circumstances" (Pomeranz's expression) of primary products and commodities that British traders sold in the world market. In India, market-based textile production and distribution systems were supplanted by production at prices and conditions of work dictated by the EEIC (Prakash, 2009). Rising productivity in Britain significantly lowered the prices of exported textiles, displacing Asian handicrafts in world markets. Parthasarathi (2009) evidences the displacement of Indian goods by British goods in the Persian Gulf, Sumatra, and the Malacca Strait, all of which had previously been important export markets. Under political conditions prohibiting import substitution and preventing technology appropriation, British cotton cloth took

40

an increasing share of the domestic Indian market. Bairoch, referring to the domestic market substitution of Indian cottons by British products, speaks of a "process of almost complete deindustrialization in the textile industry" as well as of other industries such as iron and steel, until beginnings of re-industrialization at the end of the nineteenth century (Bairoch, 1997: 853–55). This may be too broad a statement in light of evidence of continuing Indian cloth exports, but there was certainly a per-capita decline, since Indian textile production did not follow the rate of population growth. The Indian share of domestic cloth consumption fell as British cloths flooded domestic markets: in the latter half of the century South Indian textile exports grew somewhat, but imports were multiplied tenfold (Parthasarathi, 2009: 430). The reversal is also evidenced by the changing composition of Indian exports: exports of raw cotton, insignificant in the early nineteenth century, rose steadily to meet British demand during and after the U.S. Civil War, reaching 440,000 tons by the end of the century. Following the first British–Chinese Opium War (1839–1842), British India also became the main world producer and exporter of opium. By mid-century, the value of Indian opium exports was significantly higher than the value of subcontinental cloth exports.

Richards's (2002) analysis of longterm data sets shows that from 1840 to 1859 opium made up 29.8 percent of all Indian exports in value, and 21 percent between 1859 and 1879. Opium also accounted for a significant part of government revenue after the Treaty of Nanking, averaging 11 percent from 1839 to 1849, 17 percent from 1849 to 1859, 16 percent from 1869 to 1879 and 13 percent from 1879 to 1889. Between 1790 and 1839 the average was 6 percent. From the 1840s to the 1880s, opium constituted the second largest source of government revenue behind land taxes (Richards: 160–61). In a 1853 article in the *New York Daily Tribune*, Marx noted that the "British government [of India] depends for full one-seventh of its revenue on the sale of opium to the Chinese while a considerable proportion of the Indian demand for British manufactures depends on the production of that opium in India" (Marx, 1963). Opium in fact played a wider role as "one of those vital commodities whose circulation sustained imperial flows of tribute, investment, exchange and trade within the British empire and in the nineteenth century world economy" (Richards: 163). Bairoch estimates that opium accounted for 8 percent of the value of total "Third World" exports in 1860, more than twice the value of total textile exports. While its role in Indian trade declined in the last decades of the nineteenth century, in Southeast Asia opium became a major source of government revenue

41

for the Dutch colonial regime in the Netherlands-Indies and in French Indochina (Murray, 1980; Trocki, 1999).

The opium trade was merely one component of an emerging global system of production and commerce that reshaped Asian economies to meet the financial and industrial needs of core countries, colonial governments, and private companies. The changing international division of labor stimulated new global migratory patterns of forced, semi-free and free labor. After the abolition of slavery in the British Empire (1833), millions of South Asians, Chinese, and Southeast Asians were recruited into overseas indentured labor, working in plantations, mines, and transport construction in various parts of the expanding Euro-Atlantic imperial systems. Approximately 2 million Asians, more than half from southern India, were imported into the sugar cane plantations of the European empires, overwhelmingly as indentured laborers. Up to 12 million migrants from India and China moved to colonial Southeast Asia and South Asia "under various forms of hybrid and semi-free arrangements, including some which were not far removed from the African slave trade" (Look Lai, 2007).[5] In the Southeast Asian colonies, British, Dutch, and French governments imposed forced export regimes using local and transnational indentured laborers who were disciplined through punitive contract laws and recurrent repression. Siam alone managed to escape direct rule, but the monarchy was compelled to sign unequal treaties with Britain in 1855 (the "Bowring Treaty"),[6] the privileges of which were then extended to France and the United States in 1856, modelled on the 1842 British–Chinese Treaty of Nanking, giving the European and neo-European states extraterritoriality and non-reciprocal trade rights. As Dixon points out, Siamese foreign trade came almost entirely under the control of Western companies and the largest indigenous manufactures, textiles and sugar processing, were replaced by imports. "Between 1870 and 1913 the value of cotton textile imports, mainly from Britain, increased sevenfold. . . . By the late nineteenth century Thailand had become almost entirely dependent on rice exports . . . to feed mainly immigrant plantation workers elsewhere in Asia" (Dixon, 88).

East Asia's largest unitary states, China and Japan, contemporaneously came under sustained coercive pressure and were forced to relinquish some of their sovereignty and open their markets. The following section is devoted to their responses to the existential challenge posed by Euro-Atlantic intrusion and the way in which imperialism and war shaped their modern state- and nation-building efforts. Mercantilist elite groups, convinced of the need to build national wealth and power to break out of the cage of the unequal treaties, came to the fore in both countries with different levels of success. Unlike the Meiji reformers in Japan whose political centralization and economic modernization efforts rapidly transformed the archipelago into an industrial and military power, and who went on to play a determining role in the collapse of the *ancien régime* in China, the Qing state failed in its "self-strengthening" efforts.

Building modern armies and states

The Qing and the Tokugawa states were both swept away in the late nineteenth century, the first by a combination of intense internal and external pressures that led to its 1911 collapse, the second by a revolution from on top (1868) that aimed to avert submersion by building a strong modern state. The demise of the Qing state was a protracted process. The imperial state did not succumb to Western intrusion, but its sovereignty was curbed and it lost control of the tributary regional system that had held up for centuries during the first (1839–1842) and second (1856–1860) Opium Wars. The treaty port system established after the wars ended China's tariff autonomy and gave, through most-favored-nation clauses, extraterritorial privileges and rights to all the colonial powers. The 1842 Treaty of Nanking between China and Britain was followed in 1844 by similar trade treaties with France and the United States; the terms of the 1858 Treaty of Tientsin—signed by Britain, France, Russia, and the United States and expanding the port system and giving foreign traders access to China's interior market— were extended to Portugal, Denmark, Holland, Spain, Belgium, and Italy. The Western powers never managed to dominate the domestic market or entirely take over Chinese domestic or overseas trading networks, but China became caged in tightening constraints.

Limited sovereignty challenged the state at a time when it was confronted with a series of natural disasters and threatened by massive domestic rebellions—the Taiping, Nian, and Miao rebellions in the southern, northern, and central regions that began in the early 1850s and lasted until the late 1860s.[7] The imperial state financed the Taiping war by collecting duties in Treaty ports through the Customs Service, which was jointly run with European officials interested in maintaining stable flows of revenue. It also imposed new levies on internal trade (the *likin* tax on interprovincial trade) outside of the purview of the Treaty powers that remained in force after war's end. At the same time, reformists sought to modernize the armed forces through the "self-strengthening" effort of the early 1860s.[8] The self-strengthening program aimed to appropriate Western technologies and organizational know-how to build capacities of resistance and create a modern state. The effort was, however, initiated from a position of weakness: "At a time when foreign troops occupy the Imperial Capital, we certainly cannot fight, not even to defend ourselves. Both fighting and appeasing are to our disadvantage. The inevitable conclusion is that we must adopt appeasement as a temporary measure and the preparation for defence as our long-term policy" (Imperial Memorial cited in Chen: 1980: 75). Significant but ultimately ineffectual efforts were made over the next three decades to follow the Meiji path and build a modern industrial base and a defense industry: coal mines were opened, the steel industry was encouraged, modern weapons were imported, arsenals were set up, military and civilian shipbuilding was expanded and some railroads were built. But, as Jerome Chen (1980) shows in his tightly argued study of state economic policies in the late imperial period, these efforts were ill-designed and unsystematic: due to a divided imperial administration, they were never made the core of a coherent national policy, and proved insufficient to deal with growing external pressures and threats. The modern industrial sector remained small and weak until the First World War, when import-substitution industrialization took off under the post-imperial state (Nolan, 1993; Pomeranz, 1993).

In the 1870s and 1880s China was challenged by Russian intervention into Chinese Turkestan, and her already much weakened traditional tributary system in East Asia fell apart: the annexation by Japan of Liuqiu and the loss of suzerainty over Korea in 1874, China's defeat by France in Annam (1884–1885), and the integration of Burma into British India after the third Anglo-Burmese War (1885). The turning point was the Qing defeat in the First Sino-Japanese War (1894–1895), whose after-effects challenged China's unity. Through the Treaty of Shimonoseki China definitely renounced its suzerainty over Korea and ceded Taiwan and parts of the Liaodong Peninsula to Japan. Favorable tax and investment conditions were given to Japanese traders and investors in China, including in the manufacturing sector, giving them advantages over their Chinese counterparts. These rights were automatically extended to the Europeans and the United States, and de facto spheres of imperial influence were constituted. The impact of the war on public finances was critically important. The indemnities prescribed by the Treaty (230 million Kuping taels or $170 million) were five times greater than the combined indemnities paid after the Opium Wars. China saw its foreign debt multiplied sevenfold and turned to Britain, France, Germany, and Russia for government-backed loans that competing European governments used for political and economic advantage (mining and railway concessions and direct supervision and direction of the customs service). In his classic study of late-nineteenth-century European finance, Herbert Feis notes: "The loans required to pay the Japanese indemnity had thus hurried the mortgaging of the Chinese Empire. They exposed China to necessities which were made the occasion of claims to territory and privileges" (1974: 439–40). Customs revenue served as guarantee for the loans that "created a common interest in maintaining the Qing Dynasty," the "course of greater wisdom (being) not to risk the slaying of the golden goose for it was laying eggs for all" (Van de Ven, 2014: 10).

In 1900–1901, the imperial powers jointly suppressed the proto-nationalist Boxer Rebellion, imposing indemnities (£67.5 million or 450 million silver taels) greater than annual Chinese tax revenue, and trapping the country in long-term debt dependency (payments continued on and off until 1939). The victors took control of Chinese fiscal resources, with maritime customs revenue as well as other tax revenue pledged for the payment of war debt. The Maritime Customs Service became a *"caisse de la dette*, a debt collection agency for foreign financial interests and countries receiving Boxer Indemnity payments" (Van de Hens: 9). From 1895 until its collapse, in Chen's stark assessment, "the empire was to sink to the status of a pariah state, poverty stricken, disease ridden, defenceless, and gasping for life" (Chen, 1980: 137). Chinese nationalism in its conservative and revolutionary incarnations came into being out of this cauldron. It took another and much greater war with Japan, under totally different international circumstances, and a civil war in which the Chinese Communist Party (CCP) prevailed over the Kuomintang, for the modern state to finally emerge.

Japanese imperialism

Japanese imperialism was both a reaction to and part of the movement of late-modern empire-building that accompanied the Industrial Revolution. External pressures on Japan intensified in the 1830s and 1840s. The threat in the early 1850s of the use of force by the United States to pry open the country to American trade forced Japan to sign the 1858 Ansei Five Power Treaties, modelled on the Chinese treaty port system. The Treaties subjected Japanese trade policy to international control. Five ports were opened to trade, Japan lost its tariff autonomy, import duties were set at low levels, and foreign residents in trading ports were given extraterritorial status and allowed to enter Edo and Osaka. Because of Japanese resistance, the treaties proved not as deeply corrosive to Japanese sovereignty as the unequal treaties imposed on China after the Second Opium War, or as detrimental as the Bowring Treaty with Siam in their economic effects.

A decade after the Treaties, the Meiji reformers, who were driven by a deep sense of national crisis and who displayed a "terrible intensity (over the opening of the country) and driving out the barbarians" (Irokawa, 1988: 7), overthrew the *ancien régime*, founding a centralized bureaucratic state that initiated a sustained modernization effort from on top to "enrich the country and strengthen the army." Forced industrialization constituted a response to forced internationalization (Fukuzawa Yukichi compared the expansion of the West to the epidemic spread of contagious disease, the exposure to which would stimulate Japanese immunities). The Meiji state- and nation-building program involved technology appropriation, mass education, and industrial promotion. A systematic effort was undertaken to appropriate Western technologies of power and adapt them to Japanese institutions: teams of officials, researchers and buyers were deployed to study Western institutional systems and military organizations, to purchase relevant technologies, and recruit specialized personnel (exemplified by the 1872 trans-ministerial Iwakura Mission to Europe and the United States). The new state built the nation from on top through mandatory mass education with a strong nationalist accent that rapidly generated near-universal literacy. The rate of primary school attendance doubled between 1880 and 1900; by 1910, 98 per cent of 6- to 13-year-olds were attending schools, a higher rate than in Europe or even the United States (enrolment rates for 5- to 19-year-olds in the U.S. was 51 per cent in 1900).

The foundations of the economic revolution that unfolded in the last decades of the nineteenth century had been laid during the late Tokugawa period due to the import substitution effects of relative economic isolation. The development of a national market and the production of primary commodities (silk, cotton, rice, tea, etc) as well as manufactured products created favourable conditions for trade expansion when the ports were opened, with the West but also with Asia. In the early years of the Restoration the sale of commodities to the West, primarily the United States, stimulated rural production and brought in foreign exchange for the purchase of modern technologies and for domestic investment. The institutional framework for industrialization was provided by a state that was "alert and sensitive . . . (to) nineteenth and twentieth century discoveries in science and technology" (Irokawa, 1988: 71), used scarce capital resources to promote strategic industries (mining, iron and steel, shipping, weapons), and encouraged import-substitution in manufacturing sectors such as the cotton industry. The state offered incentives to the large merchant-industrial conglomerates (*zaibatsu*) that consolidated at the time. In sectors combining commercial and strategic interests, such as shipyards and shipbuilding, it launched a "comprehensive development programme" (Chida and Davies, 2012: 4) in which Japan first imported ships at the technological frontier from Britain, and then moved to domestic reproduction and autonomous production. As Irokawa Daikichi argues, the state's focus on power to the exclusion of all else left out popular well-being: "technological advances [were] to a great extent seen as an instrument of national policy with political, commercial and class implications. . . . Japan built a first rank military power through the sacrifices of workers and farmers" (Irokawa, 1988: 71). The mobilization nonetheless generated remarkable overall economic results: Japanese growth rates at the end of the century averaged 9 percent per annum and the share of merchandise exports more than doubled between 1890 to 1913, from 5 to 12.5 percent. The textile industry greatly expanded during the decade: the average annual output of yarn tripled and silk filatures grew rapidly in number and in size. Having recovered full tariff autonomy in 1911, during and after the First World War Japan moved from light to heavy industries (steel, shipbuilding, chemicals, railways, machines, weapons) supported by the state Industrial Bank and protected by high import tariffs. Between 1890 and 1913, the number and gross tonnage of domestically built steamships rose dramatically: Japanese shipyards built 9 steamships on average annually between 1870 and 1879, 22 between 1880 and 1889, 40 between 1890 and 1899, nearly 80 between 1900 and 1909, and 161 from then until the end of the First World War. Domestic production equalled imports in 1913 and largely exceeded them in 1918, when the country built 516 steamships with a gross tonnage of 598,691 tons (derived from Chida and Davies, 2012). Harootunian sums up the industrial surge during and after the First World War: Japan was transformed "into an industrial power equal to most European nations . . . ahead of societies like Italy and the Soviet Union" (Harootonian, 2000: xi).

New international trade linkages contemporaneously came into being. The United States was the country's primary trading partner until the Great Depression, absorbing more than a third of Japanese exports on average between 1890 and 1929 and accounting for a growing share of Japan's industrial and oil imports—14.85 percent on average between 1895 and 1914, 26.3 percent between 1915 and 1929 (Beasley, 1987). As Sugihara has documented (Sugihara, 1990), the last decades of the nineteenth century also witnessed the emergence of a Japan-centric division of labor in Asia, in which Japan imported primary commodities from Southeast Asia and India and exported manufactured products via Chinese and India trading networks. His findings show not only a rapid growth of Japan's total international trade (from £11.81 million in 1883 to £35.21 million in 1898, £151.46 million in 1913, and £488.92 million in 1928) but also a significant rise of Asia's share in total trade (from 23.5 percent in 1883 to 48 percent in 1898, 51.86 percent in 1913, and 53 percent in 1928). Japan became the largest intra-Asian trader, its overall share rising from 4 percent in 1883 to 30 percent in 1928—more than double India's share and nearly twice that of China. The archipelago became the "workshop of Asia," importing raw materials and exporting manufactured products—a trading pattern prefiguring the division of labor between Japan and Southeast Asia in the 1960s. Between 1890–4 and 1925–9, the share of primary products in total Japanese exports declined from 25.7 percent to 6.6 percent, while the share of primary products and food in total imports rose from 32.2 to 59.1 percent (Beasley, 1987: 126).

In conjunction with industrialization came two other inextricably linked features of modernity: nationalism and imperialism. A "more ambitious and totalizing vision of 'Japaneseness' [took hold] than had existed in the Tokugawa period" (Morris-Suzuki, 1998). Nationalist movements and identities were mobilized by the state, that pressed the cultural assimilation of the Ainu and the Okinawan native populations in Hokkaido and Okinawa, and instilled "nationalist and imperialist ideology through its control of education and the media" (Duara, 2009: 25). Nationalism had various expressions: following his tripartite scheme of cultural hierarchy that placed Japan in the semi-developed middle between Asian "barbarism" and western "civilization," Fukuzawa argued that Japan had to "quit Asia" to "make a great nation, strong in military might, prosperous in trade", and acquire the "best possible means of guaranteeing the safety and integrity of Japan from rapacious and unscrupulous foreigners" (quoted in Beasley, 1987: 30–31). His vision of national identity defined Japan against the West but also in distinction from China and the "old ways." Another vision was the idea of a Japanese civilizing mission in Asia. Pan-Asian nationalism proposed an alternative narrative of resistance to Western encroachment based on the idea of the cultural unity of Asia that gained some purchase in nationalist anticolonial circles in China, South Asia, and Southeast Asia. The two discourses cohabited uneasily in debates during late-nineteenth and early-twentieth century imperialist expansion over the "tutelage" of China and the establishment of a Japanese "sphere of co-prosperity." Prasenjit Duara aptly captures the ambiguity of the Japanese position: "The Japanese leadership, anxious to gain recognition from the Western powers by creating an empire in the contiguous region, also felt victimized by these very powers and identified with their weaker 'Asiatic brethren'" (2009: 25).

Working within the Western-dominated inter-imperial system or breaking out of it by creating a separate Asian empire became the core question and tension of Japanese international policy until the 1930s, when the second option gradually came to prevail. From the 1890s through the First World War, Japan sought a space and place in the imperialist club. Having defeated China in 1895, the archipelago had become an important if still subordinate actor in the Great Power competition over China and the Far East. Forced by Russia, France, and Germany to give up some of its territorial gains (Port Arthur and the Liaotung Peninsula), Japan allied with Britain to contain Russian ambitions in the Far East. British capital, in harmony with the policies of the British imperial state, flowed to Japan to finance the costs of the war. Larger capital flows followed the 1902 Anglo-Japanese agreement and helped to finance the subsequent Russo-Japanese War (1904–1905), rendering "vital aid" to the arms industry, railway development, and the acquisition and economic takeover of Korea (made into a Protectorate in 1905 and annexed in 1910) and Manchuria. "Japan," summarizes Feis, "proved capable of using to good advantage the capital of Europe. Its government succeeded in the threefold task of promoting industrial development, extending and reinforcing Japanese economic interests in Korea and China, and adjusting its plans to the political rivalries of the European continent. All three were connected. Western Europe financed its armaments, its wars, and its economic development" (Feis, 1974: 429). Until the Great Depression, the United States played a crucial role as a market and as a provider of capital equipment. In 1905 the British officially recognized Japan's "paramount political, military and economic interests" in Korea. The United States made no objections (Beasley: 89), insisting only that the Open Door be preserved throughout China, in keeping with U.S. commercial interests. Through victory in war, Japan had forced its way into the ranks of the "civilized" world: as one Japanese diplomat put the matter bluntly around 1899: "We show ourselves at least your equals in scientific butchery and are at once admitted to your council tables as civilized men" (cited in Koskenniemi, 2004: 84).

Deepening linkages with the Atlantic powers and integration into the world economic system did not satisfactorily resolve the question of equality, however: Japan fought on the Allies' side in the First World War in the hope and expectation of equal status and some of the spoils of war. Though it did acquire some German concessions in Shandong and some of Germany's colonial holdings in the northern Pacific at Versailles (1919), it did not achieve equal status. The Japanese demand to have a clause on racial equality inserted in the covenant of the League of Nations was rejected out of hand by Britain and the United States. The 1921–1922 Washington Naval Conference limited the size of the Japanese Navy to maintain U.S. and British naval predominance in the Pacific, a policy reiterated at the 1930 London Naval Conference. The Chinese Republic had also joined the war on the Allies' side in the hope of recovering sovereignty; it sent hundreds of thousands of Chinese to support the war effort in Europe. The relatively favorable terms of the settlement for Japan, as far as China was concerned, fuelled Chinese revolutionary nationalist ferment, sparking the May Fourth Movement and prompting Sun Yat-sen's 1924 warning: "Japan today has become acquainted with Western civilization of the rule of Might but retains the characteristics of the Oriental civilization of the rule of Right. Now the question remains whether Japan will be the hawk of the Western civilization . . . or the tower of strength of the Orient" (quoted in Jansen, 1954: 211).

The breakdown of world trade and of world order during the Great Depression resolved the question. Facing a deep domestic social and economic crisis, starvation in the countryside, and rising political disorder, the Showa state moved to establish an exclusive Japanese-centric Asian order in East Asia. This would create new trade outlets and help the country break out of tightening resource constraints (Iriye, 1972). Japan conquered Manchuria (1931), quit the League of Nations (1933), and launched its full-scale invasion of China in 1937. A new empire was constructed that differed in its economic logic from the 1890s imperial system. Until the 1920s the Japanese empire followed general colonial core-periphery patterns. Korea, Taiwan and Manchuria had been made into complementary but subaltern and dependent components of the Japanese economy, exporting food and raw materials to Japan and importing manufactured goods. Together they accounted for a significant share of Japanese exports (one-sixth of Japanese exports prior to the First World War and more than one-fifth in the late 1920s) and met Japan's food needs. Beasley estimates that food constituted 80 percent of Taiwan's exports and over 60 percent of Korean exports to Japan prior to the Great Depression, playing "a major part in sustaining Japan's modern economy by providing cheap food for a growing urban population" (Beasley, 1987: 131). At the end of the 1920s one-sixth of rice consumption was covered by colonial imports. The effort to construct a self-sufficient Asian empire altered this logic. The Japanese state developed "a specific economic plan" for a two-tier empire:

> The countries of north-east Asia, comprising Japan, Korea, Manchukuo, north China, and Taiwan, were to constitute a region in which heavy industry was to be developed. It would be Japan-centered in the sense that the home islands would be the principal source of capital, technology, and managerial skills but there would also be a measure of industrial decentralization. The rest of the area brought under Japanese rule—most of China and South-east Asia, plus the islands of the south-west Pacific—would serve the industrial heartland as a source of export earnings and raw materials. (Beasley, 1987: 255)

Industrialization in Korea, Manchuria, and, to a lesser extent, Taiwan was designed to consolidate the core of the empire and prepare for war. They were made into a "fortress" deeply integrated in Japan's industrial system, leading to a different pattern of specialization than during the prewar period. Building on an existing autochthonous industrial base, Japanese public and private investment in Manchuria increased fivefold between 1931 and 1941: in railways, mining, roads, iron and steel, and electric power to supplement heavy industry in Japan. The state provided the capital and ran or oversaw most of the heavy industry firms, while *zaibatsu* (Mitsui, Mitsubishi) invested in chemicals, machinery, textiles, and foodstuffs. "By the end of the war, the southern part of Manchukuo was quite heavily industrialized" (Beasley, 217). Korea became an industrial bulwark of the new empire: by 1936 "heavy industry accounted for 28 percent of total industrial production in Korea," with more than half a million Koreans employed in industry. Wartime needs accelerated the trend, leading to a tripling of the industrial workforce (Cumings, 1999: 76).

This abrupt transformation involved extraordinary social and symbolic violence. In Korea, imperial Japan suppressed the population

51

through a totalitarian system of repression and control. Intense industrial and infrastructure development went hand in hand with subjugation. During the "imperialization" phase after 1936, efforts to erase
indigenous culture included banning the use of Korean in schools,
forced name changes, and mandatory Shinto worship. During the war,
"millions were forcibly relocated to Japan, Manchuria, and northern
Korea for hard labor in mines and factories—or, in the worst case,
for sexual slavery" (Cumings: 74). The wartime empire in Southeast
Asia, which supplied food and primary materials worked by forced
labor, experienced great colonial violence. Military expansion in
Southeast Asia after 1941 (as well as in China) had been framed
as a pan-Asian project of "coexistence and co-prosperity," aiming
for the liberation of Asia from Western colonial rule. Unlike earlier
pan-Asian discourses that gained broad adherence among nationalist
forces that viewed Meiji Japan as a model for how to achieve independence and modernity, the wartime claim was emptied of meaning
by racialism and the "trail of unspeakable cruelty and rapacity [left
by] the emperor's soldiers and sailors" in China and Southeast Asia
(Dower, 2000: 22). There were some supporters, such as Subhas
Chandra Bose's Indian National Army or the Burmese National
Army. But, as Cumings puts it: "You had to go all the way to Burma
to find an Asian people that bought Japan's wartime ideology perhaps
because it looked good only at a great distance . . . Imperial Japan's
ideologues failed miserably at a subjective program for being both
Asian and modern at the same time" (Cumings, 1999: 210).

Japanese imperialism did succeed in shaping the future of Asia in
important if unexpected ways. First, its vast but inherently unsustainable[9] territorial expansion hastened the end of European empires in
Asia—not by liberating Asian peoples subjected to European misrule,
but by evidencing the latter's weaknesses and undermining their
authority and grip. Second, Japan's prewar institutional system and
state-building efforts provided a model for the East Asian authoritarian capitalist developmental states that successfully modernized in
the postwar period. Japanese developmentalism deeply influenced
Taiwan's postbellum economic system and "indelibly marked South
Korean development in the 1960s and 1970s" (Cumings, 1999: 75).
Among the keenest observers of East Asia there is a consensus on
this point (Beasley, 1987; Cumings, 1999; Duara, 2009; Atul Kohli,
1999; Woo-Cumings, 1999). The Park Chung-hee and Kuomintang
regimes in South Korea and Taiwan nationalized and adapted the
Japanese industrial and commercial system, reproducing Japan's
"ruthless use of state power" (Kohli's appropriate formulation) to

modernize their economies in compressed fashion from on top. For contingent strategic reasons, both regimes enjoyed the support of the new predominant power in East Asia, the United States. Japanese modernization and Japanese imperialism also had a deep impact on China. Republican conceptions of modernization and state-building were influenced by the Meiji experience. The later Japanese empire stimulated Chinese nationalism and an armed mass-based independence movement that fused nationalism and communist egalitarianism to build its own Soviet-styled developmental state. Influences stretch to the present: Chinese state capitalism owes a great deal to borrowings from the Japanese modernization experience in the nineteenth and twentieth centuries (Chapter 5). The following two chapters are devoted to post-1945 industrialization and state formation in East Asia. They highlight the interaction between exogenous and endogenous factors favoring Japan's economic renaissance after the war, and examine the subsequent movement of state-led industrialization in Northeast and Southeast Asia.

—— 3 ——

WAR-MAKING AND STATE-MAKING
AFTER 1945

East Asian developmentalism was shaped by imperialism, revolution, counterrevolution, and war, a long history of violence that can be broadly periodized into three interlinked and overlapping historical sequences: the movement of Euro-Atlantic conquest and intrusion throughout the nineteenth century; the fifty-year Japanese imperial moment that began with the First Sino-Japanese war of 1895 and ended in Japan's defeat and the collapse of the empire in 1945; and the regional civil wars, external interventions, and counterinsurgency campaigns after 1945—from the Chinese civil war (1945–1949), through the Korean and Vietnam wars, until the Vietnamese intervention against the Khmer Rouge in Cambodia in 1979 and China's war against Vietnam in its immediate aftermath. If 1945 marks the renunciation of war as a mechanism of resolution of intra-European conflicts (though not the end of European armed interventions in the colonial and postcolonial peripheries), war did not cease in East Asia after Japan's defeat. The region became the primary battlefield of the post-1945 competition in the "Third World" between the United States, the Soviet Union, the declining but still standing European imperial powers, and the People's Republic of China—an era that is quite improperly called the Cold War.

The remarkable yet insufficiently recognized historical reality is that East Asia, more so than any other region of the Third World, was nearly constantly at war between 1945 and 1979. In sharp contrast to the armed peace in divided Europe, East Asia became the main theater of post-1945 war-making. Insofar as the United States and the Soviet Union did not clash directly with each other, the post-1945 global strategic configuration can be characterized as a "cold peace" between the two main victors of the Second World War. But "Cold

54

War" is a Eurocentric misnomer for the lengthy period (1950–1990) during which over 34 million people[1] died during wars large and "small" in the colonial and postcolonial peripheries. Over 11 million of these deaths occurred in East Asia (17 million when Chinese civil war casualties are included). To be sure, the not-so-cold Cold War was about bipolar competition, the arms race, and the constitution and consolidation of military-industrial complexes and national security states. But what it "was really about for Americans [was] interventions in the Third World, from Korea through Iran, Guatemala and Cuba to the debacle in Vietnam" (Cumings, 1992: 90), which a neoconservative U.S. academic during the late 1960s characterized as "routine imperial wars" fought "at the remote frontier of empire . . . to uphold minimum world order" (for a discussion of U.S. imperial purpose see Golub, 2010). For the Soviet Union, though to a more limited extent than the United States, it was symmetrically about covert and overt interventions in the Third World. For the Dutch, French, and British colonial states it was about preserving empire as long as they could and regaining some maneuvering room in the new Atlantic system overwhelmingly dominated by the United States. For East Asians who were swept up in revolution, counterrevolution, and armed conflict, it was a continuation under new historical conditions of the mass violence that had originated with European empire, continued with Japan's imperial expansion, and persisted well beyond the collapse of both of the latter after the Second World War.

Seeking vainly to restore their prewar status and arrest the tide of history, the European imperial states in a position to do so briefly re-established colonial rule in Southeast Asia after Japan's defeat, repressing or warring against national independence movements with indirect or direct support from the United States. When the Europeans were ultimately forced to withdraw in the face of determined resistance and unsustainable costs, the U.S. became the primary external actor in regional armed conflicts, whose casualty toll was staggering. Though statistics vary according to different sources, the death toll in post-1945 interstate wars and civil wars in which Europe and the United States were overtly or covertly involved is appalling. Approximately 600,000 people, military and civilian, were killed during France's Indochina War (1946–1954), for which the United States provided significant though ultimately ineffective support; anywhere between 3.5 million to 4.5 million people during the Korean War (1950–1953), one million in North Korea alone; two to three million during the United States' Vietnam War (1963–1975); many hundreds of thousands, possibly as many as one million, during the

Indonesia civil war (the 1965 seizure of power by General Suharto and the subsequent liquidation of the Communist Party by the Indonesian Armed Forces); around 200,000 during Indonesia's invasion of East Timor in 1975, which was sanctioned by the United States; and tens of thousands in the suppression of insurgencies in Malaya, Thailand, and the Philippines. To these horrific figures one must add the millions who died in Cambodia at the hands of the Khmer Rouge regime backed by China,[2] which emerged out of the destruction and chaos of the Vietnam War and which received tacit diplomatic support from the United States as a "counterweight to North Vietnam,"[3] and the hundreds of thousands of Vietnamese and Chinese soldiers who were killed during China's fierce but failed "punitive" war against Vietnam in 1979 that followed the latter's successful intervention against the Khmer Rouge. When the 6.2 million deaths during the Chinese civil war (1945–1949) are included, total war casualties in East Asia after 1945 are significantly higher than those of the First World War.

This chapter focuses on the world level or systemic dimension of post-Second World War developmentalism in East Asia, in particular the role played by the United States in capitalist Northeast and Southeast Asia's post-Second World War trajectory. The argument derives from Charles Tilly's important observation that if states make wars, wars make states. Discussing early modern European nation-state formation, Tilly argues that war was the handmaiden of the nascent nation-state: war-making and conquest induced centralization and the acquisition by rulers of a domestic monopoly of legitimate violence, which in turn provided the means to extract resources from nationalized populations under their territorial control. "Pursuit of war involved [power holders] willy-nilly in extraction of resources for war-making from the populations over which they had control and in the promotion of capital accumulation by those who could help them borrow and buy. War-making, extraction, and capital accumulation interacted to shape European State making" (Tilly, 1985: 172). A competitive European interstate system emerged out of the violent delineation of inner and outer state space—the construction of sovereignty.

In East Asia, post-1945 war-making shaped and consolidated competitive capitalist and socialist developmental states that were modelled either on the Meiji state or the Soviet Union, all of which were led by nationalists who sought in different ways to build modern nation-states out of the debris of empire. The constancy of armed conflict, rather than supposedly culturally distinct ways of being and doing, accounts for the authoritarian state forms and dirigist

56

economic orientations that emerged in the region prior to and following the Second World War. If Western imperialism shaped the national consciousness, the state form, and the expansionist pathway taken by the Meiji state, constant war-making conditioned state formation in the region after 1945.

The Meiji model

Late modern Asian state- and nation-building emerged out of European imperial globalization in the nineteenth century. By generating new competitive pressures and resource imperatives, the European Industrial Revolution globalized conquest, extraction, and accumulation, while also accentuating centralization and fostering vast and deep bureaucracies for the management of capitalism (Weber, 2005), including those required for the overseas colonial territories. As part of the general movement of colonial expansion, energized by industrialization and fuelled by hardening visions of cultural and racial hierarchy, the European nation-states projected their interstate rivalries and violence onto the rest of the world: the long period of relative interstate peace in Europe following the Napoleonic Wars that coincided with the development of modern capitalism was accompanied by "an almost incessant series of open wars" (Polanyi, 1972: 6) in Asia, the Middle East, and Africa. Wars of conquest and the daily experience of violence, domination, and subalternness inherent to the colonial project (Wesseling, 1997), gave rise to modern nationalisms and movements of resistance in Asia, as well as in other societies of the postcolonial periphery. These movements selectively appropriated features of Western "modernity" that could serve as instruments to end Western domination and restore or achieve political and economic autonomy.

Japan's late industrialization and modern state formation were, as we saw in the last chapter, the combined features of a uniquely successful response to deepening European intrusion in Asia and intensifying pressures from Europe and the United States in the latter half of the nineteenth century. Japan's industrialization and military successes showed a way out of subordination for other colonized societies, and seemed to offer the possibility of achieving political autonomy and technical modernity without compromising historically constituted identities.[4] Notwithstanding Japan's own late-nineteenth-century colonial expansion in Taiwan and Korea, many Asian nationalist leaders and movements, from Sun Yat-sen to Burmese and Indian

57

nationalists, looked to the Meiji state as a model for their own anti-colonial, state-building, and developmental efforts. "The example of Japan acted as a leaven for the Indian national movement, as a source of inspiration. . . . What had been possible in Japan during the Meiji restoration ought to be possible in colonial India as well. Japan had proved to early Indian nationalists that Asian nations need not be colonized by the West in order to modernize" (Van Bijlert, 2003: 38). They could invent their own autonomous paths. Indeed, some Indian radical nationalists, notably from Bengal, considered Meiji empire-building in Korea, Taiwan, and China as a counterweight to the West and a step toward pan-Asian unity.[5] After 1917, burgeoning communist movements and socialist-inclined nationalists looked to the Soviet Union as an alternate state-building and industrialization model, and as a source of international anticolonial solidarity. The clash between these alternate paths to independence and development shaped subsequent regional history.

The increasingly predatory character of Japanese imperialism in China and, during the war, in Southeast Asia undermined Japan's claim that it was acting in the interest of all Asians by building an empire of its own, thus alienating many though not all anticolonial nationalists (Narangoa and Cribb, 2003).[6] But, as we noted in the last chapter, Japan's territorial expansion in China and Southeast Asia had nonetheless served an important purpose by exposing the vulnerability of the European empires and loosening their grip. As a British diplomat noted in 1951: "Japan lost a horrible war but gained its great objective of the 1930s: to eliminate most Western power from Asia" (paraphrased by LaFeber, 1997: 307). To be precise, Japan not only helped to precipitate Europe's end of empire but also propelled the United States' emergence as the dominant power in East Asia— outcomes that ultimately and ironically made possible the restoration of the archipelago's prewar status as the premier economy in the region, and its emergence as a world economic power.

The weakening of the European imperial states gave a powerful impetus to Independence movements throughout Asia. From India to Vietnam and through Burma and Malaya, mass-based nationalist and/or revolutionary social forces, some of them armed and trained by the Japanese military during the war, challenged the remaining European colonial empires and sought to create strong independent developmental states. "From left to right, from Malayan communist to Indian businessman, everyone believed that planning and state intervention was the way of the future. Production and organization for war, whether by the Americans, the British Empire or the

Japanese, had given people a belief in the state's competence which would become almost a religion" (Bayly and Harper, 2004: 464). As subsequent Asian economic development would demonstrate, notably in East Asia, that "religion" was not enchanted: it had strong purchase on social reality, transforming a number of resource-poor formerly peripheral East Asian countries into modern industrial societies in the space of a few generations, and launching or stimulating industrialization in countries such as India. In China, two structurally similar but politically opposed authoritarian developmental states emerged out of the long anticolonial struggle and the 1945–1949 civil war on both sides of the Taiwan Strait. In Korea, likewise, rival developmental states were forged through war in the North and South. The anticommunist states in Northeast and Southeast Asia reappropriated and nationalized core features of the Japanese developmental state, whereas the People's Republic of China and North Korea chose the Soviet path to "forced development" and accelerated industrialization.

The Japanese rather than the Soviet developmental "model" ultimately prevailed in East Asia, including in China after the state capitalist turn in the late 1970s and the 1980s (Chapter 5). The third option, economic liberalism, was impracticable under revolutionary postwar conditions and a global situation that sociologist C. Wright Mills in 1956 acutely described as "an emergency without foreseeable end [in which] war or a high state of war preparedness is felt to be the normal and seemingly permanent condition" (Mills, 2000: 184).[7] Liberalism was never a serious option for regional capitalist states or for their hegemonic patron, the United States: war-making to avert revolution and assert U.S. regional predominance meant that the visible rather than the invisible hand, the state rather than the market, would have to guide urgent economic reconstruction and development. For reasons related to the global commitments and strategic vision of the post-1945 power elite, the United States ended up promoting statism and developmentalism in capitalist East Asia, however much this was at odds with liberal theory and official discourse, in a region in which it was constantly at war. Japan, South Korea, Taiwan, Singapore, and other Southeast Asian allies such as Thailand were able to profit to varying degrees from their enmeshment in the United States' globalized security system, and their willing involvement, mostly as resource providers and/or production and service centers, in the U.S.' anticommunist and counter-revolutionary wars in Asia. Conservative nationalist leaders, who converged with the United States' general strategic aims but who aimed to restore their own autonomy, more or less capably grasped the opportunities of what Japanese officials in the late 1940s described as the emerging "era of State capitalism" (Dower, 2000: 538). The discussion that follows puts U.S. choices and decisions in context and then examines the ways in which U.S. war-making shaped state-making in capitalist Northeast Asia.

The United States' East Asian frontier

The role played by the United States in East Asian developmentalism flowed from its aim to preserve and consolidate the country's new position as a dominant state with worldwide economic interests, and nearly global strategic reach, in a postwar world in revolutionary upheaval. The Second World War led to the definitive recentering of the world capitalist economy from London to New York, a movement that had been building since the late nineteenth century, when the United States became the world's leading manufacturing economy. It also opened the way for vast new international commitments and the internationalization of the new U.S. military-industrial apparatus. These outcomes had been anticipated by influential segments of elite opinion well before the U.S. became involved in combat in Asia and in Europe. They had envisioned that "a vast revolution in the balance of power" would occur that would make the United States "a dominant power in the world," supplanting Europe at the center and apex of a new international order (Golub, 2010). In 1940, Henry Luce famously coined the term the "American Century." After the tides of battle turned decisively in the Allies' favor in Europe and East Asia in 1942–3, this vision took concrete shape. U.S. political and military leaders began to think of the productive western and eastern regions of Eurasia as new "strategic frontiers." As Melvin Leffler has argued and documented, military planners supported by the White House "devised elaborate plans for [a post-war] overseas base system . . . [that] were defined as the nation's strategic frontier [and that] presupposed American hegemony over the Atlantic and Pacific oceans." The military and economic dimensions of the emerging configuration of power were inextricably linked. The internationalized security structure would undergird the U.S.-centered world capitalist system by securing worldwide access to raw materials and markets. In East Asia, the "Philippines were the key to Southeast Asia, Okinawa to the Yellow Sea, the Sea of Japan, and the industrial heartland of northeast Asia. From these bases on America's 'strategic frontier,' the

60

United States could preserve its access to vital raw materials in Asia, deny these resources to a prospective enemy, help preserve peace and stability in troubled areas, safeguard critical sea lanes, and, if necessary, conduct an air offensive against the industrial infrastructure of any Asiatic power, including the Soviet Union" (Leffler, 1984: 351).

The U.S. obtained its worldwide base system in 1945. Yet the critical global problems in the immediate postwar period were not military or strategic but rather social and economic. The United States had benefitted greatly from the war, which made possible the mobilization of idle capacity and vast economic resources. At war's end the U.S. economy accounted for half of world output and nearly half of world trade. The U.S. enjoyed crucial comparative advantages in agriculture and manufacturing, notably in the most advanced technologies, and had become the world's sole creditor. On the other shores of the Atlantic and the Pacific, the European and East Asian economies lay in ruins. In Europe, as Keynes noted at the time, Great Britain was threatened with a financial Dunkirk that was only avoided thanks to the 1946 conditional U.S. loan of 3.5 billion dollars that saved London but tethered the country to the United States. France, Europe's second-largest imperial state, was likewise tottering on the brink of bankruptcy and was in the midst of deep political and social polarization. Powerful mass-based communist parties had emerged from the anti-Nazi and anti-fascist resistance in France, Italy, and Greece. Occupied Germany was on the verge of economic and social collapse. In East Asia, revolutionary conditions were more advanced: mass unrest loomed in Japan where the economy had been shattered and the country faced famine. In Korea, now under U.S. tutelage like Japan, worker and peasant uprisings almost immediately challenged the postwar U.S. order. In Vietnam, where famine in the countryside during the Japanese-French regime had killed hundreds of thousands of people, deeply rooted revolutionary social forces led by Ho Chi Minh fused anticolonial nationalism and communist egalitarianism and proclaimed independence. In China, where the anticolonial war against Japan had morphed into full-scale civil war, the Chinese Communist Party likewise blended nationalism and egalitarianism in its victorious march to power.

The prospect of "famine, disease, anarchy and revolution" (Leffler, 1984: 363) posed two fundamental problems for U.S. policymakers as far as East Asia was concerned. The first was what to do with Japan and its former colonies, now under U.S. trusteeship; the second was how to deal with the European colonial empires that had been shaken by the war. Both problems were dealt with, the first far more successfully than the second, by abandoning the anticolonial and democratizing aims enunciated during the war and integrating capitalist East Asia in a "great crescent" of anticommunist containment stretching from Japan and its former colonies through Southeast Asia to the Middle East. The core strategic concept, articulated in a series of National Security Council directives, and made public in a speech by Dean Acheson in May 1947 in which he warned of "economic catastrophe" in Europe and East Asia and stressed the need to revive the "economic workshops" of Europe and East Asia, was to link raw materials production zones in the Gulf and Southeast Asia to the industrial centers and subcenters of the world capitalist economy in order to promote Europe's recovery and Japan's reconstruction. Japan, like the Federal Republic of Germany in Europe, were to be "satellites", as a 1949 report of the State Department's Policy Planning Staff put the matter, of the United States, without autonomy or identity. Germany would again become the industrial engine of Europe, Japan of East Asia. In effect, the U.S. aimed to revive Japan's prewar economic empire with the reconstitution of a regional division of labor linking South Korea, Taiwan, and Southeast Asia to the archipelago to meet its need for raw materials and markets. At the same time, in the context of revolutionary upheaval, the U.S. acted to briefly restore European empire in Southeast Asia.

European empires and illiberal states

Under Roosevelt, the United States had in principle imagined the dismantling of the French empire, and its placement under trusteeship. A more gradual decolonization of the other European empires was also envisaged, through a system of international mandates akin to the one set up by the League of Nations of 1919. Article 3 of the Atlantic Charter (1941), imposed on Churchill by Roosevelt, which was in continuity with the Fourteen Points of Woodrow Wilson stipulating "the right of all peoples to choose the form of government under which they will live," expressed U.S. preferences in the early phases of the Second World War. While the European colonial powers aimed to restore imperial authority after the war, the U.S. sought to fold them into a new U.S. order and have them follow the U.S. example when it committed to decolonize the Philippines and prepare the conditions for postcolonial self-government. The corollary of this objective was a policy of declarative and material support for the movements in East Asia fighting Japanese imperialism, including sustained contact with communist forces in China and Vietnam.[8]

In practice U.S. policy was far more ambiguous, since Washington sought to gain the favors of nationalist anticolonial forces, while simultaneously relying on the European imperial states that those forces wished to overthrow to help win the war in the Pacific. While the Roosevelt administration frequently invoked self-determination as an ideal aim, it was very careful not to stimulate revolutionary trends in colonial areas. Throughout the war the U.S. played a balancing act, leading nationalists to believe that it supported independence while assuring their wartime European allies, including the Dutch and French governments in exile, that they would recover colonial sovereignty. Senior planners resolved as early as 1943 not to "seek to destroy any existing empire or to dictate to other countries concerning colonial administration" (O'Sullivan, 2007: 105). As former Secretary of State Cordell Hull noted after the war, the U.S. never pressed "Britain, France or the Netherlands for an immediate grant of self government to their colonies . . . in view of the fact that we were seeking the closest possible cooperation with them in Europe. We could not alienate them in the Orient and expect to work with them in Europe." Working with the European imperial states was seen as crucial to the revival of the world capitalist economy and the consolidation of the U.S. position as the world's leading manufacturing and trading nation. Expressing a widespread but minority left-liberal view within U.S. state institutions, an American critic acutely observed in 1944: "Because of our silence we are tacitly committed to the support of an imperial system which will inevitably come to an end. . . . We appear to millions of Asiatics to be fighting [not only to defeat Japan] but to restore colonialism in Asia. . . . Failure to clarify our position in unequivocal terms may bring us into a future alignment where we shall be ranged with a dying imperialism against a united and vigorous Asia" (Salisbury, 1944: 237).[9]

The contradiction immediately resurfaced in the postwar period and was soon resolved in favor of the dying imperialism. Wartime anticolonialism gave way to a policy of propping up the French and British empires and associating them in a subordinate position in the counterrevolutionary wars and global containment effort that became the cornerstone of postwar U.S. policy. While the U.S. State Department noted "a lack of French understanding" and "dangerously outmoded colonial outlook and methods" in Indochina, it nonetheless sought to reassure the French government in 1947 that "we have fully recognized France's sovereign position in that area and do not wish to have it appear that we are in any way endeavouring to undermine that position" (Pentagon Papers, Vol. 1, 1971).

The U.S. tacitly condoned French misappropriation of European Recovery Program funds for the colonial war effort and, after Mao's victory in the Chinese civil war and the outbreak of the Korean War, funded over three-quarters of the French war effort until France's 1954 defeat at Dien Bien Phu—the second major European defeat at Asian hands after Japan's victory over Russia in 1905. As the U.S. Defense Department Study on U.S.–Vietnam Relations (known as The Pentagon Papers) shows, by 1956 the U.S. was already well on its way to supplanting France in Vietnam. Until 1948 the U.S. also turned a blind eye to Dutch government misuse of Marshall Plan aid in its failed attempt to restore the Dutch empire by force in Indonesia. As far as Great Britain was concerned, "the cold war worked generally to the advantage of the British empire. Despite its tradition of anticolonialism, the United States buoyed up the British colonial system for cold war purposes until the mid-1960s. American dollars helped sustain British power overseas by underwriting the balance of payment costs of British forces in NATO and, indirectly, the expensive British garrisons in the colonies. . . . The cold war thus gave the British empire an extended lease on life" (Roger Louis, 1999: 29). In its effort to contain rising communist influence in Asia and Europe, the United States ended up supporting faltering European imperial regimes that were recognized by lucid observers as contributing to revolutionary ferment.

Democratization in Japan, South Korea, and Taiwan endured the same fate as decolonization in Southeast Asia. Unlike Europe, where economic redevelopment was generally (though not always) associated with liberal-democratic politics, the United States' regional order in Northeast and Southeast Asia was primarily founded on illiberal states, linked and subordinated to the U.S. emerging national security state. During the Second World War, U.S. policy makers had planned to destroy the foundations of Japanese militarism by dismantling the social and economic institutions on which it had been based, decentralizing the political system, and sustaining the emergence of a strong Japanese civil society (trade unions, political associations, and so on) along classical liberal-democratic lines. In the initial phases of the occupation, "the Americans imposed a root-and-branch agenda of 'demilitarization and democratization' that was in every sense a remarkable display of arrogant idealism—both self-righteous and genuinely visionary. Then, well before their departure [in 1952], they reversed course and began rearming their erstwhile enemy as a subordinate Cold War partner in cooperation with the less liberal elements of the society" (Dower, 2000: 23). The purges of wartime officials

64

and the bureaucracy were stopped, as were plans for the dismantling of the industrial conglomerates that had supported the war effort (the *zaibatsu*). The United States simultaneously bolstered authoritarian conservative nationalist regimes in South Korea and Taiwan, which gained a firm hold on power, remaining in place until democratization in the late 1980s and early 1990s, respectively. In capitalist Southeast Asia, where anticommunist counterinsurgency wars were being waged, military dictatorships (Thailand, Indonesia) and authoritarian regimes (Philippines, Singapore) sustained by the United States became the norm.

Political liberalism and democratic idealism didn't mesh with U.S. situational imperatives and its hegemonic ambitions. Neither did economic liberalism. U.S. officials acknowledged in the late 1940s: "We could point to the economic benefits of Capitalism but these benefits are concentrated rather than widespread, and, at present, are genuinely suspect throughout Europe and in many other parts of the world" (Leffler, 1984: 369–70). The economic dimension of the reverse course in Japan was a pronounced shift from wartime visions of free trade and market mechanisms toward state capitalism and the concomitant revival of the bureaucratic system required to guide economic redevelopment. Well prior to the Korean War, the U.S. occupation authorities in Japan, who "ruled over their domain as neocolonial overlords" (Dower, 2000: 27) but had to rely on the Japanese bureaucracy to restart the completely devastated economy,[10] pushed for what General Douglas MacArthur, Supreme Commander of Allied Forces in the Pacific (SCAP), called "integrated approach across the entire economic front"—a statement that U.S. allies interpreted as meaning that the situation demanded that "free enterprise should be replaced by a directed economy" (Dower, 2000: 534). The approach suited conservative Japanese leaders animated by "intense [economic] nationalism" (LaFeber, 1997: 269) who were seeking to restore the country's economic autonomy and avoid economic colonization by reinventing and ultimately improving upon the institutional system and overall economic approach that had propelled Japan's industrialization in the late nineteenth and early twentieth centuries. Coinciding overall purposes overcame divergences over economic policy, and the United States ended up "parenting . . . the new mercantilist state" and reviving the wartime bureaucracy that the "Japanese [shrewdly] perpetuated to protect their new capitalism" after the end of the occupation in 1952. The result was a "greater centralization of economic authority than had been achieved at the peak of Japan's mobilization for war" and the institutionalization for a time of the most "restrictive foreign trade and foreign exchange control system ever devised by a major free nation" (Dower, 2000: 544–46).

Korean and Vietnam War booms

U.S. regional war-making proved a decisive factor in Japan's economic revival, South Korea and Taiwan's subsequent industrialization, and the consolidation or construction of strong developmental states. The Korean War generated a war boom that made possible the remobilization and redeployment of Japan's industry. The Vietnam War, in like manner, played a critical role in South Korea and Taiwan's industrialization. To a lesser extent, U.S. allies in Southeast Asia (Singapore, Thailand, Indonesia, Philippines) were incorporated in the United States' security system and became the recipients of U.S. infrastructure investments and military aid linked to services provided for the Vietnam War and for domestic counterinsurgency campaigns. From 1948 to 1962, with a marked acceleration after 1950, U.S. military and civilian aid in the form of grants and loans to capitalist East Asia totalled $18.9 billion (in 1960 dollars, or $149 billion in 2014 dollars), far less than the military and civilian aid packages to Europe during and after the Marshall Plan, but nearly five times more than U.S. aid flows directed to Latin America, and ten times more than flows to Africa ($0.8 billion). From the contemporary U.S. perspective, these expenditures were indispensable investments designed to secure "control of every wave in the Pacific Ocean," in Dean Rusk's memorable words. By lifting domestic political constraints and opening the way for the institutionalization of the internationalized power structures analyzed by Mills, the Korean War created a "tremendous if unexpected opportunity" to consolidate the United States' strategic positions in East Asia, making "possible the realization of NSC-68's vast plans to control these and other ocean waves" (LaFeber, 1997: 283).

If the Korean War thus "came along and saved us [the United States]," in Secretary of State Dean Acheson's formulation, it proved decisive for the mobilization and modernization of Japanese industrial capacity through U.S. "special procurements" programs that fuelled the country's economic recovery. Between 1950 and 1953, U.S. "special procurements" from Japan to support the war effort in Korea reached $2.3 billion, "a sum that exceeded the total amount of aid received from the United States between 1945 and 1951." An additional $1.7 billion flowed into Japan between 1954 and 1956 as

66

part of "new special procurements" (Dower, 2000: 542). In current U.S. dollars, special U.S. procurements between 1950 and 1956 totalled $40 billion. Special procurements stimulated infrastructure redevelopment and an array of industrial sectors, from

> metals products . . . to fossil fuels and machine oils, cloth and finished textile goods, medicines, vehicles, primary metal products, raw materials (excluding food and energy sources), non-metallic minerals, electric machines and installation parts, clothing and shoes, building components (including plumbing and heating), lumber and cork products, nonelectrical machinery, drink and tobacco, paper and paper products, food and rubber products . . . ammunition, light weapons, and napalm bombs . . . (and) facilities for a new influx of American military personnel and their families. (Dower, 2000: 541–42)

The war also created the opportunity for Japan to revive and modernize its heavy industry, for instance the shipbuilding sector that had matured after the First Sino-Japanese War, most of the facilities for which had been undamaged and which were rapidly remobilized to meet U.S. and world needs. By 1959, overall tonnage had recovered to 1937 levels and doubled in the following five years, meeting both military and commercial needs. By the end of the 1960s, Japan had become the world leader in shipbuilding (Chida and Davies, 2012). For Japanese postwar leaders, the Korean War was thus truly a "gift of the gods," in the oft-cited words of Japanese Prime Minister Yoshida Shigeru, making Japan into an indispensable hub in the U.S. regional political economy, leading to a sudden and (relatively speaking) extremely important increase of U.S. demand, matched by considerable U.S. financial flows. The most significant general effect was that it gave Japanese policymakers the latitude to reinstitutionalize and reinvent prewar economic statist policies and institutions that would otherwise not have found their place so happily in the post-1945 U.S.-centered capitalist world order.

Planned "free" economies

In much the same way that classical economic liberalism was shelved in Japan for overriding security reasons, and notwithstanding the complaints of some multinational U.S. business interests, the United States quickly abandoned laissez-faire economic reform policies in Taiwan and Korea, frontline states that were seen as essential to Japan's economic stability and prosperity and to the containment of China, hence to the United States' regional strategy and its global interests.

After assuming control of Japan's former colonies, the U.S. had initially aimed to reconstitute the basic features of the prewar colonial economic system in which Korea and Taiwan would become suppliers of rice and raw materials to Japan, and importers of Japanese light manufactured products. These plans, designed to reduce the U.S. economic "burden" by creating a partially self-sufficient Northeast Asian economic network, were not realized. South Korea refused to play the subordinate role that was implied in the suggested arrangement and, like Taiwan after the Kuomintang (KMT) came to power, chose instead to pursue autonomous industrialization, successfully playing on U.S. security concerns to extract vital resources for as long as possible from the new regional hegemon.[11] Despite early misgivings on the other shore of the Pacific, with recurrent complaints by free traders over the Asian allies' economic policies, situational imperatives consistently trumped ideology and purely commercial interests: as in Japan, the United States ended up supporting and indeed stimulating statism after 1950 in South Korea and Taiwan. Plethoric armed forces had to be kept up. The national success of allies needed to be demonstrated in the face of rival communist states that were industrializing with some success. North Korea achieved industrial growth rates that surpassed South Korea's in the 1950s and early 1960s due to a "pre-war industrial infrastructure more developed than that of South Korea," assistance from other communist countries, and the sacrifices of the population (Armstrong, 2010). Growth was also significant in Maoist China until the Great Leap Forward. Decried in theory, though very successfully implemented in the United States itself during the Second World War, state capitalism and military Keynesianism were the only serious alternatives to state socialism under conditions of permanent emergency.

While Japan harnessed the special procurements program to rapidly rebuild industrial capacity, the United States showered South Korea and Taiwan in the 1950s with various forms of economic and military aid that were not conditional on liberal economics, much less liberal politics. Between 1951 and 1960, U.S. economic grants to South Korea alone totalled $2.35 billion, to which one has to add military aid and expenditures for U.S. forces stationed in the country (Jung-en Woo estimates that annual average flows during the decade were close to $1 billion). Economic aid accounted for a significant share of GDP and for nearly all of the country's foreign exchange earnings in the 1950s. For lack of any private sector alternatives in what was still a very poor war-torn country (the country had an average per capita income of around $100 in 1950, a level comparable to countries such as Egypt or Nigeria), the inevitable result was a concentration of resources in programs that were run by the South Korean state. State-building effects of U.S. aid were even more tangible in Taiwan, where the KMT government, with the support of local U.S. aid officials, channelled U.S. aid to the public sector enterprises it had constituted through the confiscation of Japanese companies built during the colonial period. In effect, "the KMT perpetuated the Japanese-controlled wartime economy and industries, though on a larger scale due to massive U.S. aid which supported the influx of Chinese refugees and 600,000 Chinese soldiers" (Hsiao and Hsiao, 2000).

While aid to the KMT state prior to the Korean War was negligible, from 1950 to 1960 U.S. aid flows in the form of economic and military assistance exploded, reaching nearly $3 billion by the end of the decade: $2.75 billion in outright grants, and $140 million in loans. Military and military-related programs designed to bolster the U.S. regional defense structure accounted for 61 percent of the aid. More important from the standpoint of state capacity, the focus of economic aid was on investment in the "rehabilitation and expansion" of Taiwan's infrastructure and public sector industries (electricity, railroads, mining, communications, and so on) or public services such as compulsory education. Special funds, jointly managed by the KMT government and the U.S., were set up to "assist strategic industries or finance institutions to establish pioneering programs, and to support urgent projects for the overall national economic construction and social development" (Lee and Chang, 2014). At the same time, U.S. financial aid was used to import raw materials and capital goods from the U.S., primarily, but also, increasingly, from Japan. As in the case of South Korea, aid solved the foreign exchange problem of the 1960s and permitted Taiwan's controlled reintegration into international trade, though with a limited number of partners. As Nick Cullather nicely shows in his study of U.S. aid to Taiwan, the U.S. Economic Cooperation Administration (ECA) not only pragmatically molded itself to Taiwanese government preferences for a "planned free economy" explicitly modelled by officials on the Meiji state, but also "supported state-oriented policies systematically." This reinforced Taiwan's statist direction:

> By shoring up collapsing state enterprises, pioneering new methods of state control, strengthening the institutional base for planning, and co-opting groups—mainly the military—that opposed or disrupted change. ECA officials . . . restored state-owned factories to prewar production levels and collaborated with Chinese planners in creating the textile industry, one of the early triumphs of the Taiwan miracle. (Cullather, 1996: 9)

U.S. engineers, the ECA, and Taiwanese officials worked together to devise a program in which the U.S. furnished raw cotton to mills that produced yarn, cloth, and garments. These were bought by government agencies and sold through government distribution networks, generating proceeds in local currency for U.S.-supplied goods. Production levels, prices, employment, and profits were set by the state. As a result, "textile manufacturing catapulted ahead of Taiwan's other industries . . . KMT officials were using it as a model for how the state could incubate new industries by controlling imports and prices. The ECA had shown the KMT how to defy the laws of the market" (1996: 9). Tolerance and indeed encouragement of statism at the highest levels of the U.S. government was founded on the strategic assessment that the Republic of China's armed forces might, like South Korea's, find useful employment "in the event of a general conflagration," an eventuality that happily did not arise, but the prospect of which justified continued massive assistance after the Korean War until the mid-1960s (combined economic and military assistance totalled just over $1 billion between 1961 and 1967). When U.S. aid was officially terminated in 1965, Japan, a leading trade partner of Taiwan's that was already well advanced in its postwar economic ascent, took on the primary role in aid and investment on the island. Aside from two nasty but ultimately inconsequential skirmishes with the People's Republic of China in 1954 and 1955 in the Taiwan strait, and lucrative but relatively small-scale clandestine operations with U.S. intelligence agencies financed by the opium trade prior to and during the Vietnam War (1963–1973),[12] the KMT army was mostly unemployed during the U.S. wars in East Asia, from which the state and the economy nonetheless profited greatly.

The South Korean military on the other hand became deeply involved in the U.S. war in Vietnam. Just as the Korean War proved a "gift of the gods" for Japan, the U.S. massive and fateful escalation in Vietnam after the Tonkin Gulf Resolution (1964) occurred at the right time for the Park Chung-hee regime, which was under growing pressure from Washington to wean itself from U.S. aid and look to Japan instead for trade and investment. In 1962, South Korea still stood near the bottom of the world development hierarchy (ranked ninety-ninth by the World Bank at the time). Twelve years later, toward the end of the Vietnam War, South Korea had risen to the sixty-first rank and GDP per capita had been multiplied threefold. In 1965, Park Chung-hee signed the unpopular normalization treaty with Japan, overriding intense parliamentary and popular opposition, and simultaneously committed combat troops to Vietnam, at

U.S. request.[13] The "deployment of Korean troops to Vietnam . . . aimed not only at securing U.S. approval of [Park's] regime but also at maximizing the economic and security opportunities . . . by tailoring Korean goals to fit U.S. Cold War policy in East Asia" (Kim H-A, 2004: 102). Between 1965 and 1973, over 310,000 South Korean troops were deployed to Vietnam, more than other U.S. allies such as Australia or New Zealand, directly and indirectly financed by the United States (and, to a lesser extent, by Japan). As part of the deal, set out by the Brown Memorandum (March 4, 1966), the U.S. not only covered the "net additional costs of the deployment of Korean forces and of mobilizing and maintaining the activated reserve . . . and support elements," but also procured supplies from Korea for the overall military and Agency for International Development effort in Vietnam. The Memorandum committed the U.S. to increase technical assistance for export promotion and to provide new A.I.D. loans "to support economic development in the Republic of Korea."

The Vietnam War opened the way for a decisive phase of South Korean economic expansion, U.S. financing amounting to 2.8 percent of GDP in 1968. Total direct U.S. payments have been estimated at more than $1 billion between 1965 and 1970, but the impact of the war on Korean GDP was larger than that figure would suggest, in that it stimulated Korean industry and marked "the coming of age for some of Korea's largest conglomerates" that became involved in infrastructure projects in capitalist Southeast Asia (Woo, 1991: 94–87). As Jung-en Woo remarks: "the total cost to the United States of equipping and paying [Korean forces] was peanuts compared to what it would be for a comparable number of Americans," but those peanuts "went a long way to finance Korea's takeoff, and also to indulge Park Chung Hee into solidifying his dictatorial grip" (Woo, 1991: 93).[14] Capital transfers accounted for 70 percent of earnings, leading to a significant growth in South Korea's foreign exchange holdings, which increased steadily through the late 1960s. The outcome was a burst of growth: GDP growth averaged 12 percent per annum in the late 1960s, against 7 percent from 1962 to 1965, and around 4 percent during the Rhee years. The industrial production index rose from 100 in 1965 to 210 in 1968. According to a Korean analyst writing at the time, South Korea received the shot in the arm it needed to emulate Japan's success:

Both in terms of immediate and long-term effects on the nation's economy, the Vietnam war represents the watershed of the economic growth, just as the Korean war helped Japan leap into the expansionary

71

stage from its recovery period ... a new self-confidence and public buoyancy has begun to emerge. The new optimism is often expressed in the slogan "We can do it," meaning that Korea can duplicate what Japan has achieved during and since the Korean War ... on the strength of the Vietnam War, South Korea has now turned the corner towards a self-sustaining economy. (Kim S.J., 1970: 522)

The problem of peace

The rest of capitalist East Asia also benefited economically to varying degrees from U.S. procurement contracts for the war effort in Vietnam. Despite deep public opposition to the conflict and some misgivings within government about being too closely aligned with a war against other Asians so soon after the Second World War, Japan acceded under pressure to U.S. demands to use the country as a staging area for U.S. military operations in Vietnam. Though proportionally far less important than the Korean war procurements, which accounted for 63 percent of total Japanese exports in value, U.S. demand for goods and services to prosecute the war in Vietnam between 1965 and 1973 proved significant by stimulating the Japanese economy at a moment when it was facing a downturn. The Bank of Japan estimates that direct procurements (sales to the United States and South Vietnam) reached $292 million in 1967, rising to $467 million in 1970. Direct procurements were the visible component of Japan's economic involvement in the Vietnam War. In addition to this, "$150 million or perhaps even twice that in [publicly unrecorded] purchases of politically sensitive goods like weapons" that transited via Korea, Taiwan, and Southeast Asia have to be added to the total. Japan profited even more from exports of consumer products to "these countries because of general wartime prosperity ... [and from] exports to America to satisfy its boom time demand for consumer products." Overall, at the macroeconomic level, the war accelerated "Japan's recovery from the slump in 1965" (Havens, 1987: 86–95).[15]

The most significant effect for the subsequent developmental history of Southeast Asia, as Thomas Havens points out, was the regionalization of Japanese capital flows ($355 million of investment in 1969) and the major increase of Overseas Development Assistance (ODA) to the Association of South East Asian Nation (ASEAN) countries ($100–200 million in the late 1960s). By the early 1970s Japan had became the second largest investor in Southeast Asia, primarily in raw materials extraction for Japanese industry, as well as the leading purveyor of official development aid that was designed to promote

72

Japanese manufactured exports. The Southeast Asian capitalist states, all of which were characterized by authoritarian political systems and all of which were engaged in counterinsurgency campaigns against domestic revolutionary opposition, thus became the recipients of both U.S. and Japanese investment and military or trade-related aid. Singapore, which gained independence in 1965, became the Southeast Asian subcenter of U.S. ship and aircraft maintenance and repair, as well as a recipient of significant Japanese multinational investment. Thailand, the main staging area of regional clandestine operations since the 1950s and the main base of the U.S. Air Force during the Vietnam War, received over $3 billion in aid and income from the U.S. between the mid-1950s and the end of the war, and became one of the major areas of Japanese investment in Southeast Asia in the late 1960s and the 1970s. Thai national income more than doubled between 1960 and 1968, stimulated by U.S. military expenditure for base and infrastructure construction as well as soldiers' expenditures that created a "rest and recreation" industry. (Among other perverse gender and class side effects, war-making led to the development in Thailand and other parts of Southeast Asia of a vast sex industry for U.S. troops, serviced by lower-class women, that later morphed into the globalized Southeast Asian sex tourism industry.)[16] On average, U.S. spending between 1965 and 1972 amounted to 4 percent of Thai GNP and approximately 26 percent of the total value of exports. At their peak in 1968, U.S. expenditures accounted for 5.6 percent of national income and 40 percent of exports (Ouyyanont, 2001). Indonesia's "military modernization" (Simson, 2010) under General Suharto, whose blood-soaked seizure of power coincided with the U.S. escalation in Vietnam, likewise received substantial U.S. economic support and a good deal of Japanese investment.[17]

The question for East Asian states that had become deeply dependent on wartime U.S. financial flows was how to "withstand the inevitable reverberation which will result from peace" (Kim, 1970: 523). That problem was answered in part in the 1970s and 1980s through the restoration under post-imperial conditions of Japan's early twentieth-century role as the gravitational center of the regional economy. Japanese investment and aid to Southeast Asia had grown steadily in the 1960s. Nearly half of Japanese capital flows to developing countries by 1970 went to South Korea (17.3 percent), the Philippines (8.7 percent), Indonesia (7.4 percent), Taiwan (7.3 percent) and Thailand (5.5 percent). These flows constituted around 20 percent of growing Japanese global investment and were proportionally very significant for Southeast Asian recipients. While the

U.S. was spending lives and vast amounts of capital in a failed and extraordinarily destructive effort to subdue revolutionary nationalism in Vietnam, Japan seized the opportunity to restore its position in the region and reconstitute its hierarchical pre-1945 economic network, this time as a trading state rather than an empire. As Woo remarks, U.S. and Japanese aims, while not identical, were convergent and "regional hegemony was shared": "the Japanese desire to augment the market in Asia finally merged with American concern for the security and cohesion of non-communist Southeast Asia" (Woo, 1991: 90–91). The ASEAN countries benefited quite substantially from their integration into Japan's economic orbit. Japanese investments increased markedly in the 1970s and 1980s and were increasingly concentrated in the manufacturing sector. Thailand became a textile, chemical, automobile, metal, electrical, and electronics producer and assembler. Since the late 1980s Thailand has become the largest automobile production and assembly base for Japan in the region.

In sum, the regional development movement in capitalist East Asia after the Second World War is largely (though not solely) to be explained by the particular global circumstances that allowed for Japan's swift economic recovery, South Korea and Taiwan's subsequent industrial modernization, and the integration of the ASEAN countries into the U.S.' and then Japan's regional political economies. Given preexisting human capital and industrial capabilities, it is likely that Japan would have eventually recovered from the Second World War even in the absence of these factors, though far more slowly and with far greater difficulty. But there is no question that the extraordinary transmutation of total defeat into economic "victory" in the postwar period would not have been possible in the absence of a deep U.S. commitment to contain communism in Asia. Ironically enough, by nurturing developmental states that later became efficient industrial competitors, the U.S. unwittingly created the conditions for East Asia's rise as a contending center of the world capitalist economy.

Indeed, U.S. concerns shifted markedly in the 1980s when it became apparent that East Asian economic cohesion had gone quite a bit further than the U.S. had wanted or anticipated, due to a very large increase of Japanese industrial investments and the rapid growth of intraregional trade flows: the regional economic system led by Japan that Washington had consistently promoted in earlier decades came to be seen as a serious economic challenge, and a political problem insofar as it lessened the region's dependence on the United States, and hence the latter's ability to assert its policy preferences, shape frameworks, and obtain favorable outcomes. In the 1980s, Japan became a net world creditor and the leading creditor of the United States, which had become a net debtor for the first time since the late nineteenth century. East Asia's single market-trade dependence on the United States simultaneously began to decrease. In prior decades, the five most developed East Asian capitalist economies (Japan, South Korea, Taiwan, Hong Kong, and Singapore) had, in Robert Wade's sharp formulation, been "addicted to the American market" (Wade, 1990: 34). In the mid-1980s, the U.S. market still "absorbed more than one third of all Japan's exports, about forty percent of South Korea's exports, and forty four percent of Taiwan's exports" (Woo-Cumings, 1993: 149). Since then, however, deepening regionalization and China's emergence in the 1990s as a gravitational center of the regional economy have altered this configuration. The United States share of Japanese merchandise exports has fallen to 17.8 percent, while China's has risen to 18.1 percent; the U.S. share of South Korean exports has likewise fallen to 10.7 percent. Similar trends are observable in Thailand, Indonesia, Malaysia, and Singapore (WTO). These statistics do not tell the whole story of current East Asian trade patterns, since exports to China include components of manufactured products ultimately destined for the world market. However, the vulnerability induced by bilateral market dependence on the U.S. has clearly significantly decreased. The problem for East Asian countries today is how to manage the next stages of regionalization in an increasingly politically polarized environment, and how to overcome persisting uneven development.

— 4 —

DEVELOPMENTAL STATES AND FLYING GEESE

The post-1945 East Asian developmental state (a concept coined by Chalmers Johnson in his groundbreaking *MITI and the Japanese Miracle*, 1982) emerged in a global ideational environment very much unlike the past decades of neoliberal intellectual and policy ascendancy, one in which it was broadly accepted that the state played a legitimate and indeed indispensable role in economic and social development. Notwithstanding variations in policies and outlooks reflecting different institutional and political traditions, interventionist states and governed markets became a worldwide norm in the aftermath of the Second World War. In the Euro-Atlantic countries, one of the lessons, gradually unlearned since the 1970s, of the catastrophes of the first half of the twentieth century had been that markets left to their own devices exposed societies to acute social strains, creating the conditions for international conflict (Polanyi, 1972). While the United States pushed for the gradual liberalization of international trade through the General Agreement on Tariffs and Trade (GATT), in keeping with its postwar commercial interests, it was understood that the "capacity of states had to be preserved to defend their economies against external disturbances that would be injurious to employment and welfare" (Graz, 1999: xi), and to avoid or at least dampen revolutionary class conflict. This postwar understanding translated throughout the core capitalist countries into Keynesian welfare states, some of which, France most notably,[1] proved to be highly successful developmental states. It was also reflected in the international institutional architecture set up at Bretton Woods (Graz, 1999; Ruggie, 1982).

In the postcolonial South, it was universally taken for granted that the state had to be the determining agent of economic and social transformation. Like their counterparts in Africa (Nkrumah) and the Middle East (Nasser), the generation of socialist and nationalist anticolonial leaders that came to power in Asia after the war (Nehru, Sukarno, Mao Zedong and Chou en Lai, Chiang Kai-shek, and so on) all looked to state-led industrialization as the way out of subordination, dependency, and "underdevelopment." The contemporary appeal of the Soviet Union as an apparently successful model of accelerated industrialization, and revolution in China, made it all the more imperative for the United States to support conservative nationalist developmental states in regions of the global South considered strategically significant. Like the Federal Republic of Germany, though in quite a different regional environment shaped by revolutionary armed struggles and civil wars, Japan as well as its former colonies were incorporated in the internationalized security system of the United States, in which they prospered. While the U.S. hegemonic regime constrained their foreign policy autonomy, they had the freedom to choose their own set of economic institutions, and were given significant aid and mostly unhindered access, at least during the first decades of the postwar period, to the U.S. market (Hong Kong benefited from similar unrestricted access to the United Kingdom market). Bilateral market relations with an overwhelmingly dominant trade partner generated single-market dependencies, limiting their range of options and generating vulnerabilities to changes of U.S. economic policy. This became apparent when the U.S. shifted in the 1970s to unilateral monetary and managed-trade policies. But the global circumstances of the early postwar era also created the conditions of possibility for the implementation of state-led industrialization strategies that generated sustained growth and historically rapid industrial-technological catch-up. If they lacked international autonomy, the Northeast Asian developers "were left alone to pursue their economic development—which was highly nationalistic and state-led—even gaining preferential resources and treatment from the USA as a quid pro quo for security arrangements" (Kohli, 2009: 403). Johnson put the matter rather bluntly but accurately when writing, years after the publication of *MITI*: Japan lost "a big war to the right people at the right time" in world history (Johnson, 1999: 40).

The success of Japan, South Korea, Taiwan, or Singapore cannot be accounted for solely by global systemic factors. Economic modernity did not erupt *ex nihilo* thanks to a benevolent *hegemon*, like Athena out of Zeus' head. Developmental success as measured by gradually rising living standards, movement up the technological ladder, and upward international economic mobility, resulted from the interaction of global and endogenous factors: the local reinvention of historically constituted bureaucratic state forms that went on to structure and direct economic change, with the aim not simply to accumulate wealth but to engage in national renewal. If it deviates sharply from the ideal-typical "night watchman" state of classical liberalism, and the equilibrium models of neoclassical economic theory, the postwar East Asian developmental state should be understood as one among a number of capitalist developmental state forms whose specificities derive from the region's historical trajectory. The discussion in this chapter focuses on the political and social dimensions of East Asian developmentalism, rather than on the techniques of intervention, market governance, and institutional set-ups that have been exhaustively studied elsewhere (Evans, 1995; Wade, 1990; Woo-Cumings, 1999; Amsden, 2001). After reviewing the general question of the East Asian developmental state and its sources of legitimacy, it moves to discuss the regional diffusion of industrialization and the creation of a Japan-centric regional economic system in the 1970s and 1980s, and the sustainability of developmentalism in light of Japan's economic stagnation since the early 1990s and the 1997–1998 regional financial crisis.

Bureaucratic authoritarian regimes

Bruce Cumings (1999) helpfully defines East Asian developmental states as Bureaucratic Authoritarian Industrializing Regimes (BAIRs) with common characteristics: 1) A highly centralized bureaucratic administrative machine that arose out of two merged state cultures: the governing structures of the East Asian *ancien régime* (the Confucian state with its civil service structure), and late-nineteenth-century dirigiste European state forms appropriated in part by the Meiji elites; 2) Policies of education of the masses aiming to create a productive, disciplined, and docile workforce, allowing only restricted access to higher education to avoid politicization and expressions of dissent; 3) A system of management, surveillance, and control of the masses, ranging from intensive and tight forms of control and repression in South Korea and Taiwan, inherited from the Japanese prewar colonial system and reproduced by postwar states until democratization in the late 1980s, to the more politically liberal, but nonetheless not entirely pluralistic, postwar Japanese one-party state system; 4) A cult of the patriarchal state, the state being represented as having a national "essence" and incarnating the nation; 5) A political economy resting on industrial policies, administrative guidance of the economy, and neomercantilist international trade policies. Many of these features can be found to a greater or lesser degree in non-Asian late industrializing states (the authoritarian control of the masses in Latin America, for instance, or mass education and state interventionism in the German economy in the late nineteenth and twentieth centuries). The fundamental and still much-debated problem in a comparative perspective is how in the case of Northeast Asia these factors combined to produce extraordinary economic success.

Johnson's starting question coincided with renewed social scientific interest in the state in the 1980s,[2] and remains relevant today in light of China's re-emergence and worried debates in Western capitals about the uncertain future of the "liberal world order" erected in 1945. Johnson sought to identify the variables distinguishing the successful postwar Asian capitalist states that achieved in-depth economic modernization from both the liberal regulation state and the centrally planned command economies. The term "developmental state" designated relatively autonomous bureaucratic machines that designed and promoted a project of national development, purposefully intervening in and piloting the economy to produce industrializing outcomes, self-sustaining growth, and cumulative absolute and relative gains. These states are understood as having "a coherent and cohesive state apparatus" (Evans, 1995: 225) and strong state capacity: the ability not merely to "administer territory effectively" (Skocpol, in Evans, 1985), but to set strategic goals and initiate and steer socioeconomic change. State capacity is manifest in the ability to extract revenue and resources from society, to mobilize those resources to intervene effectively and in a *transformative manner* in key sectors, to provide essential public goods (education, health, welfare, defence, and so on), and to foster societal adhesion to the overriding goal or sets of goals set by state managers, which are presented as a national project and said to be coterminous with the national interest. Strong state capacity thus presumes that the state has sufficient autonomy to avoid being captured by private oligarchic interests, while at the same time having an institutional structure and administrative machine that is embedded in society and can translate strategic goals into effective change through selective and designed interventionism and appropriate public policies. Using Michael Mann's categories, strong state capacity presupposes that the state is endowed both with "despotic" power, or the "range of actions which the elite is empowered to undertake without routine institutionalized negotiation with civil society groups," and "infrastructural power" or deep state penetration into society (Mann, 1984). Peter Evans synthesizes the two in his conceptualization of "embedded autonomy" (Evans, 1995).

Drawing on the distinction between market and planned economies, and on the Japanese Ministry of International Trade and Industry's (MITI) own concept of a "plan-oriented market economy system," Johnson argued that the East Asian developers were "plan rational" states whose visible bureaucratic hand did not overwhelm or suppress markets but rather set "substantive social and economic goals" (Johnson, 1982: 19), creating or nurturing chosen strategic sectors through a pragmatic and adaptive use of policy instruments appropriate to different sequences of industrialization. The bureaucratic 'rationality' at work differs from the rationality of utility-maximizing individual agents in neoclassical theory and the "plan ideological" system, in Johnson's terms, of communist states. Penned at a moment when the United States was experiencing a prolonged moment of economic troubles, and Latin America was passing through a crisis of regional development, the problem was to account for Japan's "extraordinary and unpredictable" economic growth after the Pacific War, and the successful spread of its model to other parts of capitalist East Asia.

Japan had not only rapidly recovered prewar levels of manufacturing output and GDP, but also underwent dynamic and sustained growth over three decades that made it into the world's second largest economy by the late 1970s. Between 1946 and 1976 the Japanese economy grew at an annual average growth rate of more than 8 percent, compared to 6 percent on average for the world as a whole, and 5 per cent in Europe. During the period, the country became a manufacturing giant, its share of world manufacturing output rising from around 2.5 percent, equivalent to its share in the late nineteenth century (2.4 percent), to over 10 percent. Japan became the world's leading shipbuilder, and the second largest automobile producer, with a world share that rose from 1 percent to 23 percent. Japanese GDP was merely one third as large as France's in the early 1950s. By the late 1970s it was twice as large, and reached half that of the United States. Starting from lower levels, South Korea and Taiwan followed structurally similar developmental state models, obtaining similar high-intensity growth. South Korea's GDP grew at an annualized average of 9 percent in the 1960s and 1970s, and by nearly 10 percent during the 1980s and the first half of the 1990s prior to the 1997–1998 Asian financial crisis. Taiwan's GDP growth averaged 10 percent per annum from the 1960s to the late 1990s. With a few exceptions such as the Philippines, the more shallowly industrialized capitalist countries of Southeast Asia, most of which had been former European colonies, were drawn by Japan into the movement and experienced sustained intense growth.

The Japanese growth dynamic was made possible by the mobilization of preexisting social capabilities (institutions, industrial know-how, human capital). As we saw in the previous chapter, it was facilitated by unexpectedly favorable international circumstances. To re-emerge out of the destructions of the Second World War, the bureaucratic state initiated and managed a process of accelerated development (Johnson calls this "forced development") that, in contrast to Soviet or Latin American statist development, led to qualitative society-wide social and economic transformation. Forced development was a continuation, under new conditions and with different aims, of Japan's prewar and wartime economic mobilization, which had generated the administrative capabilities and scientific and industrial know-how that resurfaced after defeat. The developmental state that re-emerged out of the ruins of war thus drew on capabilities, knowledge, and experience built during the industrialization drive of the Meiji state at the end of the nineteenth century and the prewar mobilization of the 1930s. The bureaucratic administrative machine resumed control and leadership of the reconstruction effort. Prewar manufacturing experience, administrative capabilities, knowledge, and technological know-how accumulated over long periods in sectors such as textiles, shipbuilding, steel, and railways (and the arms industry), were drawn upon by the state bureaucracy as part of a national project of revival. Korea's industrialization in the prewar and war period, discussed in Chapter 3, provided similar foundations for the country's takeoff in the 1960s and 70s. As Alice Amsden emphasizes: "the depth of pre-war manufacturing experience" was a "necessary condition for post-war industrial expansion," distinguishing the successful postwar East Asian industrializers and a handful of Latin American states from other postcolonial countries that lacked it (Amsden, 2001: 121).

The United States' 1947 "reverse course" not only authorized but encouraged state managers to reproduce and improve the prewar system of administrative guidance of the economy, allowing them to engineer economic transformation and pursue the single-minded objective of protecting and growing the Japanese economy, and to rally society around a reindustrialization project. The array of institutions and the instruments of policy intervention that had been tried during the late 1920s and 1930s, reinvented for that purpose, constituted "a formidable set of institutions for promoting economic growth" (Johnson, 1982: 12). The policy frameworks and instruments designed by the Ministry of International Trade and Industry (MITI) involved a mix of policies and instruments that were flexibly adapted to changing circumstances: import substitution and export promotion measures, the selective allocation of scarce capital by the Japan Development Bank, making foreign exchange and technologies available to promising industries, trade-promoting tax subsidies, and the protection of a large state sector. Export-oriented industrialization was never a singular or dominant policy and was always implemented while retaining various instruments of tariff and non-tariff protection. In like manner, South Korea and Taiwan maintained relatively high tariffs and an "extensive array of non-tariff protective measures in selected sectors" until the mid-1970s, while industry benefited from export promotion measures.

The East Asian developmental state cannot be understood simply as a bureaucratic machine possessing its own rationality, acting outside of or above politics and social conflict. Johnson, as well as other authors, reads them as "quasi-revolutionary regimes" that aim to resolve situations of crisis (underdevelopment, late development and dependency, or defeat in war) through top-down mobilizations of society akin to those required in conditions of national emergency or wartime. Distinguishing between successful and unsuccessful developmental states, Johnson writes: "In the true developmental state . . . the bureaucratic rulers possess a particular kind of legitimacy that allows them to be more experimental and undoctrinaire than in the typical authoritarian regime. This is the legitimacy that comes from devotion to a widely believed-in revolutionary project"—in this case the "overriding objective (of) economic development" that would have been "present among the Japanese people after the war, the Korean people after Syngman Rhee, among the Chinese elites and the Taiwanese after Chiang Kai-shek acknowledged that he was not going home again, among the Singaporians after the Malaya Emergency and their expulsion from Malaysia, among the residents of Hong Kong after they fled communism, and among Chinese city dwellers after the Cultural Revolution" (Johnson, 1999: 52–53). Some holders of power, such as President Park Chung-hee (1961–1979), who presided over South Korea's industrialization, clearly enunciated their objectives in these terms: "I want to emphasize and re-emphasize that the key factor in the May Sixteenth Military Revolution (1961) was to effect an industrial revolution in Korea. Since the primary objective of the revolution was to achieve a national renaissance, the revolution envisaged political, social and cultural reforms as well. My chief concern, however, was economic revolution" (Park Chung-hee, 1963: 177).

82

Authoritarianism was the corollary of this "revolutionary" project. The autonomy of East Asian states would thus have allowed them to lift the decision-making obstacles encountered in pluralist political systems (fractious politics and dispersed authority) through the top-down mobilization of the population around economic objectives presented as vital to national survival. Yet the question remains how political and ideological mobilization in a highly repressive context was able to obtain popular adhesion to state goals. What founded the legitimacy of the state? Johnson's formulation in this regard is problematic: the unhelpful use of "true" to distinguish successful industrializers from less successful ones makes for a dichotomous reading that overlooks the industrial advances, however limited, of other prewar and postwar postcolonial states. More important, it suffers from a lack of specificity concerning how societal "devotion" to a "revolutionary" project which was coercively managed from on top and was not based on the powerful socialist ideals and hopes that had mobilized the masses elsewhere, and that entailed significant and lasting sacrifices—curtailment of political and labor freedoms, repression of consumption, and more[3]—was achieved. If "the power of the developmental state grew both out of the barrel of the gun and its ability to convince the population of its political, economic and moral mandate" (Woo-Cumings, 1999: 17), force and compliance better captures the nature of state–society relations than "devotion," a term that inadvertently veers toward the cultural explanations that Johnson otherwise explicitly and rightly rejects. Broad popular preference for industrialization and other economic improvements to increase well-being is hardly specific to East Asia. While Japan moved gradually toward democratization, though in a nonpluralistic political system characterized by the durable hegemony of the conservative Liberal Democratic Party (LDP), forced-paced industrialization in the cases of South Korea and Taiwan occurred at the expense of civil society, which was politically suppressed and silenced for many decades but was given the "right" (over time) to reap some of the gains of economic growth.

Building elite consensus across intersecting political and business interests is one thing. The ability of one-party states or authoritarian regimes to establish a hegemonic vision and generate compliance to wrenching economic and social change across social classes is quite another. State violence of varying intensity to discipline society and deal with the social turbulence accompanying industrialization, urbanization, and changes of class structure, has of course been a constant of all national capitalist transformations since the British industrial revolution. South Korea, nonetheless, stands out for extraordinarily brutal state coercion, from the fierce military suppression by the United States and its local relays of the mass peasant and workers' movements of the immediate postwar period, to the 1980 Kwangju massacre in which hundreds if not thousands of people were killed by the army, and beyond until democratization in the late 1980s and early 1990s (Minns, 2001). In Taiwan, thousands were killed during the 1947 popular uprising by the new KMT state, which enforced martial law ruthlessly for nearly four decades until democratization in the late 1980s. The Korean and Taiwanese "miracles" were built on enforced social docility achieved through the coercive mobilization of labor in the context of repression and silencing of social and political opposition. Over time, economic gains generated consent for developmentalism, though not to authoritarian rule. Two factors of state legitimation stand out: nationalism and the relatively fair distributional outcomes of growth.

Developmental nationalism

In Japan and South Korea, the state framed industrialization as a national project, fusing developmentalism and nationalism to rally populations behind official objectives and hence legitimate the state (the ethnic divide in Taiwan meant that nationalist KMT discourse regarding China could not operate in the same way). Laura Hein writes,

> Japan developed a distinctive and powerful version of developmental nationalism in the first decade after World War II.... Most Japanese regarded economic performance as definitive of national identity to an unusual degree, treating the economy as a cultural marker and assuming that culture functioned as an economic engine. In fact, ideas about the economy (as well as economic thought itself) operated as imaginative bridges that connected the Japanese and their nation to the rest of the modern world even as they constructed Japanese uniqueness. (2008: 448)

In South Korea, developmental nationalism served as a derivative of anticolonial nationalism, which was constantly mobilized in the North. General Park's statement cited earlier underscores the fusion in official South Korean discourse of the nation ("national renaissance"), the state, and development.

The mix of authoritarian politics and nationalist ideological mobilization led Atul Kohli in the first draft of his comparative study

84

State-Led Development in the Global Periphery to characterize the East Asian developmental state form as "neo-fascist," a term he dropped in favor of the notion of "cohesive-capitalist states" (Kohli, 2004: 19). This ideal type is not entirely satisfactory, however, as the author himself remarks. The concepts overlap uneasily given the similarity, if not identity, in his view, between cohesive and fascist states: "such cohesive-capitalist states resemble fascist states of yore, and thus are not very desirable political forms. Nevertheless, it is these states that have succeeded in generating considerable power to pursue rapid industrialization in the developing world" (22). They (and one presumes the current Chinese state) would thus be success-ful neofascist states. Besides the problems of definition and historical comparison it raises, is not clear how this helps to grasp the character of the Northeast Asian developmental state.

Insofar as it reflects an underlying aim of national (re)construc-tion or national renewal, not merely the quest to accumulate wealth, development has always been at its core a political project. Spurred by a troubled regional history of empire, subjugation, and war, Northeast Asian late-industrializers engaged in a race to catch up, gain upward economic mobility, and create some manoeuvring room for themselves in the regional and international systems. Catch-up, of course, is always relative to a dominant country or group of countries. The primary aim of the Meiji reformers who founded the modern Japanese state in the late nineteenth century was to avoid Japan's political submersion and overcome economic entrapment (the unequal treaties) by catching up with Europe and the United States, and becoming an empire pursuing its own regional *mission civilisa-trice*. After defeat, power political aspirations were, to use Hein's apposite term, "sublimated" in the developmental nationalism that succeeded, unlike the militarism of the 1930s, in making Japan into an economic giant, though not a world power properly speaking. As Dower emphasizes: "the only real avenue of postwar national-ism left to the Japanese leadership was economic. National pride—acute, wounded, wedded to a profound sense of vulnerability—lay behind the single-minded pursuit of economic growth that created a momentary superpower a mere quarter-century after humiliating defeat" (2000: 564). Reflecting their colonial experience as well as their positions in the post-1950 U.S. regional order, the objective of the South Korean and Taiwanese regimes was to catch up with Japan and buttress themselves in the face of rival Korean and Chinese com-munist states that were engaged in their own versions of forced-paced industrialization. The consistently enunciated aim of the Chinese leadership since 1978 has likewise been to catch up with the developed capitalist world, notably Japan and the United States, and, in more recent formulations, to "restore" China's early-modern position as the predominant power of East Asia (Chapter 5).

For postwar Japan, revival could not and did not imply regional, much less global political-power aims. If the late nineteenth- and early twentieth-century Japanese state sought power and wealth in the context of sharpening interimperial competition, postwar Japan (like the Federal Republic of Germany) abandoned power politics by adopting a U.S.-inspired constitution outlawing war as a means of settlement of interstate disputes, folding itself into the United States' regional political economy. (Since the 1990s this posture has been gradually evolving. Official pacifism has been losing traction and is unlikely to prove lasting given intensifying tensions and territorial disputes with the People's Republic of China over the Diaoyu/Senkaku islands and expressions of rising nationalism fuelled by competing historical narratives.) The other East Asian developing states likewise became subordinate semisovereign components in the U.S. security system, with precious little foreign policy autonomy. Notwithstanding its rhetoric of regime change in Mainland China, the Kuomintang never constituted a serious challenge to the Maoist regime, whose historical legitimacy derived from the anticolonial struggle against Japan as well as the cohesion born out of its revolutionary-egalitarian politics. Nor could South Korea hope to effect regime change in the North. Developmental nationalism became the means through which leaders and state managers could legitimate their rule by framing growth as a national project and channelling aspirations into international economic competition.

Social fairness and development

The relatively equitable distributional outcomes of accelerated development proved essential in legitimating the authoritarian state. One of the historically unusual features of the capitalist Northeast Asian developmental process (Japan, Taiwan, South Korea), which disconfirms the long-held assumption that sustained growth in its early phases is always correlated with high levels of social inequality (Kuznets, 1955), has been intense and sustained growth with relatively equal income and wealth dispersion. The World Bank underlined this feature of the "East Asian Miracle" in its well-known 1993 report that veered uneasily away from neoclassical orthodoxy. Under Japanese prodding, the Bank acknowledged the role of state

86

intervention and noted that sustained growth had been accompanied by declining income inequality and significant poverty reduction: "The high performing Asian economies have achieved unusually low and declining levels of inequality, contrary to historical experience and contemporary evidence in other regions" (World Bank, 1993: 29). To explain deviation from the supposed historic norm, the Brookings Institution later argued that relatively fair social outcomes reflected the need to meet the internal and external challenges posed by egalitarian socialist movements and avoid the rise of mass insurgencies: "Broadly similar historical circumstances led [regimes] to pursue shared growth as a strategy for legitimating its rule. The threat of communist takeover, made credible by a successful peasant-based communist revolution in China, induced regime leaders to pay close attention to the needs of the rural poor and the working class" (Campos and Root, 1996: 3). The contextualization is certainly pertinent, and there is no question that in the absence of political or social freedoms and the presence of potentially revolutionary mass movements, regime stability rested not merely on generating growth but on distributing its benefits relatively fairly.

The other side of the equation, as Joseph Stiglitz emphasises, is that relative socioeconomic fairness stimulated sustained growth: "Government policies that promoted greater equality contributed in no small measure to the remarkable growth (of the East Asian countries)." Because of public policies that increased domestic demand (land reform, universal education, lifetime employment, and so on) and that "contributed to political stability…high rates of growth provided resources that could be used to promote equality, just as the high degree of equality helped sustain the high rates of growth" (Stiglitz, 1996: 167–69). Amsden makes the same compelling point, emphasizing effects in both agricultural and industrial sectors: "Post-war land reforms in Japan, Korea, Taiwan…created some of the world's most equally distributed economies." At the same time, "countries that invested heavily in national firms and national skills—China, India, Korea, and Taiwan—*all* had relatively equal income distributions. A national economy may be regarded as an organic whole. The greater income inequality (by social class, race, religion, or region), the more that organic whole is fractured, and the more difficult it is to mobilize support for national business enterprises and firm-specific national skills. After World War II, greater equality induced a relatively large flow of resources from primary product production to manufacturing and also resolved a *policy paradox* in industry's favor" (Amsden, 2001: 18). (Social inequality is a crucial issue in China today, where the legitimacy of the Party-state rests on its capacity to maintain the growth momentum begun in the early 1980s, and will in the future depend on broadening its benefits beyond the new middle and upper classes and reducing disparities.)

In Japan, spectacular growth rates and increases in real income after 1955 were accompanied by a sharp decrease in inequality and the eradication of extreme poverty. While income inequality had been pronounced in the late nineteenth and early twentieth centuries, postwar public policies shifted the picture considerably. In a study of historical inequality trends in Japan, Moriguchi and Saez point to three postwar equality-promoting redistributive policies:

> First, the land reform in 1947–1950 mandated landlords to sell their farmland to tenants, eliminating virtually all large- and medium-sized landowners. As a result, the percentage of land cultivated by tenants declined sharply from 46% in 1941 to 9% in 1955. Due to hyperinflation, compensation paid to landowners in real terms was a mere fraction of the land value. Second, to finance large deficits, the government imposed [an] extremely heavy and highly progressive property tax (*zaisan zei*) from 1946 to 1951. The property tax affected approximately 13 percent of all households in Japan in the initial year, and taxed away on average 33 percent of their properties. For the top 5,000 households, more than 70 percent of their properties were transferred to the government. Third, under the dissolution of *zaibatsu* in 1946–1948, not only were ex- and current directors of *zaibatsu* firms expelled, but also their stocks were confiscated and redistributed to a large number of employees and other investors at a market price. Consequently, these three measures transferred a significant amount of assets (that is, land, stocks, and other household properties) from the higher to lower end of the distribution. (Moriguchi and Saez, 2008: 727)

During the high-growth decades that followed the Korean War until the 1973 oil price shock, "shared growth" was achieved through full employment and a social bargain based on lifetime employment in firms, a practice that constituted an indirect but generalized system of welfare that differed from the European welfare state but had similar protective effects (Bouissou, 2003). Postwar land reform in South Korea and Taiwan likewise played a crucial role in reducing poverty and social inequalities and opening the way for industrialization. "Korea, like Japan and Taiwan, shows relatively equitable income and land distribution during its rapid industrial growth. . . . This is a radical departure from 1945, when big landlords, 3 percent of the rural population, owned 60 percent of the land, while a vast 80 percent of the rural population were either landless tenants or semitenants (who both owned and leased) with little land ... this reversal from a highly unequal to a fairly equitable social structure primarily stems from land reform, first by the American military government in 1948 and second by the Korean government in 1950." Land reform not only reduced inequalities—in South Korea the Gini Land Index fell from 0.73 in 1945 to 0.38 in the 1960s—but proved essential to industrialization. It "removed a centuries-old stumbling-block to the rise of capitalist production relations by destroying a landlord centred agrarian class structure," thereby enhancing state autonomy, generating a pool of surplus labor for industry, and removing a "major source of rural unrest" (Shin, 1998: 1313/14).

International and domestic structures

In a comparative perspective, capitalist Northeast Asia's experience contrasts in this respect with the situation of Latin American countries, many of which witnessed significant industrial gains and sustained growth prior to and right after the Second World War thanks to import substitution industrialization strategies that were far more successful than the neoclassical and neoliberal narratives would have it (Amsden, 2007), but proved unwilling and unable to accomplish in-depth social transformation that would have created the conditions for comprehensive development. Differing social structures and institutional systems, on the one hand, and different patterns of external dependency on the other, constitute core variables accounting for these divergent developmental trajectories. Levels of socioeconomic inequality among the most extreme worldwide—concentration of land ownership, income, and wealth—have meant that relatively strong GDP growth in Brazil, Argentina, Mexico, and other capitalist Latin American countries in the 1950s and 1960s failed to generate the same kind of society-wide developmental outcomes achieved in Northeast Asia, as measured in rising general living standards and broad access to public goods such as quality education and health.

Reflecting the persistence of oligarchic social and economic structures inherited from the colonial era, which were reproduced after independence in the early nineteenth century, as well as "deeply engrained patterns of social exclusion and discrimination" founded on ethnicity and race (Ferreira et al., 2004: 121), socioeconomic inequalities in Latin America were and remain more pronounced than in Northeast Asia and even in some very large Southeast Asian countries such as Indonesia.[4] The Northeast Asian developmental states have income dispersions, as measured by the Gini coefficient, that are slightly higher than the European Union average after taxes and transfers (0.3), but significantly lower than the United States' (0.380). Latin American countries, however, with few exceptions suffer from income inequality levels akin to those in Sub-Saharan Africa, a world region that is generally characterized by the absence of modern bureaucratic states and by the prevalence of weak and/ or predatory states. Levels of land distribution inequality are among the world's highest: based on the last available 1990 Food and Agriculture Organization (FAO) census, the median landholding Gini coefficient in Latin America was 0.85 (1990 census), against 0.48 in East Asia in aggregate, with much lower levels in the Northeast Asian developmental states (South Korea's landholding coefficient averaged slightly above 0.3 between 1960 and 2000). Though greater landholding equality does not automatically translate into higher productivities, and land redistribution has weaker overall economic effects in highly urbanized societies, it is widely recognized that, like other equality-promoting measures, it generates greater social cohesion and has wider empowerment effects on the poor, favoring industrialization and broader development (Sen, 1999). Oligarchic land ownership structures, and high levels of income inequality resembling Latin America's, help to explain the persistent growth gap between the Philippines, for instance, and its neighbors.[5]

Latin America's external environment tended to reinforce rather than change existing social structures. An uneasy proximity with the United States has, since the mid-nineteenth century, shaped the Latin American political economy in a dependent direction, a situation that the various *dependencia* theoretical frameworks cogently explain. Whereas the United States encouraged land reform in Northeast Asia in the immediate postwar period, and promoted developmental states that shielded themselves substantially from world market forces, there were no overriding strategic incentives to change landowning or income distribution patterns in Latin America. To the contrary, U.S. hemispheric economic policy was long driven by agricultural and resource-extractive multinationals that had a vested interest in the preservation of oligarchic social structures, and whose investments were protected and enforced through both overt and covert U.S. political pressures. On this point, Kohli rightly emphasizes the relative superiority of the "nationalist capitalist model of development" pursued by states in Asia with a "measure of national autonomy from global constraints" over the "dependent capitalist economies characterized by heavy dependence on external forces" prevalent in Latin America (Kohli, 2009: 387). In short, variations of outcomes reflect the interaction between domestic social structures and systemic or international factors and pressures.

Flying geese

East Asian development is also singular in that it was significantly favored by Japan's role as a regional economic driver. I emphasized in the introductory chapter of this book that the intensity, spatial scope, and duration of the developmental dynamic begun in Japan after the Second World War meant that a general *movement* has been at work, unfolding over time and space to nearly all of East Asia. Regional economic integration, which should be distinguished from regionalism as a political or ideological project, has steadily deepened since the 1970s, leading to a concatenated regional division of labor embedded in wider transnational production and supply chains. Regionalization was driven until the late 1980s by successive waves of Japanese industrial relocations to the NICs and to Southeast Asia, a process promoted by purposeful political efforts to create the foundations of a Japan-centered political economy. This led to a diffusion of industrialization and a general, albeit uneven, rise up the development ladder in East Asia. Since the late 1990s the gravitational center of regionalization has shifted to China, which was already enmeshed in the regional economy through historically constituted Chinese commercial networks, and which has become a hub of regional growth and of new regional and transnational chains of production, trade, and investment.

The sequential diffusion of industrialization from a dominant capital-intensive growth center to more labor-intensive economies, leading to regional division of labor whose different components experience sequential upgrading, has been characterized by Japanese scholars as "interdependence among regionally clustered economies" (Kasahara, 2004). This concept of East Asian regionalization derives from Kaname Akamatsu's work on changes in the productive profiles of late industrializers seeking to catch up with more industrially advanced countries. He argues that the former moved in staggered stages from imports of manufactured products, to import-substitution production, and then to the export of manufactured products, thanks to technology appropriation, learning, and appropriate public policies. He famously likened this three-stage process of rationalization and diversification of production to a flying geese formation in which wild geese fly in orderly ranks behind a lead goose: "Wild geese fly in

91

orderly ranks forming an inverse V, just as airplanes fly in formation. This flying pattern of wild geese is metaphorically applied to three time-series curves each denoting import, domestic production, and export of the manufactured goods in less advanced countries."

Akamatsu applied this framework to the propagation of industrialization in a regional setting: "with regard to a wild-geese-flying pattern sequence, the underdeveloped nations are aligned successively behind the advanced industrial nations in the order of their different stages of growth in a wild-geese-flying pattern. . . . The less-advanced 'wild geese' are chasing those ahead of them, some gradually and others rapidly, following the course of industrial development in a wild-geese-flying pattern" (Akamatsu, 1961: 208). In this extrapolation from the domestic product cycle model of a single late industrializer seeking to catch up with more developed countries, a regional division of labor constitutes itself around a dominant center that shapes the industrial pathways of "followers." As the lead economy moves toward a technological and production frontier, diffusion proceeds through relocations of lower value-added production manufacturing to less developed economies incorporated in the regional cluster. The latter develop new social capacities, hence potential for ascent, through the accumulation of capital and the acquisition of knowledge and know-how. The hypothesis was that under certain framework conditions coherent regional formations constitute themselves, generating productive complementarities.

Insofar as it leads to upward international mobility for all incorporated countries, the framework suggests that outcomes are distinct from the contra-developmental dependencies observed in exploitative colonial core–periphery relations, or indeed in market-determined outcomes deriving from the mechanisms of static comparative advantage. Like product-cycle sequencing inside a country, the countries integrated in such formations are described as passing through successive phases of industrialization, moving from traditional crafts to light industry, to heavy industrialization, and ultimately to frontier technologies. The process of catch-up therefore leads to constant internal restructuring based on dynamic comparative advantage, in which the different economies inserted in the regional network displace their dominant productive activities from one technical level and mode of productive organization to another. As the more technologically advanced countries move up the value chain, this induces a relocation of lower value-added production toward countries with labor-intensive profiles, which in turn are swept up in logics of internal restructuring.

At the time that Akamatsu was writing, the hypothesis had not really been tested. Japan's post-1945 moves to reconstitute a regional economic system took off in the mid- to late 1960s. To overcome the political obstacles resulting from empire and war, Japanese firms worked through long-established local business groups, notably entrepreneurial Chinese networks. By the late 1960s and early 1970s, however, Japan accounted for a significant share of foreign direct investment and development aid flows to Northeast and Southeast Asian capitalist countries. Japanese investments and development aid became significant in Southeast Asia, with nearly half of FDI and 45 percent of total aid going to the ASEAN countries stemming from Japan from 1969 to 1981. The deepening of regionalization in the 1980s was spurred by new international pressures and changing global monetary circumstances. Japanese overseas development assistance tripled from $703 million in 1980 to $2.18 billion in 1989. A new wave of investments occurred as a result of the coordinated response of Japanese multinational companies and of government to the 60 percent appreciation of the yen after the Plaza Accords of 1985, which pushed multinational Japanese manufacturing firms to relocate activities worldwide to restore their price competitiveness, notably in the rest of East Asia. (East Asian regionalization was thus unwittingly stimulated by the United States, which pushed through the Plaza Accords to restore the price competitiveness of U.S. industry.)

The relocation movement to the rest of East Asia, including China, was promoted at political level by influential public figures. Former foreign minister Saburo Okita presented the emerging division of labor in the "Pacific region" as the expression of a "flying geese pattern of development" or "catch-up development.". He distinguished the latter from the "vertical division of labor such as prevailed in the nineteenth century to define relations between the industrialized country and the resource-supplying country or between the suzerain and the colony. In the Pacific region, for example, the United States developed first as the lead country. Beginning in the late nineteenth century, Japan began to play catch-up development in the non-durable consumer goods, durable consumer goods, and capital goods sectors in that order. Now the Asian NICs and the ASEAN countries are following in Japan's footsteps" (quoted in Kojima, 2000). In 1987, the Japanese government announced a New Asian Industries Development Plan, offering "investment incentives for selected Japanese industries to relocate to ASEAN countries" involving a "large number of [participating] government agencies" (Katzenstein, 1993).

By 1991 Japan had become the leading investor in Asia, ahead of the United States in, by order of importance: electric, electronics, and information technology; chemicals; metals; textiles; and transport equipment. The further appreciation of the yen in the first half of the 1990s accentuated the relocation trend. Between 1986 and 1995, the share of Japanese manufacturing FDI in the developing countries of ASEAN (ASEAN 4: Indonesia, Thailand, Malaysia, Philippines) and China, as a percentage of global Japanese manufacturing FDI, rose from 6 to 35 percent (subsequently falling to 19.9 percent in 2000). After a brief decline in the early 1990s, FDI flows to the NICs also grew between 1993 and 1997. Between 1985 and 2000, Japanese investment in the NICs totalled 1,892 billion yen, with a further 3,541 billion yen invested in the ASEAN 4, and 1,551 in China (of which 1,326 billion was allocated between 1993 and 2000, after a sharp two-year decline following the Tiananmen events). At the same time, subsidiaries of Japanese multinational firms implanted in the rest of Asia invested heavily in infrastructure and equipment to resolve bottlenecks hindering growth and exports (Pottier, 2003; Katzenstein and Rouse, 1993; Pempel, 1999). Investments in China, which were negligible in the 1980s, expanded rapidly in the 1990s and have massively increased over the past two decades. As a result, regional production chains were constructed linking the highly capital-intensive countries of East Asia with each other and with those having more labor-intensive profiles. Japanese investment in developing Southeast Asia has been supplemented since the 1980s by flows from Korea, Taiwan, Hong Kong, and Singapore, as the latter moved up the technology and value chains.

Fluid hierarchies or dependency?

The flying geese hypothesis is thus both a development theory and a theory of regional economic integration through the "orderly trans-formation of economic activities among participating economies" and the "orderly transfer of industrial activities among national economies along the regional hierarchy" (Kasahara, 2004: 8). It stipulates absolute gains of participating economies, a hypothesis empirically confirmed by strong growth, rising overall living stand-ards, and declining poverty in third- and fourth-wave countries. More controversially, it suggests that hierarchies within the regional economic system are fluid. Relative gains are possible through learning, technological appropriation, and structural changes of productive profiles (Ozawa, 2005). While this has indeed occurred in the cases of

94

South Korea, Taiwan, Singapore, and Hong Kong, it is not yet estab-lished that similar sustainable outcomes will be possible in middle-income Southeast Asian countries that remain heavily dependent on external investment, technology, and know-how. Critics (Bernard and Ravenhill, 1995) rightly pointed in the 1990s to persisting Southeast Asian dependencies: "the diffusion of manufacturing in East Asia has increasingly been characterized by shifting hierarchical networks of production linked both backward to Japanese innovation and forward to American markets for the export of finished goods" (Bernard and Ravenhill, 1995: 172). The dependency has not been of an enclave type, however, in which locally captured surplus is trans-ferred out of the producer country, without technological diffusion or local accumulation of knowledge and capital. Nor have Japanese investments been solely concentrated in industries requiring only low skills and limited local inputs, as in the "MNC economies" discussed in dependency theory. As Claude Pottier shows in his analysis of regional variations in the globalization of production, the integration of regional economies in the Japanese productive system encouraged an "evolution towards higher value-added activities in the NIEs [and] direct transfers of evolved technologies towards the ASEAN-4 and China" (Pottier, 2003: 118). While Southeast Asian modernization remains well behind South Korea's or Taiwan's, it has generated capacities to "implement evolved foreign technologies and cannot therefore be characterized as 'technology-less'."

> The international division of labour put into place by Japanese multi-nationals in East Asia remains very hierarchical. For the most part, the Research and Development activities and the launching of new products remain concentrated in Japan. But the activity of production in East Asia cannot be completely separated from the activity of development, including in the low wage countries of ASEAN. . . . The relocation of Japanese manufacturing industry in Asia concerns all categories of wage earners: workers, employees, technicians and engineers. (136)

The question nonetheless remains whether Southeast Asian devel-opers, for whom growth was made possible in no small part by bureaucratic-state institutions of their own (Amsden, 2001), are in a position to replicate the achievements of the NICs and move from their current intermediate position in the regional economic hierarchy toward more systematic improvements of general living standards, and endogenous scientific and technological mastery. This would require a shift from the dominance of a few large business groups toward greater economic pluralism, the development of rural areas, significant infrastructure improvements, sustainable urbanization, increased investment in R&D, and systematic efforts to reduce social inequalities that polarize society. Southeast Asian societies are characterized by high levels of inequality, with Gini coefficients of 53.6 for Thailand, 44.8 for the Philippines, 46.2 for Malaysia, and 47.8 for Singapore. Indonesia stands out as a fairer society in terms of income distribution, with a Gini coefficient of 36.8 in 2009.

In many cases, the sociopolitical conditions for further upgrading are missing. Sociopolitical polarization has become a significant problem in Thailand, a major hub of Japanese regional production networks, and one of the most economically dynamic countries of ASEAN until recently. The economic transformations of past decades have generated sharp sociopolitical tensions as new social classes and forces have emerged, demanding a greater share in the country's gains and political voice. The sociological changes associated with industrialization—the rise of a working class and the insertion of the peasantry into transnational production and trade networks—have not been matched by institutional or political change: democratization since 1992 has been superficial at best, with repeated military interventions in domestic politics to uphold a basically feudal social order. Since 2006, political violence has intensified, reflecting the tension that has emerged between the traditional and still dominant semifeudal system of authority that has governed the country since the 1930s, in which interlocked aristocratic, business, and military elites and castes reproduce themselves through opaque networks of influence and power, on the one hand, and new social actors (subaltern but increasingly self-conscious segments of society as well as newer business groups) on the other. Industrial capitalism and deepening insertion into global flows have undermined the old sociopolitical order, but a new one has yet to emerge. Worsening domestic political conditions (the military coup d'état of May 2014 and the installation of what properly should be called a despotic regime) are coupled with uncertainties regarding the international economic and political-strategic environment in which ASEAN finds itself. Even if Thailand is more troubled than its neighbors, the developmental path forward for developing Southeast Asia is far from clear. The ASEAN's growing enmeshment in the emergent Sinocentric trade system generates ambiguous effects: China serves as an export market but also acts as a competitor in the low and middle parts of the value chain.

Crises and the future of developmentalism

Japan's prolonged economic stagnation since the financial crisis of the early 1990s and the 1997–1998 regional financial crisis raise broader questions about the sustainability of East Asian developmentalism and the future of regionalization. Theory is value-laden, and it is important to distinguish between prescriptive critiques that reject state-led development a priori and more thoughtful analyses of its strengths and limits. The former, primarily from Western authors and the International Financial Institutions (IFI), reflect normative concerns about the challenge East Asian developmentalism posed (and poses) to the intellectual hegemony of liberal theory and its foundational assumptions about actor rationality and market optimality, policy concerns over the strategic implications of the emergence of an increasingly autonomous East Asian regional economic system, and cultural concerns about Western decline and "alien" success.

Japan was integrated into the postwar U.S. system on the understanding that "Japan's sun was to rise high but not too high; high enough to cause trade problems for the [Western] allies in declining industries" (Cumings, 1999: 213) but certainly not so high as to become a competing center of the world capitalist economy. In the 1980s and early 1990s, Japan's industrial performances, and concerns over the "sharp growth of Japanese influence and power in Asia" (Katzenstein, 1993: 73), created deep unease in the United States (and Europe) where angst over decline had become pervasive (Golub, 2010). Samuel Huntington warned of an "economic cold war" between the U.S. and Japan: "The issue for the United States is whether it can meet the economic challenge from Japan as successfully as it did the political and military challenge from the Soviet Union. If it cannot ... the United States would no longer be the world's only superpower and would be simply a major power like all others" (Huntington, 1991: 16). Lawrence Summers expressed the same view when affirming, "an Asian economic bloc with Japan at its apex is in the making. This raises the possibility that the majority of American people who now feel that Japan is a greater threat to the U.S. than the Soviet Union are right" (quoted in Katz: 1998: 9). Japan's economic success, according to Robert Gilpin's contemporaneous assessment, constituted a challenge to the Western-centered world order. Noting a "considerable shift" of the center of economic power toward East Asia, he wrote: "The magnitude of the task for the world economy to absorb the emerging Asian and other developing economies may perhaps be best appreciated by considering the continuing and far from resolved challenges posed for the United States and Western Europe in adjusting to the extraordinarily rapidly growing economic power of Japan. If these other rich economies have found it difficult to come to terms with Japan's highly productive millions of workers, it will certainly be even more daunting to make room in the world economy for China's hundreds of millions. . . . But for the immediate future, the foremost challenge to the international status quo comes from Japan and its astounding economic success" (Gilpin, 1995: 12). Joseph Nye wrote, somewhat more cautiously: Japan's "form of communitarian capitalism, its prowess in process technology, and its broad inroads in several high technology sectors directly challenge the economic competitiveness of many of the United States' most strategic industries [and provide] an attractive economic model for industrializing countries in Asia . . . to emulate" (Nye, 1993: 1–2).

A reversal of perceptions occurred when Japan plunged into a long period of economic stagnation after the financial bubble burst in the overinvested FIRE (Finance, Insurance, Real Estate) sector. Irrational fears of Japanese economic supremacy gave way to equally unfounded claims that the bureaucratic-state system that had been at the source of Japan's success was suddenly revealed as the structural cause of the country's crisis. It would have demonstrated, in the condescending words of a U.S. author, that the "Japanese model was not a different type of capitalism but a holdover from an earlier stage of capitalism. It is the spectacle of a country vainly trying to carry into maturity economic patterns better suited to its adolescence" (Katz, 1998: 6). The subtext of this orientalist caricature conveyed the idea that the East Asian latecomers to modernity had been put back in their rightful ancillary place. At the time, Woo-Cumings pointedly noted: "The East Asian countries are perceived to be in but not of the world, free-riding on defense, and predatory in economics . . . the contemporary rancor of representatives of this view indicates a frustration about Asians getting off the reservation and doing their own thing, so to speak" (Woo-Cumings, 1993: 139). The acute 1997–1998 regional financial crisis, rooted in capital account liberalization that led to unsustainable debt accumulation in Southeast Asia and South Korea, considerably amplified this set of perceptions. "One of the most important consequences of the crisis," Marc Beeson wrote, "was to subject the entire East Asian development experience to a rapid and generally unfavourable reappraisal." The theoretical critique was prescriptive:

The distinctive role of the region's interventionist political elites was the object of particular attention as what were formerly seen as "strong" states were now depicted as centers of self-serving "crony capitalism." This remarkable change in the conventional wisdom about East Asian modes of governance was mirrored in, and drove, an externally imposed reform agenda—designed primarily by the International Monetary Fund with encouragement from the United States—which was intended to completely reconfigure much that was distinctive about East Asian developmental states. (Beeson, 2004: 30–31)

U.S. and European behavior during the crisis clearly suggests the intent to dismantle the institutional systems that had made East Asia's re-emergence possible. In its early phases, the U.S. Treasury brutally and myopically vetoed a Japanese proposal to create an Asian Monetary Fund (AMF) that would have pooled regional financial resources and provided urgently needed liquidity to Southeast and Northeast Asian countries facing massive and time-compressed capital outflows, for fear that it might become the institutional kernel of an autonomous regional financial system rivalling the International Monetary Fund (IMF). The IMF waited on the sidelines until it became clear that chain reaction effects were spreading to the heart of the world financial system and then imposed draconian fiscal policies that transformed a liquidity crisis into a solvency crisis (Stiglitz, 2002), the adjustment costs of which were transferred exclusively to debtor countries (and hence their populations). Structural adjustment programs—privatization and market liberalization—struck at the heart of the institutional set-up of the developmental state (Golub, 1997). In the United States, the crisis was interpreted as a defining moment in the balance of world economic power: it would first have

> ravaged the credibility of a supposedly distinctive East Asian or Japanese model of economic growth based on cooperation between conglomerates ... and astute government officials. Collapsing Asian markets revealed the crony capitalism beneath the surface of East Asia's "developmental state". . . . [Second,] falling growth rates and mounting losses in dollars jeopardized the resources and self-confidence that leaders of the Sinic world would need were they to challenge the West. Third, the crisis damaged the Asian leg in the tripod model favored by those who expected power after the Cold War to coalesce around three regional blocs, each with its respective hinterland and hub. (Emmerson, 1998)

According to Alan Greenspan, then chairman of the U.S. Federal Reserve, the crisis represented a defeat of state-led modernization models and an "important milestone in . . . a significant and seemingly inexorable trend toward market capitalism" (Greenspan, 1998). In East Asia, however, Western behavior was interpreted as predatory, part of a design to weaken state autonomy and use the opportunity to acquire valuable local assets at much depreciated prices. Eisuke Sakakibara, Japan's deputy finance minister at the time, rejected suggestions that it was properly speaking an "Asian crisis"; rather, it would have been the expression of a "global crisis of capitalism" (Golub, 2010).

These clashing interpretations shaped subsequent evolutions, notably by stimulating nationalist backlashes in East Asia that translated into a "counterweight strategy" to reduce regional vulnerability to exogenous pressures and shocks, and gain greater autonomy by building up currency reserves, loosening the control of the IFIs on the region, and setting up mechanisms of regional monetary protection (Dieter and Higgott, 2002; Golub, 2010). A flurry of initiatives followed: the 2000 bilateral swap arrangements among central banks that were conceived as a first step toward the creation of a regional financial institutional to pool currency reserves (the "Cheng Mai initiative"); the 2003 ASEAN+3 (China, Korea, and Japan) decision to establish an Asian Bond Fund, initially capitalized with $1 billion and designed to channel reserves held by Asian central banks back into the region rather than to global markets; the 2005–2006 exploratory discussions at the Asian Development Bank (ADB) to set up an Asian Currency Unit (ACU) indexed on participating currencies and aiming to harmonize regional monetary policies; and the 2008 announcement by Finance ministers from thirteen Asian countries to build on the Cheng Mai initiative and create a $80 billion fund to cushion regional currencies in the event of global market swings. Some of these initiatives have not matured: the ACU idea, for instance, was dropped due to strong U.S. pressures on Japan, which had initially supported the proposal. The broader goal of gaining autonomy from the IFIs did gain traction, however, as did the idea of gradually replacing the U.S. dollar as an instrument of intraregional trade settlement and investment.[6] Institution-building is currently maturing, as seen in the 2014 creation, at China's initiative, of the Asian International Investment Bank (AIIB) (discussed in the concluding chapter of the book).

With hindsight, contrary to some expectations that the region would become ensnared in new dependency relations in a global economy dominated by the United States (Berger, 1999), East Asia gained greater economic and financial autonomy from the United

States and the IFIs than at any time in their postwar history. Marc Weisbrodt argues: "The Asian crisis set in motion a process in which the IMF has lost most of its power over middle-income countries. This is a sea change in the developing world, and it is likely to be the most lasting impact of the crisis" (Weisbrodt, 2007). By stimulating nationalist responses against what was perceived as Western intrusiveness, the crisis paradoxically advanced regionalization by expanding it to new domains.

China's new regional role

The effects on developmentalism per se have been more ambiguous. Careful scholarly critiques have pointed to the problem of sustaining developmentalist policies and statist economic institutions in a globalized world economy structured around transnational production and value chains. The crisis raised the "big question whether the distinctive forms of capitalism found in the region, of which the DS is such a prominent part, can survive in the face of sustained reformist and competitive pressures ... the intense pressure to conform with pervasive international regulatory standards and liberalise key sectors of the domestic economy, like finance, has set in train major structural changes which may fundamentally undercut the capabilities of developmental states" (Beeson, 2004: 35).

The evidence at regional level is mixed. Japan and South Korea, in particular, have shifted from interventionism and administrative guidance toward neoclassical regulatory regimes (to varying degrees). Japan, the most important economy of the region at the time, which had engaged in gradual and cautious financial market liberalization in the 1980s, undertook complete liberalization (the 1996–2001 "big bang") and has yet to pull out of the cycle of stagnation and weak growth that began in the early 1990s. In the aftermath of the 1998 crisis, South Korea acceded to IMF demands to liberalize the capital account, abolished restrictions on foreign mergers and acquisitions, and attempted but failed to privatize health care in the face of significant resistance. The liberalization of financial markets created new vulnerabilities that became apparent during the 2008 global financial crisis, leading to reregulation and the restoration of capital controls in 2010 (Cho, 2013). In Indonesia, which experienced a depression in 1997–1998, the state sold off public sector companies at a recovery rate of merely 20 percent, against 47 in Korea, leading to a weakening of the country's manufacturing base. Capital account liberalization was also implemented in Thailand in 1998 but, unlike Korea where significant parts of the banking system were sold to foreign capital, economic nationalism came to the fore in 2001 with a turn toward protectionism, limits on foreign ownership of sectors such as telecommunications, government subsidies for health care, and withholding requirements for foreign currency purchases other than those designed for trade and domestic investment. In this case, the crisis led to expanded state action and attempts to protect national industrial and financial sectors. Malaysia preserved itself from the worst effects of the crisis by establishing capital controls, suffering proportionally less than its neighbors. Though Korea and Thailand recovered from the crisis relatively quickly, the economic and social costs of the crisis proved significant. Indonesia took much longer to recover. In the more mature economies, the nature of state intervention has changed, with a significant shift from interventionism and administrative guidance to neoclassical regulatory functions.

The other significant outcome of the crisis was that Japan lost its position as the gravitational center of East Asian regionalization. By being denied leadership during the AMF episode, and folding under U.S. pressure, Japan lost the ability to steer regional economic policy, leading to a decisive shift of the center of regional gravity to China. China, a bureaucratic industrializing authoritarian state and by far the largest of the East Asian geese, emerged as the main beneficiary of the 1997–1998 crisis. Protected by capital controls from financial contagion, she played a crucial role in regional recovery (after having been one of its multiple causes due to the competitive pressures exerted on Southeast Asia by Chinese exports and an undervalued currency). In contrast to the Japanese economy, which stalled during the decade, China remained on a strong growth trajectory: Chinese annual GDP growth averaged 9.3 per cent between 1997 and 2007 against Japan's 1.2 per cent. China played an important supportive role in reviving economic activity in the region by absorbing a growing share of regional exports. The choice not to depreciate the renminbi (RMB) in 1998, despite the wave of regional currency depreciations, proved a crucial decision, avoiding a cascade of further competitive currency depreciations in the region. While the U.S. shortsightedly quashed Japanese efforts at regional leadership, China was able to demonstrate "responsibility and leadership through its policy choices" (Naughton, 1999: 209).

In the aftermath of the crisis, trade and investment flows between China and the rest of Asia grew significantly, proving an important factor in regional recovery. The share of NIC and ASEAN exports to China rose, respectively, from 17.5 percent and 8.9 percent in 1990, to 25.4 and 11.1 percent in 2006. Since the late 1990s, regional Asian trade with China has been growing faster than Asian trade with the United States: Japan's imports from China already exceed those from the U.S. and Japanese exports to China have been steadily rising. The same trend is evident in South Korean, Thai, Malaysian, and Singaporean trade flows. A 2007 IMF study noted that

> China has displaced the United States as the largest export market for an increasing number of Asian countries. It has also been pivotal in boosting intraregional trade and Foreign Direct Investment (FDI), particularly in the form of intermediate goods channelled through multinationals as part of cross-border chains. . . . The potential expansion of China's domestic market creates opportunities for the regional economies, for example, to produce higher-tech goods that China is unlikely to be able to produce domestically in the near future. (Cui, 2007).

At the end of the 2000s, Chinese officials attributed the "launch of (Chinese-centered) East Asian cooperation to the Asian Financial Crisis of 1997. The process of the East Asian cooperation has been consolidated day by day since then [and is now] based on a multi-layered, multi-faceted structure."[7] Though the economic logic for Sinocentric regionalization is strong, the political foundations for such a system are rather shaky: the constitution of a Chinese-centered regional political economy has been set back by an ill-managed policy on the part of Beijing to assert its "historical rights," in effect its suzerainty, over the South China and the East China seas. China's claims have generated significant geopolitical tensions that could overcome the deep economic interdependence that has been woven between East Asia's largest developmental state and its neighbors. The next chapter takes a close look at the question of China's developmental trajectory and her relative autonomy. It argues, in contrast with contentions that the U.S. has incorporated China in a dependent position in the world capitalist system (Gindin and Panich, 2012), that the state has preserved a great deal of international autonomy.

— 5 —

CHINA'S STATE CAPITALIST MUTATION

In the late 1970s no one could have anticipated the deep transformations of the Chinese economy and Chinese social relations that have occurred since the state capitalist turn that was confirmed and amplified in the 1990s. Nor was it conceivable that the most populous country of the world, which was just emerging from the political convulsions of the Cultural Revolution and was facing a severe economic crisis, would a few decades later become the world's second largest economy and an essential component of the second historical phase of capitalist globalization. It seemed rather that China was heading toward systemic breakdown, like the Soviet Union that had contemporaneously entered a phase of slow but regular economic decline that undermined the Soviet leadership and ultimately shook the foundations of the Soviet state. In contrast to the Communist Party of the Soviet Union (CPSU), however, which belatedly sought to revive the economy through hesitant and politically divisive reforms, the Communist Party of China (henceforth "the Party") successfully averted a collapse of the economy and of the state by adeptly managing the transition from totalitarian politics to "rational authoritarianism" (Nolan, 1993), and from autarkic command economics to a state-led mixed economy that became gradually integrated with regional and then global markets. Engineered by policymakers inspired by the Japanese and other capitalist East Asian developmental experiences (Heilmann and Shih, 2013; Huchet, 2014) who were following a nationalist modernization program that has deep roots in late-modern Chinese history (Kuhn, 1999), the shift has fundamentally transformed not only China's domestic socioeconomic landscape and its position in the global political economy but also the world environment itself. Borrowing François Perroux's useful concept, the country is becoming an "active unit" of the world system, a unit "whose program is not simply adapted to its environment but which adapts the environment to its program" (Perroux, 1994: 236).[1]

The overall economic outcomes of the introduction of a "socialist market economy" in the late 1970s are well known and require only cursory restatement here. China has experienced annual average growth of 9.9 percent, a sustained expansion that has increased the size of the economy from $298 billion in 1980 to $16 trillion in 2013 (in current international dollars PPP), and led to a rise of per-capita GDP (PPP) from around $300 to nearly $11,885 (IMF, 2014). In relative terms, the country's share of constantly rising world GDP (PPP) rose during the same time frame from 2.2 percent to just over 15 percent (Figure 5.1), and is expected to soon equal or surpass the world share of the United States.[2] The People's Republic, which accounted for less than 0.5 percent of world trade in the mid-1970s, has become the world's leading trading nation, ahead of the United States, Germany, and Japan, and the hub of new and increasingly dense transcontinental South–South trading networks. As detailed in other chapters of this book, China has become the epicenter of regionalization in East Asia and accounts for a growing and increasingly significant share of the international trade of nearly all the states of the global South. Sustained trade surpluses have led to the accumulation of very large foreign currency reserves (currently estimated at $3.66 trillion) that have made China into the world's second largest net creditor, just behind Japan.[3] Accelerated industrialization and large-scale urbanization have had other more problematic global economic and environmental effects: China has become the world's second consumer of primary energy, the second importer of fossil

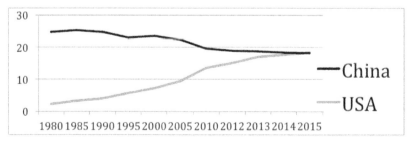

Figure 5.1. China and USA GDP as a share of world total (PPP)

Source: Derived from *World Economic Outlook*, IMF, Washington D.C., 2013.

fuels, and the first emitter of CO2 in aggregate ahead of the United States.[4]

These broad measures of change are clearly meaningful: they show China climbing the development ladder, moving from self-confinement to deep global integration, and becoming a hub of new transnational trade, investment, finance, and energy flows. But this is only part of the story of an incomplete and uneven mutation, the economic, social, and ecological sustainability of which remains open to question. Internationalization and reliance on exports for growth has generated new dependencies, hence vulnerabilities to potential exogenous economic shocks; the domestic restructuring (marketization and privatization) has led to sharp social inequalities and spatial unevenness; industrialization and large-scale urbanization to major ecological constraints. Moreover, the current export-led industrialization and growth model is reaching its limits: due to the contraction of world trade and weak global demand since the 2008 global financial crisis, China's growth rate has fallen from 13 percent to 7.5 percent (2013), and is expected to continue to slow somewhat in coming years in a world economy whose growth trajectory is projected to remain weak. These adverse global conditions underscore the need for a structural shift of the economy to balanced or ecologically and socially sustainable growth, based primarily on domestic demand and household consumption rather than the pull of world markets. The Chinese leadership, whose legitimacy is tightly bound to its economic performance, has been seeking since the mid-2000s to reorient the economy in this direction, but the turn will take time and implies a significant shift of domestic policy toward socially inclusive growth. The state, which has been the initiator and regulator of change, has proved resilient in the face of evolving domestic and international circumstances. During the different phases of the post-Maoist transformation, it has accelerated or slowed the rate of change, relaxing or reinstating centralization, refocusing planning when confronted with policy failures, and intervening forcefully in markets (the massive expansionary fiscal response to the 2008–2009 global financial crisis being a recent example). But even if the country avoids manias, panics, and crashes, the recurrent crises and social upheavals in the history of modern capitalism would suggest that major challenges lie ahead. The 1989 political and social upheaval that culminated with the events of Tiananmen may seem distant today, but deepening inequalities have bred widespread and multifaceted protest and discontent.

A hybrid developmental system

The central contention of this chapter is at odds with arguments that China has simply been folded into transnational capitalism (Robinson, 2004), as well as with neoclassical claims regarding convergence. Instead, it claims that the country's ascending economic trajectory since the end of the 1970s should be understood in the general framework of post-1950 East Asian developmentalism. China is not only the largest bureaucratic authoritarian developmental state to have emerged as part of the pattern of regional diffusion discussed in earlier chapters, but also the most consequential in terms of its global effects. Seeking a third way between Western capitalism and the failed imperative planning system of the Maoist period, the post-Mao leadership looked to the East rather than the West for modernization models that would generate growth while preserving the Party-state's power and authority. The transition to state capitalism was influenced by the example of the other East Asian developers that had successfully modernized under the guidance and control of strong bureaucratic states. Deng Xiaoping visited Japan and Singapore in 1978 and, as Sebastian Heilmann and Lea Shih show in a detailed discussion of the evolution of Chinese industrial policy, Chinese decision-makers and planners, notably Chen-Yun, selectively adopted and adapted Japanese policy approaches and experiences that were "widely seen as being closer and more compatible to the Chinese setting than most Western economies."[5] The successful Japanese system of administrative guidance and nonimperative indicative planning made the Japanese institutional setup "attractive to state-centric policy makers in China"—a perception reinforced by Japanese economists and former planning officials who, during intensive interactions with their Chinese counterparts in the 1980s, emphasized that "Japan was not a regular capitalist country but rather a distinctive type of political economy in which government guidance of markets played an indispensable role." Despite policy failures and struggles between contending coalitions over the balance to be struck between state and markets that inhibited the coherence of policy design, Japanese influence proved "deep and lasting," exerting a sway on "Chinese economic administrators in the national planning bodies from the 1980s to the present day" (Heilmann and Shih, 2013: 4–6).

However, due to different initial conditions at domestic and international levels, as well as enormous differences of scale—China's population is ten times greater than Japan's, twenty-seven times South

Korea's, and fifty-nine times Taiwan's—post-Maoist developmentalism in China has taken on a distinctly hybrid character. Core features of state–market relations of the precursor Northeast Asian developmental regimes such as a highly autonomous interventionist state, a large state sector (state-owned enterprises or SOEs, which account for a third of industrial output), administrative guidance, industrial policy, neomercantilist trade promotion, and managed currency policies, have combined with two characteristics that distinguish the Chinese experience: a higher degree of penetration by transnational capital and dependence on continuing inflows to maintain the country's extraverted growth momentum, and great social unevenness as seen in constantly rising levels of social inequality. Both issues emerged over time, resulting from policy choices made in the late 1980s and the 1990s to adapt China to the new global environment resulting from the disintegration of the Soviet empire and the collapse of the Soviet state.

Whereas Japan and the NICs were able to integrate international markets in an unusually permissive international environment, which allowed them to pursue neomercantilist policies that boosted exports while carefully limiting foreign access to the domestic market, China's export-oriented industrialization (EOI) strategy since the 1990s has relied far more on Foreign Direct Investment (FDI) by global firms that have integrated significant parts of Chinese industry in transnational manufacturing chains as part of the globalization of production process. This has generated a set of interconnected problems discussed in this chapter: the difficulty of harnessing transnational capital flows to national developmental purposes and moving up the value chain, regional development disparities, domestic mass migrations, and the constitution of new working underclasses. The other major contrast with earlier East Asian industrializers is social: while Japan, South Korea and Taiwan experienced intense growth with relative social fairness, distributional outcomes in China have been deeply inegalitarian. This is evidenced in rising income dispersion since the early 1990s: the Gini coefficient, which stood at a low 0.16 at the start of the transition (reflecting the egalitarian character of Chinese society under Mao and post-1949 land distribution policies), averaged 0.29 between 1979 and 1985, 0.325 between 1986 and 1991, 0.377 between 1992 and 1998, 0.422 between 1999 and 2007, and has hovered around 0.42 ever since (Andong Zhu and Kotz, 2011). In this regard, China resembles developing Southeast Asia more closely than it does the Japan and second-wave Northeast Asian industrializers.

The dualism of the Chinese developmental experience raises a series of interrelated analytical and normative issues that are addressed in following sections of this chapter: the question of dependent development and of technological innovation and catch-up in a world economic system dominated by transnational firms that own proprietary technologies and capture most of the value-added in transnational production chains; the problem of spatial unevenness flowing from economic internationalization and of social inequalities generated by labor-market liberalization and privatization of health and education; the challenge of mass domestic migrations and urbanization; the issue of Party-state legitimacy, which is no longer founded on revolutionary antiimperialism and social egalitarianism, but on the pursuit of wealth and national power.

Internationalization, extraversion, and dependent development

China's internationalization occurred in phases. The first sequence, bracketed by the announcement of the "open door" policy in 1978 and the Tiananmen repression of 1989, involved a controlled experimental opening to regional and international investment through the first Equity Joint Venture Law of 1979 and the creation of preferential "special economic zones" (SEZs) in the southern coastal provinces that had always been the most internationalized regions of China. The SEZs in Shenzhen, Shuhai, and Shantou in the province of Guangdong, and Xiamen in Fujian province initially attracted regional international investment in labor-intensive, export-oriented processing industries. Capital inflows from Hong Kong, Macau, Taiwan, and Singapore (HMTS) stimulated growth and raised incomes in the coastal areas, even if inflows were initially quite modest (just over $7 billion between 1979 and 1986) and were concentrated in low-value-added activities with weak technological contents. The pull exercised by the SEZ on overseas Chinese capital led to their expansion in 1984 to fourteen new coastal cities that were given SEZ status. In 1985 the government created new Development Zones in the Yangtze River Delta, the Pearl River Delta, and the Minnan region, and two years later announced the Coastal Area Development Strategy. Hainan and the Shandong and Liaodong peninsulas were "opened" in 1988. New legal frameworks authorizing and encouraging wholly owned foreign enterprises (WOFE) and joint ventures (the 1986 "Wholly Foreign-Owned Enterprise Law" and the "Regulations to Encourage Foreign Investments") attracted Japanese investment as part of the general relocation movement of Japanese industry in the late 1980s. Japanese direct investment in

109

China's manufacturing sector, nearly half in the form of joint ventures producing for the domestic market and only one-quarter for the world market, rose from a mere 4.5 percent of total Japanese investment in East Asia in 1985 to 44.7 percent a decade later (total Japanese manufacturing investment in East Asia increased sevenfold, from ¥109 billion to ¥753 billion, or around $7.5 billion, between 1985 and 1995). By the end of the decade, southern China, which had been the industrial hub of the country in the early part of the twentieth century, had effectively become a component of the regional economic system that had emerged in the 1970s and 1980s: "The inflow of export oriented manufacturing investment from Japan and the Four Tigers led to the integration of South China into the East Asian regional economic order characterized by the Japan-led Flying Geese model" (Ho-Fung Hung, 2009: 12).

During the following decade, after a three-year pause reflecting policy uncertainty at the top over the character and pace of reform in the aftermath of the Tiananmen events, the dominant leadership faction led by Deng Xiaoping accelerated and broadened the domestic restructuring begun in the 1980s, as well as the country's internationalization and integration into the world (rather than simply the regional) capitalist economy. This policy choice was officialized in 1992 at the Fourteenth Party Congress, which confirmed the ascendancy of the orientation enunciated by Deng around the time of his "imperial tour" of southern China: "if we do not carry out the reform and opening, if we do not develop the economy and improve people's standard of living, it will definitely bring (the party and the state) to a dead end. . . . If we fail to pass, there will be chaos and civil wars" (quoted in Jianyong Yue, 2010: 131).

If the "radical reform agenda" and the definitive turn toward a "socialist market economy" reflected concerns over regime stability and legitimacy, it was also crucially shaped by contemporary changes in the global landscape: the fall of the Berlin Wall (1989), the breakdown of the Soviet State (1991), the 1990 Gulf War, and the faltering of the Japanese developmental model in the aftermath of the 1990 financial crash. Together these shifts confirmed the strategic ascendancy of the United States and cleared the way for the second cycle of capitalist globalization since the late nineteenth century (Golub, 2010). While the Russian Federation underwent savage privatization and liberalization ("shock therapy"), which disarticulated the economy and provoked a deep and lasting depression, the Chinese leadership chose, in Deng's words, to "firmly stick to economic construction and continue along this line unless there is large scale foreign aggression. We should never divert our attention or allow undermining or interference in this central task" (quoted in Suisheng Zhao, 1993: 743). The geopolitical correlate of global economic integration was the need for "peaceful evolution" and accommodation with the United States, to avoid confrontations that could have derailed the economic transition. In 1992, China signed a memorandum of understanding with the U.S. acceding to the latter's demands to phase out trade protections and recognize patents and intellectual property rights.

The new global configuration posed a problem common to all postcolonial Southern countries: how, if possible, to secure national autonomy and move up the development ladder, while integrating global capital and trade circuits and submitting to the institutional disciplines and regimes set by the dominant capitalist states. China, which applied for membership in the General Agreement on Tariffs and Trade in 1986, had to wait fifteen years before being granted membership in the World Trade Organization (WTO), after having signed a series of accession obligations that were more constraining than those applied to other developing states (Susan Perry, 1998).[6] Internationalization, as measured by FDI inflows and the share of exports in GDP, increased after 1992. Net FDI inflows, which averaged $2.2 billion per annum (in current dollars) between 1984 and 1989, rose dramatically to $30.8 billion per annum on average between 1992 and 2000, and $170 billion from 2000 to 2013 (UNCTAD, 2014). Exports as a share of GDP increased from 11.6 percent between 1984 and 1991 to 19.5 percent between 1992 and 2000, with a steep rise of the ratio between 2002 and 2008 after China's accession to the WTO (34 percent on average, with a peak ratio of exports to GDP of 39 percent in 2007). Due to the contraction of world trade following the 2008 global financial crisis, the ratio fell back to 27 percent in 2009 and is currently estimated at 26 percent (World Bank, 2014).

The growing importance of FDI since the 1990s in China's export-led growth is anomalous when compared to Japan or second-wave Northeast Asian industrializers, whose export-oriented industrialization (EOI) was driven by private and public national firms in protected markets with institutional barriers to foreign investment, rather than wholly or partially owned foreign-invested enterprises (FIE). Thus, while the Chinese economy is significantly less extraverted than South Korea's, whose exports-to-GDP ratio is 56 percent (Table 5.2), wholly owned FIEs accounted for over half of total Chinese exports in the 2000s as compared to 12 percent of South Korean exports.

111

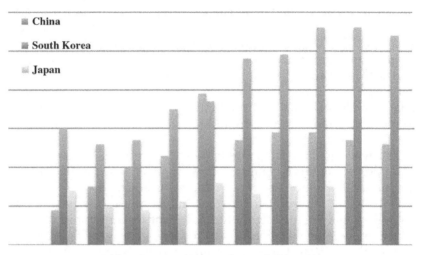

Table 5.2. Exports as a share of GDP (%)

Source: Derived from World Bank data

(It should be noted that FDI has grown quite spectacularly in South Korea since financial liberalization in the 2000s, with FDI stock rising from 4.5 percent of GDP in 1998 to 13.7 percent in 2013, a higher ratio than China's current 10.3 percent. The significant difference is that South Korea, like Japan, built its national industrial "champions" and gained upward economic and technological mobility prior to rather than after liberalization of the foreign investment regime.)

Harnessing transnational flows to national developmental purposes and climbing the value chain through technology acquisition and appropriation were the major motivations in China's opening in the 1980s. In 1980 Deng told journalists: "Technology, science and even advanced production management, which is also a kind of science, will be useful in any society or country. We intend to acquire technology, science and management skills to serve our socialist production" (quote in Yasheng Huang, 2001:149). China's reliance on FDI for this purpose raises interlinked questions about value-added capture, skills acquisition, and technological catch-up that are essential to assess autonomy and the depth of economic development. From an international political economy perspective, the distribution of value-added matters insofar as it affects state capacity: the higher the foreign value-added content of a manufactured product produced by wholly owned foreign invested enterprises (WOFIE) benefiting

112

from preferential tax regimes, the less its export will have domestic developmental effects.

FIE investments have been concentrated in the processing trade in which "China is the last section of a long global production chain that ends up assembling components from various countries into a final product" (Koopman et al., 2012: 178). There are two distinct processing trades in China: the first is predominantly concentrated in labor-intensive lower value-added sectors traditionally invested by overseas Chinese capital, such as textiles and garments, the second in the capital-intensive advanced technology sectors, notably electronics and telecommunications where FIEs account for over 85 percent of exports. In these sectors transnational firms from the most developed countries owning proprietary patents and technologies capture most of the value-added of processed goods that are destined for the world market. In the framework of preferential tariff regimes that encourage imports rather than local production of intermediate goods, the domestic content of processed exports declined during the 1990s. It was particularly low in advanced technology products such as electronics. International organizations estimate at 33 percent the total foreign-value-added (FVA) content of total gross Chinese exports, with much higher ratios in more advanced technology sectors. FVA more than tripled in the electrical equipment industry between 1995 and 2009, and more than doubled for machinery and transport equipment. There was a concurrent increase in the technological sophistication of exports, the share of value-added of electronics exports doubling since 1995 to 30 percent. The share of imported intermediate inputs used for final product assembly of electrical equipment, however, rose from 20 to 73 percent (OECD/WTO, 2013). Hence the question whether such exports in fact generate endogenous developmental effects: "If China's rising export sophistication is driven by WFOEs, we must ask how much China benefits from this rising export sophistication. If China's export structure upgrading is driven by processing trade in which firms import sophisticated intermediate inputs to assemble sophisticated final goods, we must ask if there is any skill upgrading in China's value added" (Bin Xu and Jiangyong Lu, 2009: 438).

In some cases, such as the by-now classical example of the Apple iPod studied by Linden et al. (2009), the answer is very little indeed: the designer – intellectual property owner – retailer captures over 50 percent of value added and Japanese or Korean producers of core inputs (microchips, screens) most of the rest, leaving the final part of the chain—in this case the Taiwanese company Foxconn—a small fraction of value added. Domestic Chinese value added is a mere 1.7 percent, in the form of wages paid to workers assembling the final product. The authors have applied their analysis to other Apple products with similar results. This is admittedly not a generally representative case, but FDI-related technology transfer and acquisition has until recently been quite weak. Writing in 2001, Yasheng Huang noted that there is

> little evidence that FDI inflows into China embody much hard or soft technology. . . . On average, the level of technology as embodied in the FDI [studied in surveys] was two years ahead of China's existing level even though the "technology gap" between investing countries and China was commonly perceived to be 20 years. The "technology package" was in most cases incomplete, meaning that the package included only one or two of the three components that constitute a complete technology transfer—product, process, and organizational technology. . . . Less than 25 percent of technology transfer projects incorporated all three components. (Huang, 2001: 149, 167)

Moreover, early state efforts to build autonomous national industries capable of competing in the world market proved elusive. In the early 2000s Peter Nolan noted: "In most key respects China's industrial policies of the 1980s and 1990s failed . . . despite significant progress, China's leading firms are further behind the global leaders than they were when the industrial policies began almost two decades ago" (Nolan, 2002: 130–31). More recently, Yianyong Yue has argued that the way in which China became incorporated into the world capitalist economy had generated "technologyless industrialization," or growth without development (Yue, 2010).

However, this picture appears to be changing. Some recent studies suggest that after having risen steadily in the 1990s, the overall FVA share in Chinese exports began to decrease in the 2000s. Robert Koopman, Zhi Wang, and Shang-Jin Wei estimate the FVA share in total merchandise exports fell from 46 percent in 1997 to 39.4 percent in 2007, the share in manufacturing exports from 50 percent to just above 40 percent (the difference with OECD figures stems from higher estimates of initial FVA). They find an increase in domestic value added (DVA) in most processing industries, including "sophisticated sectors" with the lowest domestic contents, that they attribute to growing FIE sourcing of intermediate inputs in China. Overall, the "number of industries with less than 50 percent domestic contents in their exports declined to 10, and their collective share in China's total exports declined to 32 percent. . . . (while) the number with a DVA share of more than 75 percent increased from 12 percent in 2002 to 25 percent . . . among these high DVA industries, besides traditional labor-intensive industries (furniture, textile, apparel) we start to see capital and skill intensive industries such as automobile, industrial machinery and rolling steel which account for one third of these high DVA sector's export" (Koopman et al., 185). Noting the Chinese government decision in 2006 to "narrow the gap in policy treatment" of FIEs relative to domestic firms and processing exports relative to normal exports, they suggest that China is undergoing "industrial upgrading" and that the share of DVA should increase in future. Since the technological sophistication of products has also been increasing, the change would indicate a simultaneous upgrading of skills and increasing technology appropriation.

These trends disconfirm the idea that internationalization has tightly caged China in a dependent-development path.[7] Unlike most global South countries and the postcommunist states of Central and Eastern Europe, China retains a large and powerful publicly owned sector embedded in the domestic market, a broad array of public research institutions and laboratories working on technological upgrading, and state institutions that still retain control of overall economic policy, as well as of "economic lifeline" enterprises. Margaret Pearson points out that changes in regulatory frameworks and economic governance, and the corporatization of state-owned industries, has not led to loss of state control of strategic sectors of the economy: the state retains "ownership of key assets, power over personnel appointments undergirding a strong patronage system, and comprehensive oversight and planning by central party-state agencies" (Pearson, 2007: 727). In important industrial sectors, the state has set frameworks that oblige foreign investors seeking market access to defer to its preferences, notably in terms of technology transfer. In the automobile industry that has been integrated into global production chains but is focused on the domestic Chinese market, the state has dictated its terms "to a very considerable degree" on the industry leading to the localization of parts and engine production as well as research and development (R&D) units within China. The Chinese government has "exerted virtually complete control . . . [and] has adopted a policy of limiting access for foreign firms, and controlling the form that their involvement can take. . . . Whereas, in many cases, TNCs are able to play off one country against another to achieve the best deal, in the Chinese case it is the state whose unique bargaining position has enabled it to play off one TNC against another" (Liu and Dicken, 2006: 1245).

The ability of the state to obtain deference by TNCs to its prefer-ences ("obligated embeddedness" in Weidong's and Dicken's formu-lation) is manifest in other industrial sectors such as High Speed Rail (HSR), where government has succeeded in imposing strict condi-tions of technology transfer by having TNCs compete over market access. Planning on HSR began in the 1990s, but the effort really took off in the 2000s. In 2004, international bids were launched in which "Chinese entities were free to choose foreign partners but foreign firms were required to pre-bid and sign technology transfer agreements with domestic manufacturers," as stipulated by the State Council, which also required that they transfer subsequent improve-ments. Many of the firms bidding offered (Bombardier) or were made to offer comprehensive technology transfer (Siemens after having been delisted during a first bid made major concessions afterwards), while others (Kawasaki) agreed to transfer key technologies that were then apparently replicated by Chinese engineers. In 2008, the "China High Speed Train United Action Plan Cooperation Agreement" of the Ministry of Science and the Ministry of Railways was announced. This led to major state infrastructure investments. It brought together universities, research institutes, national laboratories, engineering research centers, and national technology R&D programs to work on "locomotive introduction, digestion, absorption and re-innovation," to make China into a world leader in HSR. Currently, China has its own fleet of high-speed trains and has begun to sell HSR in the inter-national market. In short, "China has been able to leverage the size of its market to achieve sinification of important foreign technologies through technology transfer agreements" (Barrett, 2014: 11).

Similar efforts to endogenize technology development have been made in the aeronautics industry, though with less clear-cut success. In the 1990s, China's aerospace industry was considered "nearly 30 years behind the United States and Western Europe in terms of design, development and production skills," limited to basic design, modifi-cation, imitation, and adaptation of existing designs (USITC, 1998). Since then, China has sought to acquire know-how and technology through joint-venture agreements with global aeronautics firms such as Airbus, Bombardier, and Embraer, involving local manufactur-ing and technology transfer. Bombardier has gone further than most firms in this direction, agreeing in 2008 to transfer design authority on major supplied parts to their local partners, and giving them a role in the design and manufacture of the fuselage for the CSeries airliner (*New York Times*, 2012). By most accounts China is nonetheless still a long distance from the technological frontier in aeronautics, though

116

it has made some gains through imitation (and likely reverse engineering). Its planned national civilian airliner, the C919, is essentially a replica of the Airbus 320. Most of the advanced technology components will be produced abroad: the motors will be manufactured by the French-American firm CFM, the cockpit by General Electric Aviation System, the electrical flight commands by Honeywell. To enter the market these firms have had to localize the production of some components and establish joint ventures. In 2012, the Chinese government announced that it will set up a national agency to certify manufactured aeronautical products, previously the exclusive prerogative of the U.S. Federal Aviation Agency (FAA) and the European Air Security Agency (EASA), which will give the country greater control over technological contents (Maréchal, 2012).

The last two instances reflect the reorientation of state industrial policy under the Hu Jintao and Wen Jiabao administration (2002–2012), which broke with the sectoral and decentralized decision-making system that produced inconsistencies and fragmentation under Zhu Rongji in the 1990s, and moved to "broad-based national industrial policy making after 2004" with centralized cross-sectoral multiyear programs. Heilman and Shih interpret the shift as a major breakthrough in industrial policy, and depict a "massive effort at comprehensive guidance and coordination of China's industrial and technological upgrading" (Heilman and Shih, 2013: 14). Major efforts have indeed been put into the creation of a web of research and development institutions to make Chinese industry globally competitive. The ratio of R&D expenditures to GDP has increased from 0.5 percent in 1995 to 1.98 percent in 2012, bringing China's R&D intensity in line with OECD averages. China now ranks fourth behind the U.S., Japan and the EU in the number of patents filed. If "China has yet to approach parity with major science-producing nations in basic scientific research," the U.S. National Science Foundation notes "the [unprecedented] rapidity of China's emergence as a major S&T player." The "country's scientists and engineers are collaborating broadly with their counterparts around the globe and in Asia, and their international patenting and publishing activities, although modest, are on accelerating upward trajectories" (National Science Foundation, 2007: vii). The challenge going forward is to create a socially embedded system of innovation, linking public and private research, capable of irrigating the whole economy (Bironneau et al., 2012).

The recentralization and reinvigoration of state industrial and technological policy has generated Western complaints that the "retreat of the state has slowed and, in some industries, reversed." China would not be meeting her WTO obligations by favoring national industries and firms through nontariff protectionist barriers (*The Economist*, 2012). That may indeed be the case. But the complaint over trade and investment practices would be more persuasive if other major countries such as the United States had not weakened the WTO and undermined multilateralism through bilateral free-trade agreements that have proliferated over the past decade and a half. At any rate, compelling China or other global South states, such as India or Brazil, to abide by trade regimes historically set in the North is proving elusive. The failure of the Doha Round of trade liberalization, that was launched in 2001 but never ratified, reflects a systemic trend: the decline of the authority of the Western-dominated institutions of global economic governance since the late 1990s.

The Chinese state, in sum, has been shaped but has not been disempowered by transnational flows. Gregory Chin rightly emphasizes: "China's internationalization differs from weaker/smaller nations where the state has become an agency for adjusting the national economy to the exigencies of the global economy, and where the influence of multinational forces are overwhelming . . . [in China] the state has the capacity to shape internationalization" (Gregory Chin, 2007: 166–67). Unlike the late-nineteenth-century Chinese modernizers under the Qing who sought autonomy but ended up being "crippled mercantilists who could not protect their home economy against foreign competition" (Jerome Chen, 1980: 137), and who failed to build a modern state, the post-Mao state has managed to maintain control and conserve its relative international autonomy.

This does not mean that China's current development path is sustainable. Building a relatively autonomous industrial-technological system is a necessary but not a sufficient condition for development, which is not reducible to growth or the ability to compete on world markets. There are other determinants of development and society's well-being: distributional justice and universal access to public goods (education, health, social security, and so on) (Ha-Joon Chang, 2002; Seers, 1969; Sen, 1999; Stiglitz, 2002). These factors of social cohesion are preconditions for sustained and sustainable modernization and development. From a social and democratic philosophical perspective, they are also normative goals to be pursued irrespective of their demonstrable economic benefits. In these respects, notwithstanding an overall reduction in absolute poverty, China has moved backwards since the late 1980s. The state has only quite recently begun trying to deal with the array of social problems and tensions generated by unbalanced and unequal growth.

Unbalanced growth, social and spatial unevenness

Export-driven growth, domestic restructuring, and intense urbanization have deeply altered social relations when compared both to the Maoist period (1949–1976) and the much longer social history of preindustrial China. It is widely recognized that the very first phase of reforms in the late 1970s and early 1980s generated substantial and balanced living-standard improvements. Between 1978 and 1988, the aggregate disposable income of households grew at a higher rate than GDP growth (11.3 percent per annum versus 10.1 percent) (Zhu and Kotz, 2011). The impact in poor rural areas was particularly important: the decollectivization of land, the increase of prices of agricultural products, and the encouragement of local industry through Town and Village Enterprises (TVE) gave new autonomy to peasants, boosting agricultural productivity and reducing income differentials between urban and rural areas, a problem inherited from the urbanized heavy-industry bias of Maoism. Though the *hukou* system of the Maoist era, which disadvantaged rural populations by banning household residency for people and their descendants outside of their province of birth, remained in force, the urban–rural divide began to recede. As critical theorist Wang Hui notes:

> From a fundamental perspective [these reforms] were based on the experience of traditional Chinese land distribution and the principle of equality. . . . [They were] the negation of the state monopoly that characterized the commune system in favour of the forms of "small farmer socialism." The resulting increase in the initiative of the rural population lay in a new flexibility in production and the reduction of the urban–rural income gap rather than stemming purely from the liberalization of markets. Through the adjustment of the prices of agricultural commodities, the state was able to provide security in small local markets. (Wang Hui, 2003: 49)

Poverty, predominantly a rural phenomenon, fell significantly as a result.

The pattern of relatively balanced growth was reversed in subsequent years. Rural income gains slowed and rural–urban disparities widened considerably, disproportionately affecting women who took over family farms in rural areas. The concentration of export-oriented industries in coastal areas generated significant intraregional growth and income differentials: real per capita GDP was comparable across provinces and regions at the start of the reform period, but they diverged from the late 1980s onwards, leading to the 1–10

119

differential between poorest (Guizhou) and richest (Shanghai) areas that prevails today. At the same time, universal access to public goods was restricted by decentralization and privatization, leading to multi-tiered and unequal health and education systems affecting rural populations first and foremost. In urban areas, labor market liberalization and the restructuring and corporatization of State Owned Enterprises (SOE) generated mass unemployment. New social stratifications emerged out of these combined trends: the construction, on one hand, of an upper managerial and capital-owning class as well as new urban middle classes and, on the other, the constitution of plural underclasses due to the weakening of employment security and social protections in urban public sector enterprises, and the appearance of a vast pool of mobile cheap labor pushed out of agriculture and seeking work in cities. Mass unemployment in urban areas surged with the introduction in 1987 of a contract system for salaried employment in SOEs that weakened traditional advantages (the "iron rice bowl": lifetime jobs, welfare coverage, pensions, and so on). This was kept out of official statistics through disguised layoffs—the putting of redundant but still formally affiliated state sector workers "off-post" (*xiagang*), at subsistence or below-subsistence stipends complemented by local government social programs. Underemployment was masked during the Maoist era but the phenomenon worsened considerably in the 1990s. In the late 1990s there were around 30 million *xiagang* out of a total of 173 million urban employees.[8] With insufficient means to live, these workers were pushed into the informal economy and into competition with another growing and massive underclass segment: migrants from the poorer provinces and from rural areas.

Widening regional disparities resulting from unbalanced industrialization and rural-urban income disparities among the world's highest[9] generated push-pull factors leading to huge migratory flows from the Western and Central regions to the more dynamic urban centers, notably in coastal industrial-export centers. China's sociospatial unevenness has put tens of millions of redundant rural workers on the move (according to the United Nations Development Programme, there were 260 million migrant laborers in total in 2011, of which over 150 million had migrated from one province to another). This wage-seeking 'floating population' has been pulled into work in infrastructure, construction and the low-value-added export industries that emerged in the 1980s and 1990s as the drivers of China's post-reform industrialization. Excluded from the formal labor market by the *hukou* system and denied the social protections afforded by legal urban residency, rural migrant laborers are particularly

120

vulnerable to managerial coercion and arbitrariness (payment failures are common). Migrant factory workers, who account for 70–80 percent of the labor force in the coastal export processing zones, labor extraordinarily long workweeks, to the point of exhaustion or sometimes death, and feel as if they had been made into "little more than appendages to machines" (Ching Kwan Lee, 2007: 26). Gender is an important dimension: female workers constitute the overwhelming majority of the workforce in low valued-added processing industries (over 90 percent in the textile and electronics assembly sectors). Construction workers building China's new cities or modernizing its historic urban centers (for instance Pudong in Shanghai) likewise work without formal protections in dangerous conditions day and night. The people who have built the "miracle" are segregated from legal urban residents, living alongside but not with them in common dormitories attached to the workplace or in precarious private housing on the outskirts of cities. As Kam Wing Chan writes: "Under this system, some 700–800 million people are in effect treated as second-class citizens, deprived of the opportunity to settle legally in cities and of access to most of the basic welfare and state-provided services enjoyed by regular urban residents" (Kam Wing Chan, 2010: 357).

The authoritarian mobilization of labor to extract surplus for modernization is hardly only Chinese; indeed, it is a common feature of all the East Asian late industrializers in the late nineteenth and the twentieth centuries. Modernization under the Meiji state, as Irokawa Daikichi argues, was made by possible by the "sacrifices of workers and peasants" (Irokawa, 1988; industrialization in South Korea and Taiwan was also founded on the control and exploitation of a dominated (if unruly in the Korean case) labor force. Nor is urban dualism a specifically Chinese phenomenon: it is a core feature of contemporary urban conditions almost everywhere, including in the socially segmented global cities of the North that concentrate an important mass of ancillary workers and excluded peoples from the former colonial periphery working in subordinate positions in the economy. But the scale of rural to urban migratory flows in China makes the phenomenon unique. The other unique feature of China's transition is the rate of urbanization, a veritable anthropological mutation when seen in the longer course of the country's history. The proportion of people living in urban areas has risen from 17.9 percent in 1978 to 52.6 percent in 2011 (in 1953 13 percent of the population lived in cities). The number of urban residents increased from 191 million in the early 1980s to over 700 million today, a figure that is expected to surpass 1 billion by 2030 due to migratory movements "unprecedented in human history" (UNDP, 2013). The mutation has, like all earlier wrenching transformations of this kind, been accompanied by social turbulence.

Concerns over social unrest led the Chinese leadership in the 2000s to pay greater attention to distributional issues and to reduce growing and glaring social and spatial inequalities. After having encouraged unbalanced regional development during the late 1980s and 1990s and privatized essential public services, the state belatedly began to address the problems of social and spatial unevenness by announcing a general policy of "harmonious development" in 2005 and more specific sets of policies in 2006 designed to build a "harmonious countryside": centralized transfer payments to the poorer regions and provinces, large-scale infrastructure investments, and urbanization in rural areas in the hope and expectation that this would channel population flows while hastening modernization by gradually reducing the rural population (Ahlers and Schubert, 2009; Shenggen Fan et al., 2009). A minimum wage was introduced in 2007. The announced aim was to "ensure sustainable development of the national economy and continuous expansion of domestic demand [by] developing the rural economy and help farmers to become more affluent." Hundreds of new intermediate "eco-cities" were launched—most of which, however, remain unfinished. In 2009 and 2010 the Party began to publicly discuss amending the *hukou* system by allowing rural migrant workers the right to settle in smaller urban agglomerations. The State Council then announced in July 2014 that the *hukou* system would be gradually phased out in some urban areas, opening the way for the legalization of migrants' status in their new areas of residence, and giving them standard if minimal access to public services. On paper, 100 million migrants should obtain urban residence permits in the small and medium-size cities by 2020 but megalopolises of over 5 million inhabitants have been given the right to continue restricting residency rights. Whether this vast experiment in social engineering will help to solve rather than accentuate China's social divides is questionable. Critics point out that the policy of forced urbanization "does not appear to address the factors that underlie urban–rural income differentials. It is possible that the new urbanization program will replace the rural–urban gap with an urban–urban gap, wherein the urban population is divided between the privileged, already established urban population, and a new urban underclass composed mainly of migrants and former rural residents" (Sicular, 2013: 4). The same kind of question arises regarding the government's 2009 nationwide health care reform that doubled public spending to subsidize

122

insurance for urban and rural residents not covered by existing public or private schemes, but simultaneously increased the share of private hospitals in the system to 20 percent (Yip and Hsiao, 2014).[10] Nor is it at all clear, notwithstanding announcements of a move toward an "ecological civilization," that the conditions have been created to make the urban and industrial mutation ecologically sustainable. China's much-discussed environmental challenges are huge and globally significant: having become the world's primary industrial assembler and workshop, China has also become one of the world's largest polluters, with deleterious domestic and international effects (Shapiro, 2012).

The wrenching socioeconomic changes sketched above belie Giovanni Arrighi's idea that post-Mao China has, at least in part, been following a "natural" evolutionary development path, contrasting with Europe's "unnatural" industrialization experience (Arrighi, 2007). China has in fact reproduced some essential features of the European nineteenth-century experience: uneven development (across a differentiated continental space rather than across nation states), ecologically damaging industrialization, urbanization and rural exodus, and mass migrations (in this case within China rather than overseas). Like the European "miracle" or the nineteenth-century industrialization of the United States, China's economic re-emergence has been built on the control, mobilization, and exploitation of a huge, subordinate, and increasingly commodified and segmented labor force. As in Europe, "free" labor markets have been constituted through state intervention, not the invisible hand. It is worth recalling that, in the paradigmatic case of Great Britain, the long historical movement to industrialization and urbanization was made possible by the various parliamentary "acts of enclosure of the Commons" that ended traditional peasant rights such as farming, mowing meadows, or grazing livestock on public lands, which were then put to private use and made into pasture to meet the needs of the growing wool industry. The decisive inflection point was the New Poor Laws of 1834, which eliminated protections for the poor, and were designed in part to stimulate migration from the countryside to the textile mills of Lancashire and Yorkshire. By the mid-nineteenth century nearly a quarter of all land had been enclosed. At the same time, improvements in agricultural productivity led to redundancies in the countryside, accelerating the rural exodus and creating a new class of wage laborers who, having lost home and land, had only their labor power to sell. Discussing the dispossession of peasants in Scotland whose lands were converted to sheep farms, Marx notes

123

with biting irony how some peasants were transmuted into fishermen: "They became amphibious and lived . . . half on land half on water, and withal only half on both" (Marx, 1977).

Making peasants amphibious, or more often into landless tenants or appendages to machines, required a great deal of coercion. As E. P. Thompson writes: "The commercial expansion, the enclosure movement, the early years of the Industrial Revolution—all took place within the shadow of the gallows. . . . The eighteenth and early nineteenth century are punctuated by riot, occasioned by bread prices, turnpikes and tolls, excise, 'rescue,' strikes, new machinery, enclosures, press gangs and a score of other grievances" and quasi-insurrectionary social movements (Thompson, 1966: 61–62). The constitution of the free labor market would not have been possible without intense state intervention, not only to suppress agitation and popular dissent but also to administratively manage land, labor, and markets. "The road to the free market," writes Karl Polanyi, "was opened and kept open by an enormous increase in continuous, centrally organized and controlled interventionism. To make Adam Smith's 'simple and natural liberty' compatible with the needs of a human society was a most complicated affair. Witness the complexity of the provisions in the innumerable enclosure laws; the amount of bureaucratic control involved in the administration of the New Poor Laws which for the first time since Queen Elizabeth's reign were effectively supervised by central authority; or the increase in governmental administration entailed in the meritorious task of municipal reform" (Polanyi, 1972: 146). The Western road to the free market, it should be added, was opened and kept open at global level through the mobilization of slave and cheap immigrant labor in the colonies of exploitation and of settlement.

China's unfinished industrial and urban revolution has been far more time-compressed than that of Europe or the United States. The mass labor migrations within its continental space are structurally analogous to the nineteenth-century waves of transoceanic migration from Europe to the United States that were stimulated by push and pull factors induced by industrialization and uneven development. Mass immigration played a decisive role in industrialization and urbanization in the latter part of the century in the U.S. by creating a large pool of low-cost wage-seeking labor for the rapidly expanding economy in the northeast and northwest industrial belts. From 1860 to 1920 the ratio of immigrants to total population averaged 13 to 14 percent but was significantly higher as a share of the total work-force. In 1900, the foreign-born population represented more than one-fifth of the workforce, with many large cities primarily populated by European immigrants. Conversely, mass emigration from Europe to the New World answered a set of European demographic and sociopolitical problems generated by industrialization: urban poverty and consequent social unrest (Golub, 2010). China cannot resolve the social tensions inherent to its capitalist transformation by external-izing population flows in similar fashion: there is no new New World capable of or willing to absorb her "surplus" labor. In the late nine-teenth century Japan and the Euro-Atlantic countries found another outlet for domestic stresses in international imperial expansion. This is not a viable option in the world today. Solutions must be found within.

Sources and problems of legitimacy

The divides of uneven development pose a legitimation problem for a self-reproducing system of power that can no longer base its right to rule on the original revolutionary and anticolonial mandate of the founders of the People's Republic. The Maoist Party-state was born out of war, and a revolution that gave rise to an authoritative sociopo-litical order. It was founded on a potent mix of nationalism and com-munist egalitarianism (rooted in earlier egalitarian norms). Having restored national autonomy and dignity after a century of humiliation and violence at the hands of imperialist nations, the Party could make the claim that it was rightfully empowered to rule. It could portray its domination as necessary to secure the nation from external threat as well as to reconnect with a history of greatness by promoting industrialization-modernization (Mao's famous September 1, 1949, opening address to the First Plenary Session of the Chinese People's Political Consultative Conference, "The Chinese people have stood up," synthesized the constitutive elements of this claim). If Maoism ultimately failed to achieve its modernization objectives, it nonethe-less generated sufficiently broad popular adherence to maintain Party-state legitimacy until the economic, social, and political upheavals of the late 1960s and early 1970s. Coercion played a constant and major role, but the Party had a working-class social base on which its power and authority ultimately rested (its large peasant base had been alienated during the Great Leap Forward). The post-Mao bureau-cratic authoritarian Party-state also makes legitimacy claims based on modernization, national revival, and anti-imperialism (recast as anti-hegemonism and directed primarily at the United States). But the meanings of these concepts and the narrative underlying them have been altered: the link between egalitarianism and modernization has been severed; conservative developmental nationalism has supplanted revolutionary anti-imperialism (which always contained a nationalist subtext but was framed in universalistic terms).

As the transition to "authoritarian capitalism" matured, the Party-state gradually abandoned its historic social bases in favor of emerging constituencies, within and outside the Party, with vested interests in economic liberalization and internationalization (initially in the provinces of South China that were the early winners of the reforms and then in other favored urban areas). Ching Kwan Lee has documented how worker protests erupted in the 1980s in reaction to industrial restructuring and job precariousness with "dozens of strikes occurring in 1980 and 1981 in Wuhan, Taiyuan, Shanghai, Tianjin, Kunming, Manchuria," and cities in Hubei and Shanxi "involving coal miners, steel workers, tool-and-dye workers, and workers in machinery and electronics factories." In the latter part of the decade, even though the government had made strike action illegal by revoking the "freedom to strike" clause from the revised 1982 Constitution, "state workers' discontent intensified due to anxiety, rising unemployment, widening income gaps between managers and workers, and corruption" (Ching Kwan Lee, 2000: 79). Hundreds of strikes erupted throughout urban China in 1987 and 1988. One year later, labor grievances that had been building for years converged with longstanding student demands for public voice, crystallizing into the mass social and democratic movement of 1989 that was crushed at Tiananmen (Wang Hui, 2003). "In May and June 1989, workers in Beijing, Shanghai and other cities left the confines of the factory gates and their collective action took the forms of public protests, independent unionism and political mobilization" (Lee, 2000: 79–80). The Tiananmen events were thus the culmination of a long series of mobilizations involving a broad array of social forces, with workers playing a pivotal if often underestimated role.[11] For their part, by invoking their lineage to the 1919 May Fourth movement, the students made the claim that they, not the authoritarian state, were the legitimate heirs of China's secular modernization efforts (Wasserstrom and Perry, 1994). The social and political movements were crushed by a dominant coalition within the Party, bringing together the old guard and Deng Xiaoping,[12] that feared the prospect of a unified student-worker mobilization, which could have called into question the power and authority of the Party and the State, leading to a Soviet-style regime crisis. The policy outcome was a temporary deceleration of economic liberalization until the 1992 fourteenth Party Congress.

126

Since the 1990s, social turbulence has become widespread, with increasingly frequent if decentralized actions by an array of social actors (peasants, SOE employees, migrants, urban middle classes) across different issue areas (labor conditions and wages, land requisition, police repression, environmental protest, corruption of local officials). According to official counts, the number of "mass incidents"—collective mobilizations and protests of varying sizes and intensity—has sharply increased, from 8,700 in 1994 to 90,000 in 2006, and just under 100,000 since then (unofficial estimates put the number above 180,000). Labor and land conflicts, as well as confrontations with the police and local authorities ("riots"), together account for a majority of large-scale mobilizations, sometimes involving thousands of people. More recently, environmental issues have become a source of intensifying local protests.[13] While these decentralized and uncoordinated actions have not proved regime-threatening, they nonetheless constitute a problem for a regime whose claim to rightful rule still derives from a line of succession going back to the revolutionary founders, even if the links to the past have become tenuous. Effective legitimacy has come to depend essentially on sustained economic growth. In their calculus of power, Chinese leaders after Tiananmen have assumed that state cohesion and Party domination could be maintained and regime-threatening dissent deflected, in spite of deepening social and spatial polarization and persistent social tensions, so long as economic gains accrued to sufficiently large sectors of the population to ensure the regime's output legitimacy. Yet at the same time intensifying protests have pushed them to create some avenues to channel popular discontents, in particular by giving people access to courts through new legal regimes and a major expansion of the judiciary system. (The partially controlled Internet/social media space also is a venue for the expression of dissent.)

In all political regimes societal consent ultimately rests on the demonstration by government that it is responsive to popular grievances, and that it operates within the bounds set by institutionalized rules that govern the exercise of power and constrain its abuse for private ends. In participatory political regimes, rules-based mechanisms (elections, referenda, court systems) allowing for the regular replacement of government and the potential redress of wrongs generally guarantee regime stability. Short of tyranny, non-participatory political regimes claiming the right and not simply the power to rule also require institutionalized channels for the expression and possible redress of grievances. In a political order that severely restricts public voice and imposes harsh penalties on overt political dissent,

127

the judiciary has thus become an arena of expression of grievances over working conditions, land seizures, bureaucratic corruption, or environmental conflicts. A "rights consciousness" among diverse population groups has emerged, in part stimulated by the government's legalist emphasis on the "rule of law," which goes beyond more traditional "rules consciousness." This has translated into a proliferation of court cases over rights issues (Lianjiang Li, 2010).[14] In her important study of labor struggles in post-Mao China, *Against the Law*, Ching Kwan Lee notes:

> The communist regime, for its own legitimacy and survival may be compelled to crack down on corruption and impose serious juridical and legal reform. We cannot underestimate the determination and effectiveness of the Chinese regime's self-reform to establish a law-based government, after its radical transformation from state socialism. Another possible force of change toward a labor rule of law is the pressure generated by workers from below. Workers' expectation of legal justice may grow over time, especially as the social contract can no longer be invoked and if the central governments insists on rule by law to legitimize authoritarianism and restrain subordinate officials. (Ching Kwan Lee, 2007: 242)

This indeed seems to be the direction chosen by the Chinese leadership. The Party appears to have adopted the idea, proposed by the scholar Wei Pan, of a "consultative rule of law regime." This legalist alternative to Western models of democratization (Wei Pan, 2003) would constitute a form of political liberalization without democratization through the creation of a more efficient and more impartial judiciary system that would give stronger legal foundation to single-party rule (Suisheng Zhao, 2003 and 2006). The judiciary reforms taken so far mirror economic liberalization: a controlled system open to individual initiative. The institutionalization of strong legal regimes that effectively protect people from the arbitrary exercise of government or managerial power would unquestionably represent a major step forward. But while it may smooth social relations, the rule by law, which is still far from being effective and which is also marred by corruption, will not in itself meet the fundamental challenge of building an inclusive social order that is perceived as just.

Lastly, there is the question of post-Mao China's national project in relation to the rest of Asia and the world. Following Tiananmen, the Party moved to mobilize nationalism from on top through a Patriotic Education Campaign that "wrapped [the leadership] in the banner of nationalism" and framed its choices as a national historical project. As Suisheng Zhao writes: "The patriotic education campaign was a state-led nationalist movement, which redefined the legitimacy of the post-Tiananmen leadership in a way that would permit the Communist Party's rule to continue on the basis of a non-Communist ideology" and which made development into a "national cause" (Suisheng Zhao, 1998). Dismissed under Mao as "feudalist junk," neo-Confucianism underwent a state-sponsored revival in the mid-1990s as part of an effort to rewrite the national historical narrative and frame the present in continuity with prerevolutionary Chinese history and culture.[15] (This move coincided with the proliferation of essentialist cultural discourses on "Asian values" in other parts of East Asia extolling collective discipline and popular submission to authoritarian or semi-authoritarian paternalist political regimes.) Post-Mao "official nationalism" (Cabestan, 2005) has thus framed modernization as the primary national goal, while concurrently emphasizing the revival of traditional Chinese culture. The tension inherent in the effort to articulate linkages between economic-technological modernity and (essentialized) cultural identity echoes the way in which culture became a battleground during the Meiji and early Showa eras in Japan.

As China's relative weight in the world system has grown, developmental nationalism and cultural nationalism have been fused in discourses emphasizing the country's restoration as the predominant power of East Asia—a discourse that has been accompanied in recent years by assertive and tension-inducing claims of de facto suzerainty over the South and the East China seas. The "Chinese dream" campaign launched by President Xi Jinping in 2012, officially designed to "build a moderately prosperous society and realize national rejuvenation" and promote "national pride," is the latest expression of post-Maoist ideological *bricolage* (soon after Xi's speech the People's Liberation Army had the seamen of the *Liaoning* aircraft carrier form six Chinese characters reading "Chinese dream, military dream" and then disseminated the image on the Net). Since it is partly contingent on global factors that are outside of state control, economic performance is a fragile pillar on which to found legitimacy. And, in China as elsewhere, the instrumental invocation of culture or history, and the mobilization of oppositional nationalist sentiment against supposed external threats, cannot provide a durable foundation for rightful rule: ritual denunciations of past Japanese imperialism or of current United States "hegemonism" can only go so far in channelling popular sentiment and unifying society behind the state. The meanings and purposes that presided over anticolonialism and developmentalism—autonomy, equality, dignity, and popular emancipation—have become reduced in current nationalist discourse to the quest for wealth and power. But this begs two questions: wealth for whom, and power for what purpose?

— 6 —

LOOKING FORWARD

Globalization is characterized by contradictory yet intertwined processes of transnationalization and renationalization, integration and fragmentation, power diffusion and new power concentrations. While production and consumption have been given a truly cosmopolitan character, national segmentation remains a stubborn social fact: the imagined communities constructed along with the rise of the modern nation-state are based on historically constructed identities that resist dissolution in the global market. For reasons relating to historical experiences of subjugation or subordination, most Southern postcolonial states understandably adhere to modern conceptions of sovereignty, power, and national interest. Notwithstanding the internationalization of business and other elite social segments, so too do most Western states, not least the most powerful among them, the United States. Nationalist political forces mobilizing essentialist identities are on the rise in the European Union, where the hybrid transnational-international architecture of the Union has proved deeply deficient, and where the input and output legitimacy of transnational institutions are being called into question. Though it is too early to tell whether the increasingly brittle European experiment in transnational monetary governance will break down, economic and social strains since the 2008 world financial crisis are tearing the democratic fabric of society and setting peoples and nations apart (Burgi, 2014; Piketty, 2014; Golub, 2011). In Asia nationalism is an increasingly prominent dimension of political discourse—in India, China, and Japan in particular. Capitalist development on a world scale, as Marx envisioned, has indeed led to universal interdependence but also to fragmentation and friction through the uneven distribution of gains and losses between and within states. Today it is

131

far from clear which, if any, of the contradictory forces at work will come to dominate.

A crucial question is how the transition out of the Western-centered structure of international relations to a pluralistic and decentralized world system could be managed. The re-emergence of East Asia, and more generally of the global South, poses a significant challenge to the authority of traditional rule-makers, whose ability to set the agenda and shape the global environment is waning. The erosion of Euro-Atlantic authority is evidenced in the irrelevance of old clubs (G7) and the difficulty the traditionally dominant countries and blocs (NATO) have experienced in setting policy agendas and frameworks reflecting their preferences. It is also evidenced in the steady decline of the legitimacy and authority of the Bretton Woods institutions, notably the International Monetary Fund, whose grip on the middle-income countries of the South has loosened since the late 1990s (and in which the voice of the South is growing). The counter-systemic movement that began in the late 1990s in reaction to the IMF's coercive management of the financial crises of the decade is currently maturing, leading to new Southern international institution-building efforts. In March 2013 Brazil, Russia, India, China, and South Africa (BRICS) set up the New Development Bank (NDB), headquartered in Shanghai, with a capital base (money paid in and pledged) of $100 billion, which will combine investment and monetary functions, serving as a lending institution for infrastructure development projects, as well as a reserve facility to deal with balance of payments issues. In October 2014, China founded the Asian Infrastructure Investment Bank (AIIB), the membership of which now includes all Asian states with the exception of Japan and which, like the NDB, has a $100 billion capital base (by comparison the Japanese-led Asian Development Bank (ADB) has a capital base of $160 billion, the World Bank $220 billion).

The importance of these initiatives, which have been met with serious but ineffective resistance from the United States,[1] should not be underestimated. While China and other major countries of the South are still seeking greater decision-making voice in existing international organizations (IO), they are now creating an institutional system parallel to the Bretton Woods institutions that have underpinned world capitalism since 1945. This has huge implications: the ability to set international frameworks and maintain regimes is an essential component of power. "[May 2015] may be remembered," writes Lawrence Summers, "as the moment the United States lost its role as the underwriter of the global economic system. . . . I can think

132

of no event since Bretton Woods comparable to the combination of China's efforts to establish a major new institution and the failure of the U.S. to persuade dozens of its traditional allies . . . to stay out of it" (Summers, 2015). If the politics of re-emergence still lags behind economics, the decision to create the NDB and AIIB demonstrates the will of Southern states to "take the future into their own hands" (Stern et al., 2013).

While it is implausible that the East (China) will supplant the West (the United States) at the center and apex of a new global hierarchy, at least in the foreseeable future, there is no question that power will further diffuse along with economic rebalancing. For observers sensitive to the need to redress historic injustices, greater relative international equality is normatively desirable a priori. Yet it also implies an accentuation of interstate competition for resources, capital, technology, status, and political voice. Global rebalancing, which is still in an early phase, therefore carries significant problems and risks.

Conflicting representations and collective narratives heighten the tensions of the transition. For the historically dominant countries, notably the United States, the intellectual challenge going forward will be to accept a more modest imprint on international politics and adjust to a decentered world in which power will have to be shared. This may well prove difficult, given deeply rooted assumptions about world order, cultural hierarchy, and historical purpose—the imperial cosmology of Euro-Atlantic modernity that continues to inform the Western gaze on world politics (Golub, 2010). For elite segments in the U.S. that were looking forward to a new American Century after 1991, and who remain a potent domestic force, the prospect of power redistribution is deeply problematic. As prominent students of modern imperial history point out: "leading powers do not take readily to the idea that the end of their period of dominance is not necessarily the end of the world. Accordingly, they find it hard to envisage pluralistic alternatives to the rule of a single power" (Cain and Hopkins, 2000: 656). Power diffusion to the formerly subaltern Orient, the Other of imperial modernity, makes acceptance of change all the more difficult.

For re-emerging societies the intellectual and policy challenges are just as great. Notwithstanding common experiences of struggle to attain independence, heterogeneous interests generate collective-action problems that have bedevilled the global South since the Bandung Conference (1955). As the ambiguous relations of India or Vietnam with China evidence, deepening economic interdependence

133

has not erased a history of rivalry and mutual distrust. Real-world relations among Southern states—competitive national economic practices and political rivalries—contrast with rhetorical claims of "South–South cooperation" and "South–South solidarity." Moreover, the major actors of global rebalancing do not offer a positive intellectual alternative to the capitalist world order that they are restructuring from within. If rebalancing conforms to the historic aim of generations of anticolonial leaders and thinkers, gaining upward mobility and achieving de facto and not merely de jure equality, the way in which it is occurring has emptied the aim of its earlier progressive contents. Anticolonialism still constitutes a component of the identities and discourses of the re-emerging South, even in conservative nationalist circles in Asia that often read the current transformation in oppositional cultural terms (Asian versus Western "values"). But unlike earlier generations of postcolonial leaders and intellectuals who aimed for social revolution, or sought to invent a third way between capitalism and communism, the actors of the current shift in global power relations are claiming a central competitive place in the world capitalist system that their predecessors had attempted to either reform or supplant. The success of that claim has dampened, if not entirely submerged, the politically universalistic and socially emancipatory dimensions of the long struggle for independence, equality, and justice. This concluding chapter is devoted to these problems and normative predicaments.

Accommodating China's re-emergence

In recent decades, the United States has sought to enmesh China in the disciplines of the world capitalist economy set by the Bretton Woods institutions and the dominant Western states. The assumption guiding U.S. policy has been that incorporation into the Western world order would shape China's economic model and its political path: market opening would gradually create conditions for an evolution of the political system, while patterning the Chinese economy to meet the needs of dominant markets. Similar assumptions about the correlation of economic and political liberalism applied to postcommunist Russia. Global economic liberalization and democratization would consolidate the post-1991 "liberal world order" under U.S. leadership. In the 1990s, "U.S. leaders saw the unchecked power at their disposal as an opportunity to mold the international environment, to enhance the U.S. position even more, and to reap even greater benefits in the future," by using a mixture of persuasion and coercion to get "as many countries as possible to embrace their particular vision of a liberal-capitalist world order" (Walt, 2006: 29–30). However, the Chinese leadership's decision in the late 1970s to gradually integrate into the regional (and then the world) capitalist economy, leading to China's accession to the World Trade Organization in 2001, is now proving a major challenge to U.S. economic and political predominance. Abundant and worried critiques of the successes of authoritarian capitalism suggest that China's emerging position as a semi-autonomous core of the world capitalist economy is a far more problematic outcome for U.S. power and authority than the Japan-centric "regional bloc" that U.S. observers were so concerned about in the 1980s and early 1990s. Extensive and multifaceted economic linkages have combined with new competitive tensions and geopolitical rivalries.

The United States and China have become deeply interdependent at trade and monetary levels. The U.S. is China's second-largest export market, absorbing 16.7 percent of China's manufactured exports, and China is the U.S.' third-largest export market (around 7 percent of U.S. exports). The stock of U.S. foreign direct investment (FDI) in China totalled $51.4 billion in 2012, a figure that understates China's importance as a production platform for U.S. transnational firms working through subcontractors on the mainland. At the monetary level, the two countries are tightly linked through China's role in the financing of U.S. current account deficits. As global imbalances accentuated over the past decade and a half, with the huge and rising current account surpluses accumulated by China and other Southern states corresponding to equally huge deficits on the part of the United States, China became the leading investor in sovereign U.S. debt. China's foreign currency reserves rose from $170 billion in 2000 to over $1.54 trillion in 2007, making up more than a third of Asian reserves and nearly one-fifth of total international reserves. Since 2008, China's reserves have more than doubled, reaching $3.88 trillion in 2013 (World Bank, 2014). China currently owns 20 percent of sovereign U.S. debt—$1.239 trillion out of a total $6.217 trillion of the Treasury securities owned by foreign holders. If one adds Hong Kong to the total, China owns $1.4 trillion dollars worth of U.S. securities, placing it in a creditor position well ahead of Japan and other creditors, such as the oil-producing states (China is also thought to own part of the $1 trillion or more currently placed in offshore financial centers in the Caribbean and Europe).

A "balance of financial terror"

This curious configuration, in which a large middle-income country finances the deficits of the richest and most powerful country of the world, has generated a complex and uneasy relationship in which the U.S. dependence on external capital flows for debt financing, and hence its potential vulnerability to exogenously dictated adjustments, is matched by China's and other surplus countries' continuing dependence on the domestic U.S. market to maintain export-oriented growth trajectories. Codependency also applies with respect to the dollar, the value of which is suspended from continued inflows of capital and which surplus countries cannot suddenly divest themselves of without incurring major losses (nearly two-thirds of world currency reserves are held in U.S. dollars). Interdependence creates incentives for coordination and cooperation, but the sustainability of current global trade and financial imbalances is questionable. The rational and optimal solution would be a coordinated multilateral effort to gradually reduce imbalances by stimulating demand in surplus countries (this also applies to Germany, whose enormous trade surpluses adversely affect other EU countries and the world economy; Wolf, 2010). But given dominant competitive logics, a far less cooperative outcome is imaginable that could well lead to a new global economic crisis. In the case of China and the U.S., the threshold at which equilibrium is broken—that is, when one or another actor chooses or is forced to defect from the arrangement—is subject to contingent domestic and international circumstances. Commenting on this problem a few years ago, Lawrence Summers noted that the U.S.' "substantial dependence on foreign capital" and its "substantial current account and trade deficit" had generated a "balance of financial terror" that is fraught with dangers for the United States. One of the "troubling aspect[s] of this dependence is its geopolitical significance":

> There is surely something odd about the world's greatest power being the world's greatest debtor. In order to finance prevailing levels of consumption and investment, must the United States be as dependent as it is on the discretionary acts of what are inevitably political entities in other countries? It is true and can be argued forcefully that the incentive for Japan or China to dump treasury bills at a rapid rate is not very strong, given the consequences that it would have for their own economies. That is a powerful argument, and it is a reason a prudent person would avoid immediate concern. But it surely cannot be prudent for us as a country to rely on a kind of balance of financial terror to hold back reserve sales that would threaten our stability (Summers, 2004).

136

If the unwinding of global imbalances "happens suddenly and without control the consequences are likely to be very serious for the cyclical performance of the United States and the global economy. Ultimately, the consequences of these adjustments being mismanaged are likely to be profound for the global integration process that we all regard as so very important" (Summers, 2004). In a similar vein, the realist historian Paul Kennedy, basing himself on the history of the successive centerings and re-centerings of the world capitalist economy, writes: "no historian can resist pointing out that surplus bank savings have usually accompanied the alterations in the military-political balances of power, either running ahead of them or following them: the Lombard cities to Antwerp and Amsterdam, from there to London; from London, after a long time, to New York; and from New York. . . to where? Shanghai? Does it not matter when as a Great Power, you owe an awful lot of money to someone else. He who pays the piper will sooner or later call the tune" (Kennedy, 2010: 6–9). This is not always the case: Japan, the leading creditor of the United States from the 1980s to the late 2000s, has never called the tune or even made a serious claim to world leadership. Even if it had wished to do so, which was and is not the case, it was never seriously conceivable that a country of Japan's size, one that moreover is dependent upon the U.S. for security, would have been in a position to claim world hegemony and supplant the United States.

China is another matter, given its scale, but its creditor position generates vulnerabilities as well as strengths. It is in China's long-term interest to reduce its massive dollar holdings, which expose the country to discretionary monetary decisions of the United States. This problem became a matter of public debate in China during the 2008 crisis, which put into question the soundness of U.S. policy, the robustness of its financial system, and the performance of regulators. The Chairman of the China Banking Regulatory Commission (CBRC), Liu Minkang, told an audience at the British Museum on April 26, 2008: "Globalisation, if mismanaged, can be disruptive and even disastrous to the course of civilisation." Another official of the CBRC called for a review of the "Western consensus on the relation between the market and government." Chinese critiques intensified as the crisis spread to the rest of the world economy, depressing global demand and contracting world trade. Some commentators argued for a "de-Americanized world" as Chinese GDP growth fell suddenly and sharply (from over 10 percent prior to the crisis to 7.4 percent in 2014): "The developing and emerging market economies need to have more say in major international financial institutions including the World Bank and the International Monetary Fund so that they could better reflect the transformation of the global economic and political landscape. What may be included as a key part of an effective reform is the introduction of a new international reserve currency . . . to replace the dominant U.S. dollar" (*Xinhua*, October 13, 2013).

The decision to accelerate the internationalization of the renminbi (RMB) reflects the idea that a tripartite world monetary system would reduce exchange rate volatility and shield China from U.S. decisions and choices. (It should be noted in passing that having placed some hopes in Europe as a possible economic counterweight to the United States, the Chinese leadership is quite mystified about the pro-cyclical management of the Eurozone crisis that is leading to Japanese-style secular stagnation and a contraction of Chinese exports.) Such a tripartite system is still a long way off. The RMB's use in cross-border trade has certainly greatly expanded over the past few years: in 2013 it overtook the euro as the second most used currency in global trade finance (8.66 percent against 6.64 percent). The currency is playing a growing role in intra-Asian trade, with 20 percent of China's foreign trade now settled in RMB. Offshore centers clearing the currency have been set up in Hong Kong, Singapore, London, Taiwan, and Frankfurt. But the RMB accounts for a small share of global trade settlements that are overwhelmingly dollar-denominated. It will take quite some time before a tripartite monetary system comes into being. Between now and this hypothetical future, the essential test for China will be to move gradually from extraverted growth to a developmental regime based primarily on domestic demand and ecologically and socially sustainable development.

Geopolitical competition

Rather than taming Chinese power, integration into the world capitalist system has served to augment it. China's economic expansion has been accompanied by a significant growth of military spending, investment in naval power projection capabilities, and a new assertiveness in the South and East China seas, where China and its neighbors entertain rival territorial claims. Estimates of the PRC's military budget vary according to calculations based on current exchange rates or purchasing power parity (PPP), and are subject to uncertainties related to Chinese official statistics, but there is no question that the country is engaged in a sustained defense expansion and modernization effort. According to the authoritative Stockholm International

138

Peace Research Institute (SIPRI), defense spending has risen from $33.4 billion in 2000 to over $188 billion in 2013 (in constant U.S. 2010 dollars). This represents less than one-third of U.S. expenditures ($640 billion), but it places China well ahead of all other Asian states as well as other large spenders such as Russia or India (SIPRI, 2014). Basing themselves on PPP estimates that take domestic personnel and procurements costs into account, some analysts argue that China's defence expenditures are already over a third of that of the U.S. Moreover, unlike the Soviet Union, which exhausted itself in its long arms race with the United States, Chinese defense spending is aligned with the country's rate of growth and appears sustainable over the long run. On the assumption that China will be able to maintain a relatively strong growth trajectory, Chinese military capabilities will continue to increase in line with GDP. According to some analysts, "this will matter a great deal in terms of [China's] ability to enforce territorial claims and achieve its foreign policy objectives. In these terms, China's ability to wield international political power would seem to be very close to that of the U.S." (Robertson, 2015).

Whether international political power derives necessarily from the barrel of a gun is a debatable point. Moreover, quantitative comparisons do not give an accurate picture of the balance, since they leave out qualitative dimensions (technological advancement, force structures, training and experience, and more) that point to continuing broad U.S. military predominance well into the future. As Michael Cox stresses, strategic disparity is still great: "The military power of other states . . . does not compare [with the United States], even China's with its huge standing army (which has not fought a war since the disastrous invasion of Vietnam in 1979) and its increasingly large blue water navy that now includes one aircraft carrier [that] hardly compares with America's 11 carrier groups. . . . Taken together [the U.S.'] many allies in the region...spend more on the military forces than China" (Cox, 2012: 377). That being said, China's growing military capabilities have nonetheless generated concerns in Washington over the future balance of power in East Asia. In 2010, the Obama administration announced a "strategic pivot" to Asia, a "vast and dynamic increase in U.S. focus and depth of engagement in the region" (Cambell and Andrews, 2013), reflecting the recognition that China's rise is part of a "historic transition . . . that will unfold over decades" (USNSS, 2015), with major consequences for the United States in the twenty-first century. In recent years the U.S. has thus consolidated bilateral security ties with traditional allies (Australia, Japan, Singapore, Indonesia, Thailand, the Philippines, South Korea,

Taiwan), developed new ones with Vietnam through trade agreements and a formalized security and defense dialogue, and sought intensified defense cooperation with India.

U.S. policy is synthesized in the White House's 2015 *National Security Strategy*:

> The United States welcomes the rise of a stable, peaceful, and prosperous China. We seek to develop a constructive relationship with China that delivers benefits for our two peoples and promotes security and prosperity in Asia and around the world. We seek cooperation on shared regional and global challenges such as climate change, public health, economic growth, and the denuclearization of the Korean Peninsula. While there will be competition, we reject the inevitability of confrontation. At the same time, we will manage competition from a position of strength while insisting that China uphold international rules and norms on issues ranging from maritime security to trade and human rights. (USNSS, 2015: 24)

Or, as President Obama forthrightly and concisely put the matter in his 2015 State of the Union Address: "China wants to write the rules for the world's fastest-growing region. . . . Why would we let that happen? We should write those rules" (Obama, 2015).

The strategic pivot, which seems currently designed to avoid the constitution of a Sino-centric regional political economy, reflects longstanding U.S. strategic doctrine over the balance of power in Asia and the Pacific, and should be read in a longer historic framework. Asia and the Pacific have always loomed large in the U.S. geopolitical imagination: nineteenth-century U.S. continental expansion was coextensive with deepening commercial and military engagements in Asia and the Pacific (Cumings, 2009). The U.S. was already an important actor in Asia in the mid-nineteenth century, when it gained trading and extraterritorial rights in China under the most-favored-nation provision of the unequal treaties that followed the First Opium War,[2] and went on to coercively pressure Japan's opening to foreign trade in the early 1850s. As industrial capitalism matured in the decades after the Civil War (1861–1865) and the continental frontier closed, the U.S. looked to Asia and to China in particular, as a new and decisive space for commercial expansion. Having become the world's leading industrial power in the 1890s, and having founded an empire in Asia through the annexation of the Philippines in 1898, the U.S. saw itself dominating both shores of the Pacific: "To extend now the authority of the United States over the great Philippine Archipelago is to fence in the China Sea and secure an almost equally

140

commanding position on the other side of the Pacific—doubling our control of it and of the fabulous trade the twentieth century will see it bear. Rightly used, it enables the United States to convert the Pacific Ocean into an American lake" (Whitelaw Reid quoted in Cumings, 2009: 127). Theodore Roosevelt, one of the architects of the 1898 Spanish–American War, contemporaneously wrote: "I wish to see the United States the dominant power on the shores of the Pacific" (quoted in Beale, 1989: 76). He acted to accomplish that aim after assuming the presidency in 1901 by initiating the construction of the Panama Canal, which created a passage between the Atlantic and Pacific Oceans, by erecting the Subic Bay naval base in the Philippines, and building the Great White Fleet that made the U.S. the world's second-largest naval power.

A half-century later, following Japan's defeat, the Pacific became an "American lake" dotted with a network of floating and fixed military bases that secured U.S. control of maritime routes, and served in the wars that reshaped East Asia's post-1945 political economy (Chapter 3). The vision of the postwar foreign policy and security elites, which drew on the U.S.' earlier experience of expansion in Asia, was of lasting U.S. regional hegemony through the assertion of U.S. power. Simply, the U.S. aimed to seize "control of every wave of the Pacific Ocean" (Secretary of State Dean Rusk quoted in Lyons, 2006: 26). Though few would formulate the idea quite so hubristically today, this vision has not fundamentally changed. Writing the rules means inhibiting changes that would disturb the status quo, and challenge U.S. positions in Asia and the Pacific. "The domination by a single power," writes Henry Kissinger, "of either of Eurasia's two principal spheres—Europe or Asia—remains a good definition of strategic danger for America, Cold War or no Cold War" (Kissinger, 1994: 813). The concern is over the potential emergence of a "grouping that would have the capacity to outstrip America economically and, in the end, militarily. . . . That danger would have to be resisted even were the dominant power apparently benevolent, for if the intentions ever changed America would find itself with a grossly diminished capacity for effective resistance and a growing inability to shape events" (Kissinger, 1994).

This negative reason for maintaining the status quo is complemented by the positive claim, ubiquitously affirmed by U.S. practitioners of power and mainstream international relations theorists, that, by securing the balance of power and an open international economy, the U.S. is providing international public goods and acting de facto in the general interest. The challenge for U.S. diplomacy, writes Stephen Walt in a concise formulation of this idea, is how to get the "rest of the world to welcome U.S. primacy" by encouraging "states to see its dominant position as beneficial (or at least bearable)" and convincing them that "American power . . . will be used judiciously and for the broader benefit of mankind" (Walt, 2006: 26). The problem, of course, is that China and quite a few other Southern states have reasons to read U.S. power in a less benign light. They cannot be sure that the U.S. will act benevolently in the future any more than the U.S. can presume that its potential rivals will, all the more that the U.S. has "consistently [opposed] any state that threatened to establish regional hegemony in Europe and Asia so as to avoid facing a rival power with capabilities comparable to America's own" (Walt, 2006: 71). If many U.S. observers see China as a "revisionist" great power purposefully aiming to alter the regional and global status quo (Mead, 2014), prominent Chinese analysts symmetrically view the U.S. as "an aggressive, ambitious, self-righteous, and highly militarized 'Rome'," aiming for regime change in China (Lanxin Xiang, 2014: 116).

Chinese officials read the pivot as a policy of militarized containment and encirclement of China: The United States is "laying out forces across the Asia-Pacific region in advance to contain the rise of China . . . bolstering its five major military alliances in the Asia-Pacific region and adjusting the positioning of its five major military base clusters. Who can believe [the U.S.] is not directing this at China?" (Major General Luo Yuan quoted in Buckley, 2012). Generally speaking, since the early 1970s, when Beijing and Washington entered into a de facto security alliance directed against the Soviet Union, China has taken care to avoid major diplomatic clashes with the United States. This is evidenced, among other ways, in the PRC's cautious voting record at the United Nations Security Council (UNSC). From 1971 to 2006, the PRC used its veto power as a permanent member of the Council only twice, whereas the U.S. cast vetoes seventy-six times, the United Kingdom twenty-four times, France fourteen times, and the Soviet Union and the later Russian Federation thirteen times. China voted for eleven UNSC resolutions on Iraq after 1990 but abstained from voting Resolution 678 authorizing the use of force. On July 31, 2006, the PRC voted for UNSC Resolution 1696 that provided for sanctions against Iran directed at the latter's uranium enrichment and reprocessing efforts. In May 2014, China joined Russia in vetoing a Security Council referral of Syria to the International Criminal Court (ICC).[3] Whether this signals a broader shift in China's strategy of diplomatic restraint remains to be seen.

The Chinese leadership has developed a narrative of "peaceful rise" that would allow for a "new type of great power relations" based on conflict avoidance, economic interdependence, cooperation in global governance, and mutual respect for sovereignty.[4] The message of scholars close to the State Council is that China is a "new type of superpower" and that the country's re-emergence (or "national restoration" in Xi Jinping's formulation) will lead to shared "prosperity that has no precedent in human history" (Angang Hu, 2007: 2). In the long run, China's re-emergence will "inevitably lead to multi-polarization of the world" and no country, "not even the United States [will be able] to rule the world" (2). This discourse reflects reasonable concerns that the country's developmental trajectory could be compromised by conflict with the United States. The problem is the transition. "The last thing China needs," Orne Westad pertinently notes, "is a long-term strategic face-off with the most powerful country on earth of the kind that destroyed the Soviet Union in the 1970s and 1980s" (Westad, 2012: 464).

Military containment?

For structural realists such as John Mearsheimer, the narrative of interdependence is misleading. "China cannot rise peacefully," he has stated, and conflict lies ahead. Following deterministic assumptions about the mechanics of interstate competition under conditions of anarchy, he argues that the U.S. and China will in coming decades be pushed into "an intense security competition . . . with considerable potential for war" (Mearsheimer, 2010: 382). China's rise, he writes, "has the potential to fundamentally alter the architecture of the international system. . . . If China continues to grow economically, it will attempt to dominate Asia the way the United States dominates the Western Hemisphere." In response, the "United States . . . will go to enormous lengths to prevent China from achieving regional hegemony" by forming a regional military coalition to contain China with willing local allies. The argument rests on the theoretical assumption that all states, undifferentiated like-units socialized into a competitive international system lacking higher authorities, are caught in a security dilemma that drives them to maximize their relative power to enhance their prospects of survival. In seeking to maximize their power and minimize their insecurity, the U.S. and China would be acting rationally as they stumbled into irrational conflict. The axiological neutrality of the observer vanishes, however, when he moves to prescription. According to press reports, during a 2014 discussion of his work,

Mearsheimer expressed astonishment about "Americans and people in allied states who profess wanting to see China grow economically," formulating the hope that "China's economy falters or collapses." This would eliminate "a potentially immense security threat for the United States and its allies." Were China to "reach a GDP per capita that is comparable to Taiwan or Hong Kong today it would be a greater potential threat to the United States than anything America has previously dealt with" (Keck, 2014).[5] It is certainly refreshing to read a theoretically consistent scholar who dispenses with diplomatic niceties. But he appears not to have thought this problem carefully through: besides the incalculable global transmission effects through monetary and trade channels, a Chinese economic collapse would generate strong pressures to externalize domestic problems, with a strong likelihood of regional if not global chaos.

The regional and global conditions for a militarized containment strategy leading to China's exhaustion in a protracted arms race are not in fact in place. Contrary to what Mearsheimer and other observers seem to believe, containment is not acceptable to most Asian states. Many countries of the region indeed fear an overbearing China but, being fated to live forever in the PRC's neighborhood, do not want to be enmeshed in a great-power rivalry that could lead to regional destabilization or possibly open conflict. If a number of countries in Southeast and Northeast Asia are looking for strategic reassurance from the U.S. they are simultaneously deepening their linkages with China. As noted earlier, with the sole exception of Japan, which is currently studying the question, all Asian states have joined the AIIB and are already deeply enmeshed in Chinese trade and the domestic Chinese market. The PRC currently accounts for nearly 40 percent of Taiwanese trade, 21 percent of South Korean trade (which is more than Korean trade with the U.S. and Japan combined), 20 percent of Japanese trade, and 14 percent of ASEAN trade. In 2010 the China-ASEAN Free Trade Agreement came into effect.

Unless China severely overreaches in the South or East China seas by seizing (rather than claiming) territory through unilateral action, a possible but unlikely development, a coherent regional anti-Chinese coalition will not come into being. A pro-Chinese regional coalition is not any more likely. China's appeals to "Asianness" based on cultural proximities, and in some cases shared historical experience, have some purchase in a region allergic to universalizing Western discourses. As one Chinese official writes: some Asian countries "share the same bed [with the United States] but have different dreams" (PLA Daily, 2012). That does not mean, however, that they share Chinese dreams.

The smaller states of East Asia have not chosen sides: they are seeking through balance, as weaker states in the uncomfortable proximity of great powers are wont to do, to preserve some autonomy in the face of both Asian-Pacific giants.

Containment, advocated by sovereignists on the right of the U.S. political spectrum, would also run counter to the interests of the politically influential transnationalized segments of U.S. business that are deeply invested in China and dependent on her continuing economic and political stability. Until now U.S. geopolitical concerns have not come into contradiction with economic interests, which weigh in the strategic calculus. Since the late 1970s, U.S. state behavior toward China has been fairly consistent. After a brief freeze in the aftermath of Tiananmen (1989), the U.S. quickly restored normal diplomatic relations with China. Despite recurrent frictions over monetary policy and one potentially perilous symbolic test of strength (the 1995–1996 Taiwan Strait Crisis), bilateral relations have been mostly steady. Like nineteenth-century British leaders who more often than not acted in symbiosis with London's financial industry, which was "more international [and] extensive . . . than even the political empire of which it was the capital" (Feis, 1973: 5),[6] U.S. leaders and state managers must and do take the interests of U.S. capital into account, since the latter constitutes an important component of what C. Wright Mills dubbed the "power elite." As in London, where profit and power went hand in hand, U.S. political and economic actors are often indistinguishable, as seen in the circulatory flows between the private sector and government. There are thus strong reasons to argue that interdependence reduces the likelihood of a major political disruption.

These circumstances could change: the balance of social forces within the U.S. or in China could evolve in an aggressive nationalist direction, leading to a contradiction of interests. As Polanyi points out in his discussion of the breakdown of the nineteenth-century international system, the "peace interest" in Europe generated by capitalist development led "international capital . . . [which was bound] to be the loser in case of war," to act as a mediating agency to forestall or limit interstate conflict. The First World War made clear, however, that "power had precedence over profit. However closely their realms interpenetrated, ultimately it was war that laid down the law to business" (Polanyi, 1972: 12). The analysts who, like Kautsky, argued before the breakdown that rationality would dictate "far-sighted capitalists" to forgo national monopolistic claims in favor of transnational class interests were proven wrong. Of course, history does not mechanically repeat itself. But the object of study is moving as we observe it: we are only at the beginning of the story of China's re-emergence, and it cannot be excluded that rivalry could upset interdependence. This is not a foregone conclusion: the more likely path of Sino-U.S. relations will be a complex mix of both, with convergence in some issue areas and divergence in others.

Even if it were to become official, U.S. policy containment would not work. China, despite external vulnerabilities and major domestic challenges, is not in the same political or economic position as the Soviet Union in the 1980s: China will soon account for one-fifth of world GDP (PPP). While economic and social strains could lead to setbacks, neither the state nor the economy are about to collapse. A half-century ago, when China was in a much weaker economic and strategic position, Hans Morgenthau lucidly warned in 1965 that containment would fail, leaving only two options to U.S. policy-makers: general war or accommodation. His analysis deserves to be quoted at length:

> Even if China were threatening her neighbors primarily by military means, it would be impossible to contain her by erecting a military wall at the periphery of her empire. For China is, even in her present under-developed state, the dominant power in Asia. She is this by virtue of the quality and quantity of her population, her geographic position, her civilization, her past power remembered and her future power anticipated. Anybody who has traveled in Asia with his eyes and ears open must have been impressed by the enormous impact which the resurgence of China has made upon all manner of men, regardless of class and political conviction, from Japan to Pakistan. The issue China poses is political and cultural predominance. The United States can no more contain Chinese influence in Asia by arming South Vietnam and Thailand than China could contain American influence in the Western Hemisphere by arming, say, Nicaragua and Costa Rica. If we are convinced that we cannot live with a China predominant on the mainland of Asia, then we must strike at the heart of Chinese power—that is, rather than try to contain the power of China, we must try to destroy that power itself. Thus there is logic on the side of that small group of Americans who are convinced that war between the United States and China is inevitable and that the earlier it comes the better will be the chances for the United States to win it. (Morgenthau, 1965: 25)

The United States chose, reasonably, not to war with China. As Morgenthau noted: "To be defeated China has to be conquered. . . . If we do not want to set ourselves goals which cannot be attained with the means we are willing to employ we must learn to accommodate ourselves to the predominance of China on the Asian mainland." The logic of this assessment is much stronger today than it was in the 1960s. Given the scale of devastation that it would imply, a general Sino-U.S. war is not conceivable, unless irresistible social forces, akin to those that led to Europe's cataclysmic self-destruction, are set into motion that sweep leaders into conflicts beyond their volition and control. Since "a long and systematic attempt at destroying each other with any means short of all-out war . . . is not in the cards" (Westad, 2012: 464), and the conditions of possibility of a general war are not present, this leaves open only one option: accommodation.

Western visions of order

The ideational dimension of the problem is significant. Liberal U.S. international relations scholars have proposed an alternative to structural realist visions of inevitable conflict, where Chinese power would be tamed through China's deepening enmeshment in the regimes and disciplines of the "liberal world order" founded and managed, until now, by the West. John Ikenberry, who has figured prominently in the debate, argues that the "struggle over the rights, privileges and responsibilities of the leading states within the system" need not lead to a "volcanic struggle with the United States over global rules and leadership", since the rising powers "are finding incentives and opportunities to engage and integrate into this order, doing so to advance their own interests. For these states, the road to modernity runs through the existing international order." In other words, to continue prospering China and other re-emerging states need to fold themselves into the "liberal order" rather than challenge it. The normative aim of the argument is to convert the "coming power shift into a peaceful change on terms favourable to the United States." Through its "leadership of the Western order" and a "revived Western system," the United States can "shape the environment in which China will make critical strategic choices," ultimately leading to the "triumph" of the West (Ikenberry, 2008). In a similar vein, Joseph Nye argues that the American Century, the post-1945 period in which the U.S. was "central to the workings of the global balance of power and to the provision of global public goods," will endure for decades so long as the United States proves able, across various dimensions of power, to influence the global balance and, by "making smart strategic choices," to avoid entropy: maintaining the balance in Asia, creating alliances and institutions for global system management, and incentivizing China to become a "responsible stakeholder" in the international system (Nye, 2015).

Claims that current institutions and governance regimes serve the universal interest through the provision of international public goods are no more convincing than the historically inaccurate but oft-repeated Eurocentric claim that the Pax Britannica ushered in a cooperative liberal world order in which the "cosmopolitan interest [was] joined to the national interest of the dominant power" (Gilpin, 1987: 183). For the peoples on the receiving end of empire, the nineteenth-century European-centered world system was anything but liberal and cooperative. The post-1945 U.S.-centered world capitalist order differs in important respects from the European imperial order that it supplanted. But, as far as the plural "Third Worlds" were and are concerned, Pax Americana did not constitute the sharp break from empire that U.S. mainstream observers are wont to claim: the "contrast between a formal British or wider European colonialism and an informal American imperium should not be overstated" (Howe, 2003). Like the European-centered system, which was generally liberal in the core but illiberal in the colonial peripheries, where despotism was the norm, the Pax has been characterized by differentiated patterns of relations in the North and the South: liberalism and institutionalized cooperation prevails in the transatlantic area, but this has not been the case in Latin America, Africa, the Mideast, and Asia, which have been arenas of intervention and regular, not to say systematic, political and economic intrusion. U.S. interventions, from overt and covert military operations to coercive economic diplomacy or the imposition of economic models (the "Washington Consensus"), carried out at the bilateral level or indirectly through the medium of multilateral institutions, are animated by "a bipolar imperialist conception of the international, wherein Western states are rewarded with civilizational status and hence hyper-sovereignty (the right to intervene in uncivilized states), while Eastern polities are demoted to the status of conditional sovereignty" (Hobson, 2010: 44–45). They were and are "liberal" only insofar as they reflect classical nineteenth-century liberal conceits, articulated by such major figures as John Stuart Mill and Alexis de Tocqueville, founded on a "standard of civilization" that divides the world according to a cultural hierarchy (Mazower, 2006 and 2012; Pitts, 2006) invoking the "civilizing mission" of the West.

Nye acknowledges that the American Century was not "always benign to non-members" of the "club," such as Iran and Guatemala in the 1950s or Chile in the 1970s, but still considers that on the

148

whole it has proven itself the best possible global arrangement. But neither he nor Ikenberry take into account the legitimate Southern suspicion, fuelled by a long history of unequal relations, that universalizing Western discourses mask the interests and purposes of dominant states. Southern states are challenging the Bretton Woods institutional architecture today because of its hegemonic features and its manifest failure over many decades to promote fair distributive outcomes. Efforts by the Non Aligned Movement and the G77 in the early 1970s to found a new international economic order through a fair global bargain foundered in large part because of the obstinate and ultimately successful resistance of Europe and the U.S. (Golub, 2013). Countries having experienced the loss of autonomy and socio-economic distress resulting from IMF structural adjustment programs have little reason to believe that the current institutions and regimes of global governance reflect the general interest. Rules are not neutral. They reflect the preferences of rule-makers, who never act under a veil of ignorance regarding the way their rule-setting shapes behaviors and generates preferred outcomes. In effect, like Falconeri in *The Leopard*, Ikenberry is arguing for a change that leaves everything, or nearly everything, the same.

"The road to the East runs through the West," he writes. The idea that the former peripheries must follow the pathway and fit into the mold set by Europe and the neo-European offshoots betrays the Orientalist underpinnings of the hierarchical Western imagination of the world. As John Agnew compellingly shows, the modern geopolitical imagination was formed through the experience of international expansion that generated a new consciousness and mental map of the world as a "single if-divided . . . global space." The early-modern Western observer, "trading and conquering as well as looking," came to see the world as a "differentiated, integrated, hierarchically ordered whole" (Agnew, 1998: 16). In the nineteenth century, seeing the world became synonymous with domination as global systems of control and management of resources, people and space were put into place. Historical contingency was naturalized as destiny. In the mental map of the late modern Euro-Atlantic elites, the West became the necessary center of the world. The late-century British imperial observer, as Conrad suggestively writes in the opening lines of *Heart of Darkness*, could thus envision the Thames as "an interminable waterway . . . leading to the uttermost ends of the earth."

The new geopolitical imagination was coextensive with the emergent master narrative of modernity that traced a straight line from Athens and Rome, through the Copernican revolution and the

Enlightenment, to the scientific and material achievements of the nineteenth and twentieth centuries. It framed Western domination as the outcome of the ascending path of European Reason in history. This evolutionary schema, whose teleological core is contained in Hegel's famous statement that the "history of the world travels from East to West, for Europe is absolutely the end of History" (Hegel, 1899: 103–4), represents the West as the fount and matrix of rationality (systematic empirical cognitive enquiry), as a historic singularity and the end point of historical time. In so doing the narrative of the "rise of the West" operated and naturalized a division of the world into fixed cultural and racial hierarchies. Though the ancients divided the world between civilized and barbarous, it is only with the European Industrial Revolution that an ontological distinction emerges between moderns and pre-moderns or advanced and primitive. These distinctions hardened into a systematic narrative that pictured the "West" as the evolutionary arrow of history. The modern social sciences were built on this dualist foundation: in differing ways, Hegel, Marx, Mill, and Weber, to mention but a few of the most important intellectual figures, all start from the assumption of some form or other of Western singularity. Weber has had the most enduring influence, his *Protestant Ethic and the Spirit of Capitalism* spawning the neo-Weberian culturalists and modernization theorists of the twentieth century (Parsons, Eisenstadt, Bellah, Rostow, and the rest) and, in a decaying intellectual trajectory, their heirs (Huntington, Landes, Bloom, and Niall Ferguson). "The more extravagant ethnocentric claims," Goody aptly notes, involve not only "presenting contemporary or recent advantage as virtually permanent, but interpreting that advantage in terms of the evolving aspects of European society alone, at least since the sixteenth century and often long before" (2006: 154).

Modern Western philosophy and social theory thus participated in the construction and legitimation of the hierarchical world order that resulted from Western global expansion during the nineteenth century. The history of the world became the history of the West: the histories of the subalterns of the newly constituted colonial "peripheries" were negated, and their societies subjected to early racialized anthropological enquiry. Out of this emerged a picture of Europe as the thinking and active subject of history, and a picture of plural others as pre-historical or early-historical objects locked in tradition, enchantment, and circular time. Since direct colonization or indirect entrapment in long-distance systems of control arrested development and generated underdevelopment. Colonial expansion provided confirmation of ontological difference between colonizer and subaltern, master and slave. Difference was legalized and codified by the colonial state. Partha Chatterjee rightly emphasizes that the colonial project is the "normalizing rule of colonial difference, the preservation of the alienness of the ruling group," which represents the other "as radically different and hence incorrigibly inferior" (Chatterjee, 1993). In the colonial and neocolonial mind, travelling from North to East and South meant moving back in evolutionary time. The latter had to be conquered and civilized to accede to modernity.

The U.S. geopolitical imagination flowed from the settler experience of continuous expansion and colonization of great spaces that were to be "civilized." In the course of the country's continental and international expansion in the nineteenth and twentieth centuries, leaders developed a vision of world history and world space that, notwithstanding a specific American idiom, was founded on the same ethnocentric assumptions that fuelled European colonization. As the United States moved from the confines to the center of the late modern world system, U.S. expansion was read as the necessary outcome of an evolutionary process of imperial selection and succession, the last phase of which was the systemic recentering from London to New York. At the same time, continental expansion nurtured a geographical imagination of limitlessness, of constantly receding frontiers and unbounded possibilities (Frederick Jackson Turner's frontier thesis). The U.S. historical and geopolitical imaginations were thus fused in a destinarian narrative of national ascent to greatness (Manifest Destiny) as a world power with planetary reach and global responsibilities. Having caught up with and then supplanted Europe, the U.S. came to view itself as the center of the cosmos with other nations and societies in orbit around it (Golub, 2010). Asia and the Pacific were, as noted earlier, incorporated into the vision of westward expansion that Turner articulated. Like the continental territories that were forcibly incorporated into the United States, they were "America's frontier to be conquered, organized, and civilized" (Woo-Cumings, 1993: 139). In the late nineteenth century, Japan was accepted in the councils of the powers, but was never considered quite equal despite its industrial successes and its martial prowess.

The Orientalist gaze influenced visions of Asia in the latter part of the twentieth century. After the Second World War, Japan was ambiguously incorporated into the meta-narrative as a latecomer to modernity. In the 1960s and 1970s, modernization theorists hypothesized that Japan's rapid industrialization process was the outgrowth of a functional analogue of the Protestant ethic. Projecting the self onto the other, Bellah (1985 [1957]) searched and found the analogue in Buddhism's and Shinshu Confucianism's asceticism and this-worldliness. When neo-Weberians looked at Japan they found ... the West. A similar evolutionary bias is evidenced in the distinction posited between European and Japanese sociopolitical development, where Japanese modernization is understood as a deviation from the normal or natural course of capitalist development. The revolution from above that transformed Japan in a short time into a modern industrial and military power in the nineteenth century does not conform to the ideal-typical British model of liberal capitalist modernization driven from below through long maturation within feudal society of socioeconomic differentiation, or to the other road to modernity represented by the revolutionary rise and domination of a bourgeois class (Moore, 1966).

Like the deep currents of the oceans that shape surface motions, these understandings of the self and the other shape in subterranean ways how U.S. observers interpret contemporary historical change. Harry Harootunian notes: "temporality was always measured from one base time since, it was believed, true time was kept by the modern West. What this has meant is that so called global late developers like Japan, and indeed any colonized society, exist in a temporality different from the modern, in a suspended state of growth that still lacks full maturity and thus timeliness. It is precisely this time lag that produces the scandal of imagining modernities that are not quite modern—usually a euphemism for 'not quite white'— ... differentiated from the temporality of the modern West which, then, allow us to safely situate societies like Japan in a historical trajectory derived from another's development" (Harootunian, 2000: xvi). The current binary debate in the United States between structural realists and liberal theorists over China, focussed on the preservation of the status quo, does not admit a world of equals in which there is no longer an authoritative and dominant Western center of gravity.

Poverty of philosophy

The poverty of Western visions of world order is mirrored by the poverty of the imagination of the current generation of leaders of the postcolonial South who, with very few exceptions, lack a positive idea of "an alternative ordering of the real" (Escobar, 2004). Global rebalancing raises important questions of meaning and purpose for the West, but also for the re-emerging states that are restructuring the world capitalist system from within. The actors of the systemic shift are realizing what generations of nationalist anticolonials and postcolonials had fought for—creating more equal patterns of international relations. But the new determining roles that they are destined to play raises the question, currently unanswered, of what kind of world the new capitalist powers want to live in, now that some of them are, at last, achieving international equality. Two dimensions of the problem require comment: the heterogeneity of interests of re-emerging states and their assertion of national power aims, on one hand, and the abandonment of social justice as a normative development aim, on the other.

Heterogeneity has been a persistent problem since the Bandung Conference proclaimed Southern unity, cooperation, and solidarity as constitutive principles of postcolonial Southern politics. Despite a common sensitivity to international inequality, founded on shared experiences of subordination and exploitation during and after the era of empire, the South repeatedly failed after Bandung to achieve cooperation, much less solidarity to effect international change. National interests have always, or almost always, trumped wider collective interests (soon after Bandung, India and China warred in a classic territorial dispute). South–South cooperation and solidarity remains an important component of postcolonial state discourse, and cannot simply be dismissed as a cynical veil covering deeper commitments to *realpolitik*. But as Philip Nel and Ian Taylor argue and document in a recent eye-opening study of Indian, Brazilian, and South Africa regional trade, discourses are in tension with neomercantilist practices. Cooperation lacks form and substance: it is weakly institutionalized, and more often than not stronger states set regional and international South–South agendas reflecting parochial economic interests (Nel and Taylor, 2013). Daniel Flemes likewise notes that China, India, Brazil, and South Africa shape their regional contexts in ways that show little regard for the structural effects their policies have on immediate neighbors: "instead of building democratic and participative regional institutions, they mainly provide to their regions the specific public goods that are necessary for their own economic development. . . . Even though the Brazilian and South African foreign policy discourses suggest the opposite, their strategic approaches rest on the assumption that regional acceptance and legitimacy only matter to a very limited extent to their path to great powerhood" (Flemes, 2013: 1022).

The problem is pronounced in Asia, where the state wields the banner of conservative nationalism for purposes of domestic legitimation and the assertion of international power aims. In India there is precious little left of the progressive international perspectives of anticolonialism and the first generation of postcolonial leaders. Power politics, not cooperation and peaceful coexistence, is the operative principle of foreign policy (India is now the world's seventh-largest defense spender). The idea of the nation has concurrently undergone a regressive transformation. Hindu nationalism (Hinduvta), which developed "an alternative political culture to the dominant idiom in Indian politics," has submerged the inclusive or "universalist view of nationalism" embodied by Gandhi and, somewhat differently, Nehru (Jaffrelot, 2007). The modernizing authoritarian nationalism of the Party-state in China, discussed in Chapter 5, is less ethnocentric—even if some xenophobic strands of Chinese nationalism conflate nation and race (Cabestan, 2005)—but the mobilization of Confucian culture as an instrument of political unification and normalization of rule carries exclusionary undercurrents. Notwithstanding elements of discursive continuity with the Maoist era (solidarity with the developing world is still mobilized in Chinese foreign policy discourse), the international policies flowing from state nationalism are firmly and conservatively focused on securing national economic and strategic interests. The incremental revival of nationalism in Japan, exemplified by intense debates over becoming a "normal country" no longer bound by post-1945 self-restraints on the expression of national identity and ambitions, exemplifies similar trends. As in China, there is a new discussion, spurred by conservatives, over national "restoration" after a long political eclipse (Soeya et al., 2011). One could multiply the examples, but there is no need to belabor the point. The "leading Asian powers ... while seeking global leadership, seem to be more concerned with developing and legitimizing their national power aspirations ... than with contributing to global governance" (Acharya, 2011: 851).

The second dimension is equally problematic. Most of the major emerging or re-emerging states have, to varying degrees, embraced laissez-faire or neoliberal social models as part of their engagement in global economic competition, resulting in new social stratifications and uneven distributional outcomes. Unlike the first generation of postcolonial Southern leaders, who saw a linkage between international equality and domestic social progress, current elites have, with some important exceptions such as Brazil since the Lula administration, abandoned the normative aim of socially inclusive development. This reflects systemic pressures in part, but it also points to domestic coalitions whose dominance rests on the success of their claim to a

central competitive place in the world capitalist system. The confisca-
tion of wealth and power in the global South by thin elite segments is
not a new story, of course. Independence rarely fulfilled the promise
of social progress for the masses that was central to both revolutionary and reformist narratives before and just after Bandung. If the
first generation of leaders after independence aimed for sustained
economic *and* social development, second- and third-generation
ruling castes generally tended to reproduce the social hierarchies of
the colonial period within the postcolonial nation-state. Still, in the
1960s and early 1970s, there was a broad normative Southern consensus that international change had to be coupled to domestic social
improvements.

The constellation of political leaders, international civil servants, and theorists who initiated the drive for a New International
Economic Order (NIEO) in the 1960s and early 1970s had a coherent
forward-looking vision not only of the desirable structure of international economic relations but also of the link between international
and domestic distributive issues. They aimed to institute a new rules-
based global redistributive order that would "correct inequalities and
redress existing injustices ... eliminate the widening gap between
the developed and the developing countries and ensure steadily
accelerating economic and social development and peace and justice
for present and future generations" (UN, 1974). The *Declaration
on the Establishment of a New International Economic Order* connected the international and domestic spheres through a normative
emphasis on socioeconomic justice. Among other things, it called for
a reform of the Bretton Woods institutions, the correction of terms
of trade imbalances, the creation of frameworks of regulation and
supervision of transnational firms, the exercise of sovereign control
over resource exploitation, the facilitation of technology transfer
and the promotion of endogenous industrial development, and the
strengthening of "mutual economic, trade, financial and technical
cooperation among the developing countries." This coherent set of
measures was designed to secure the "sovereign equality of States"
and correct historically inherited disparities. But it was also directed
to achieve "even and balanced development" with a view to the "liberation" and "emancipation" of the peoples of the South. As Robert
Cox emphasizes, the challenge posed to the "intellectual hegemony of
liberal economics and its claims to an exclusive 'rationality'" ranged
into "domestic and transnational structural issues" (Cox, 1979: 258).

Absent a theoretical and philosophical alternative, the recent
embrace of the rationality of *homo economicus* and global economic

155

competition has produced uneven and unbalanced development, characterized most everywhere by sharp urban–rural divides, new social stratifications, and yawning inequalities. "To get rich is glorious" (Deng Xiaoping) may have served for a time to release pent-up energies and mobilize growth capacities in China, but the slogan hardly supports a long-term collective project. As all of the truly successful East Asian modernizers have made clear, the sustainable path to modernity runs through socially inclusive growth. This is also clearly demonstrated in Western Europe and the United States after the Second World War, where strong and sustained growth was coupled with relative social fairness. Thinking on this point is more advanced in Latin America, where critical politics and critical theory still have some sway, than in Asia. For all its realism, the Lula administration's vision of Brazil's place in world politics was founded on social and democratic principles aiming for not only a more balanced inter-state system but also for the reform of oligarchic structures from within. In South America, the regional political reaction to the "lost decade" of the 1980s and subsequent neoliberal "reforms" has taken a different route than the conservative nationalism in East Asia. As Arturo Escobar notes: "Latin America was the region that most earnestly embraced neoliberal reforms, where the model was applied the most thoroughly, and where the results were the most ambiguous" (Escobar, 2010). The response was the political affirmation of progressive social and intellectual forces that were shaped by earlier debates and struggles over non-alignment, dependency and development, and which are now seeking to construct more socially inclusive development models at the domestic level, as well as new patterns of cooperation at regional and international levels. The results on both fronts have been ambiguous, however. High, though somewhat declining, levels of social inequality underscore the difficulty of transforming longstanding domestic social structures and hierarchies in the context of continuing if diminishing external vulnerabilities and systemic constraints.

A new global bargain?

There is a continuum between domestic and international policies and outlooks. One cannot expect states led by elite formations that disregard the welfare of the majority of their own population to have regard for the welfare of their neighbors, much less defend the cosmopolitan interest. Giovanni Arrighi glimpses the hope and possibility that "the ruling groups of the global South in general, and of China and India in particular, [may] open a path capable of emancipating not just their nations but the entire world from the social and eco-logical devastations entailed in Western capitalist development. An innovation of such world-historical significance requires some aware-ness of the impossibility of bringing the benefits of modernization to the majority of the world's population unless . . . the Western devel-opmental path converges with the East Asian path" (Arrighi, 2007: 385–86). This curiously naïve statement is founded on a romanticized idea of precapitalist Smithian growth, the "natural" course of which would have been disrupted by the Industrial Revolution and the anthropocene. (This is not an appropriate space to engage in a sys-tematic critique of the problematic distinction between development paths deemed "natural" and "unnatural," but one cannot avoid the major epistemological problem posed by positing positive knowledge of what the natural is in the first instance.) It also completely misreads the current "ruling groups" of the global South, who are mostly inca-pable of emancipating their own populations, and generally unwill-ing to do so—much less the rest of the world. To the contrary, global rebalancing is occurring in a philosophical vacuum: the quest for wealth and power has constricted and impoverished the postcolonial intellectual imagination.

Arrighi is certainly right when noting the need for socially and ecologically sustainable development. But surely the problem cannot be solved, as he suggests, by simply jettisoning Enlightenment Prometheanism and adopting Mohandas Gandhi's frugality: neither the South nor the North are about to willingly give up the advantages of industrialization and move back to (idealized) premodern and early modern socioeconomic patterns. Even if a shared understanding is gradually emerging that the common human fate is bound to finding collective answers to transnational problems such as global climate change, that awareness does not translate easily into a cosmopolitan ethos that has a ready purchase on politics, since it bumps against competing rationality claims founded on national or individual self-interest. Even if we were able to dethrone *homo economicus*, it does not necessarily follow that this will give way to cooperation, much less empathy toward "strangers," or to altruism. Solutions should be found that equitably distribute the costs of mitigation of issues such as global climate change, for instance, taking into account the cos-mopolitan interest. Just how this can be accomplished and who will set the terms of the settlement remain open and extremely difficult questions (Golub and Maréchal, 2012).

157

The transition from the Western-centered world system to a plural and decentralized system poses the inescapable question of the future organization of world politics. To avoid insuperable contradictions we might start by rejecting options that are either undesirable or unattainable. The most undesirable outcome of global rebalancing would be an exacerbation of competitive struggles over power, scarce resources, and status (the structural realist scenario). At the same time, as Richard Falk argues, we need to exclude a number of undesirable or unattainable "post-Westphalian scenarios" such as the neo-liberal utopia of a self-regulating global market, the limits of which are plainly apparent, or the illusory quest for world government. The alternative he proposes is to gradually move toward "an accountable global polity" underpinned by reinforced and empowered multilateral institutions legitimated by their inclusiveness, democratic character, and normative focus on cooperation and solidarity (Falk, 2004). This may well be realizable in theory, but movement toward a strong or highly institutionalized international society has been halting at best. Unlike 1945, there is no overarching normative vision today, and there are no recognized and legitimate sources of authority to guide the transition.

Because of the erosion of its claim to world political and economic leadership in the 2000s, the United States is not in a position to set the global agenda and to "write the rules." The U.S. remains the most powerful state in the international system and retains significant structural power in the monetary, credit, and production spheres (Helleiner, 2009, 2014; Schwartz, 2009; Starrs, 2013). Nonetheless, the country's authority is contested, and its capacity to steer world politics and generate outcomes reflecting its preferences is more limited than in the 1990s or, *a fortiori*, the late 1940s. This is evidenced in a loss of leverage in various regions of the global South, but also in Europe, where U.S. efforts to persuade the European Union to stimulate demand, as part of a global strategy to deal with the world economic crisis, have fallen on deaf ears (Burgi, 2014b). While the dollar remains the world leading reserve currency by far (two-thirds of world reserves), and the U.S. ability to finance its debt in its own currency constitutes an essential component of U.S. structural power, a slow shift in global monetary relations seems inevitable as global rebalancing proceeds. Benjamin Cohen reasonably hypothesizes that the "most probable outcome is apt to be ... like the interregnum between the two World Wars, when Britain's pound sterling was in decline and the dollar on the rise but neither was dominant. Coming years ... will see the emergence of something

158

similar, with several monies in contention and none as clearly in the lead as in the recent past. The economic and political impacts of a more fragmented currency system could be considerable" (Cohen, 2009: 24). If U.S. authority has weakened, Europe is certainly not in a position to exercise world leadership. The EU's deplorable misman-agement of the current economic and social crisis has fundamentally undermined Europe's claim to be a model of transnational govern-ance. The re-emerging states of the global South do not constitute a coherent ensemble. They all face major domestic developmental chal-lenges and, while they are gaining voice, they have as yet to propose a persuasive vision of the way the new plural world, in which they will have a determining place, should work. However useful it may be as a guide to Sino-U.S. relations, China's realist vision of great-power interactions hardly qualifies as an innovation in thinking about world politics. The international institutions erected after 1945 have neither the authority nor the means to address efficiently the global or local issues of the present. This splintering of authority raises major prob-lems of collective action and suggests an urgent need to renovate the international institutional architecture and reinvent a legitimate rules-based system on which to found cooperation in future.

Is a new grand bargain at the global level possible? It would require a constellation of forward-looking leaders converging around common principles and goals, the conditions for which are not cur-rently present. The best one can reasonably expect is incremental change, institutional *bricolage*, and partial answers to various prob-lems in different issue-areas of world politics. A grand bargain would require further theoretical innovations that put to rest the supreme fiction, to borrow Edward Said's expression, of ontological difference and separation, as well as normative advances that open the way for social and democratic outcomes at global and local levels. If very little has been achieved on the latter question, and social inequalities continue to disfigure the world, there have been important scholarly advances on the first issue. Thanks to the work of world historians and critical social theorists, there is today a far better understanding that "the movement of the world does not simply operate around the capitalist system that centers on Europe; its operation is the process in which multiple worlds communicate and fight with each other, permeate into each other, and mould each other" (Wang Hui, 2005). The challenge going forward is how to mobilize that understanding to theorize the conditions for cooperation and inclusive development in the interdependent yet fragmented world that is emerging.

NOTES

1. Globalization, East Asia, and the Dynamics of Capitalist Development

1   Marx's dozens of articles devoted to the colonial issue gathered in *Marx on Colonialism* (International Publishers, 1963) provide a remarkable depiction of European expansion and the resistance that it provoked in Asia. Though much has been anachronistically said of Marx's Eurocentrism and his use of typically nineteenth-century distinctions ("civilized" and "barbarian"), his writings show acute sensitivity to the systematic violence of the colonization enterprise, and to the potential for emancipation from imperial rule resulting from the rise of national consciousness among the colonized. In his depictions, the "civilized" Europeans were barbaric in morals and practice, committing "abominations" in India and China and making torture an "organic institution of ... financial policy" (p. 146). During the First Opium War, British forces engaged in "violations of women, the spittings of children, the roastings of whole villages" (p. 147), as they later did during the First Indian War of Independence, cruelties that were "related as acts of martial vigour" in Europe. Though he envisioned East–West convergence in an evolutionary perspective, Marx saw revolutionary potential in the rise of the national consciousness of the colonized. Industrialization and, in the case of India, political nationalization through unification "imposed by the British sword," would in time create the conditions for "self-emancipation" and for Asia to cease being "the prey of the ... foreign intruder" (p. 84). Contemporary mass uprisings in colonial and semi-colonial Asia—the Taiping Rebellion (1850–1864) and the First Indian War of Independence (1857)—seemed to contain the seeds of bourgeois revolution. Moreover, interdependence meant that the rise of nationalized resistance to colonial rule would feed back to Europe. In "Revolution in China and in Europe" (1853), Marx hypothesized that the mid-century Taiping Rebellion against the Qing dynasty, stimulated by English intrusion and the weakening of imperial authority and sovereignty, would in time "react on England and through England to Europe" (p. 18) by cutting off China from the world market. This would lead to a contraction of world trade, a decline in the demand for British manufactures, a fall of British revenue due to the cut-off of opium exports to China from

160

India, and financial crisis. Global linkages meant that the "Chinese revolution will throw the spark into the overloaded mine of the present (English) industrial system and cause the explosion of the long-prepared general crisis, which, spreading abroad, will be closely followed by political revolutions on the continent [. . . It would] be a curious spectacle, that of China sending disorder into the Western World while the Western powers, by English, French and American war-steamers, are conveying 'order' to Shanghai, Nanking and the mouths of the Great Canal" (p. 21).

2 The *Declaration on the Establishment of a New International Economic Order* at the UN General Assembly in 1974 aimed to "correct inequalities and redress existing injustices . . . eliminate the widening gap between the developed and the developing countries and ensure steadily accelerating economic and social development and peace and justice for present and future generations." It offered a comprehensive program for a negotiated restructuring of world economic relations, calling for a reform of the Bretton Woods institutions and the international monetary system, the establishment and institutionalization of mechanisms to correct terms of trade imbalances between the North and the South, the implementation of preferential and nonreciprocal arrangements for "developing countries in all fields of international economic cooperation," the creation of frameworks of regulation and supervision of transnational corporations to secure the "full permanent sovereignty of every State over its natural resources and all economic activities," the right of states to nationalize foreign firms and to exercise control over resource exploitation, the facilitation of technology transfer and the promotion of endogenous technological development, the extension of assistance to the "least developed countries," as well as the strengthening of "mutual economic, trade, financial and technical cooperation among the developing countries." This coherent set of measures was designed to secure the "sovereign equality of States," correct historically inherited disparities, and achieve "even and balanced development" with a view to the "liberation" and "emancipation" of the peoples of developing nations. United Nations General Assembly, Sixth Special Session, 3201 (S-VI), *Declaration of the Establishment of a New International Economic Order*, New York, 1 May 1974.

2. EARLY-MODERN ENCOUNTERS, LATE-MODERN COLLISIONS

1 Prominent studies include: Paul Bairoch (1997); Christopher Bayly (2004); Fernand Braudel (1984); K. N. Chaudhuri (1991); Jack Goody (1996, 2006); Andre Gunder Frank (1998); Takeshi Hamashita (2008); Philip Kuhn (1999); Janet L. Abu-Lughod (1991); Kenneth Pomeranz (2000); Giorgio Riello and Tirthankar Roy (2009); R. B. Wong (1997). For useful syntheses of the literature on China see Feuerwerker (1992) and Rawski (1991).

2 The world system Braudel (1984) draws a picture of was not spatially or economically centered. Wealth and power were diffuse and were distributed relatively equally among large economic zones, coherently structured at regional level through networks of production and exchange, that he dubs *economies-mondes* or world-economies. He thus distinguishes between the

world economy and these semi-autonomous systems, "the economy of only one portion of the planet forming an economic totality."

3 Smithian growth denotes preindustrial economic development of the kind described by Adam Smith in *The Wealth of Nations*, characterized by a deepening division of labor, the expansion of market institutions, and trade and commercialization. Mokyr (1990) usefully distinguishes this pattern of growth from the self-sustaining growth deriving from continuous technological progress.

4 For discussions of the transatlantic economic system see Inikori (2002), who focuses on the extraction of surplus from African slave labor in the Americas in fuelling the British Industrial Revolution; Golub (2010), who points to the symbiotic relationship between British and United States economic development; Pomeranz (2000), who highlights the role played by New World slave labor as an important factor differentiating the development paths of the eastern and western parts of early modern Eurasia. For general overviews of the transatlantic slave trade and the British economy, see Kenneth Morgan (2000), David Eltis (2000), and Eric Williams' (1966). On the slave system in the United States, see Rothman (2005).

5 On empire and transnational migrations, see Harper and Constantine (2010); Fedorowich and Thomson (2013).

6 The "Treaty of Friendship and Commerce" annulled the 1826 treaty between Britain and Siam and fixed new import duties at 3 percent, with no duties to be paid on opium imports. The Bowring Treaty granted British subjects the right to trade freely and gave them extraterritorial rights. The application of the most-favored-nation clause extended these rights to other Western states.

7 The rebellions began in the early 1850s and fighting went on for more than a decade and a half (Taiping, 1851–1864; Nian, 1851–1868; Miao, 1854–1873), at the cost of tens of millions of lives. The Taiping Rebellion alone is estimated to have caused over 20 million casualties. The state, which was nearly toppled by the simultaneous domestic and international wars, was forced to call upon Western military support to put an end to the Taiping challenge.

8 On the self-strengthening movement, see Ssu-yu Teng and John K. Fairbank (1979).

9 After the war it became obvious, as perceptive Japanese observers already knew when the country embarked on war with the United States (as well as the Soviet Union and Britain), that a relatively small, already imperially overstretched resource-poor country could not reasonably hope to come out of the conflict victorious. In the *Origins of the Second World War in Asia and the Pacific*, Akira Iriye argues that Japanese leaders were "captives to their own illusions." He also emphasizes that they were responding to resource constraints and the United States' attempt to shape Japanese behavior by restricting energy supplies (Iriye, 1987: 124).

3. War-Making and State-Making After 1945

1 From 1945 to 1990 approximately 34 million people, civilian and military, died during armed conflicts in the colonial and postcolonial periphery, against approximately 50,000 in Europe during the Greek civil war (1946–

1949). Around 1 million were killed in Latin America during civil wars and counterinsurgency campaigns, half in Colombia and Guatemala; 2.5 million in the Middle East, the majority during the Iran–Iraq war (1980–1988) and the Iraq government's massacres of Kurds; 3.4 million in South Asia: 800,000 during the Partition in India, 1.5 million during the Bangladesh civil war and India's subsequent intervention, and 1 million in Afghanistan during the civil war and Soviet intervention; over 11 million in Sub-Saharan Africa during the wars of decolonization and the civil wars and the ethnic/religious conflicts that followed independence (3.5 million in proxy U.S.–Soviet conflicts in Angola, Mozambique, and Eritrea); and nearly 17 million in East Asia, from the Chinese civil war to China's war against Vietnam in 1979, the vast majority in the course of East–West or capitalist-communist conflicts (derived from Leitenberg, 2006).

2 After the Sino-Soviet split in the mid-1960s in the midst of the Vietnam War, which led to the secret Chinese–U.S. negotiations in the late 1960s and Richard Nixon's trip to China in 1971, the People's Republic of China gradually turned against North Vietnam, which it had previously backed. Chinese support for the Communist Party of Kampuchea (CPK) reflected the shift, as China sought to create a client communist rival to North Vietnam. In a recent study of Chinese–Khmer Rouge relations, Andrew Mertha notes: "China was involved in every aspect and at each stage of the CPK rise to power. From 1970 to 1975 Beijing provided [the coalition government between the CPK and King Sihanouk that China had brought into being] with an annual budget of $2 million as well as office space and living quarters at the Friendship Hotel in northwestern Beijing ... even the Chinese mission to Phnom Penh was physically relocated to Beijing, where the Chinese Ambassador to Cambodia, Kang Maozhao, carried out his functions as if he were on Cambodian soil. Beijing continued to provide arms, clothing, and food and even printed banknotes for use upon the CPK's assumption of power. And, as relations between the Cambodian and Vietnamese communists began to sour, China's support for the CPK insurgency correspondingly increased" (Mertha, 2014: 2–3).

3 Declassified U.S. government documents available at the National Security Archive of George Washington University show U.S. acquiescence and involvement in General Suharto's coup d'état, American intelligence involvement in the identification of left-leaning figures who were then liquidated, and support for the invasion of East Timor. See "East Timor Revisited: Ford, Kissinger and the Indonesian Invasion, 1975–76", in William Burr and Michael L. Evans (eds.), *National Security Archive Electronic Briefing Book No. 62* (Washington, D.C.: The George Washington University, December 6, 2001). http://www.gwu.edu/~nsarchiv/NSAEBB/ NSAEBB62/. Secretary of State Henry Kissinger characterized the CPK as "murderous thugs" but asked Thai leaders to convey to them "that we will be friends with them." The Nixon administration saw Cambodia as a useful "counterweight to North Vietnam." Thus: "Our strategy is to get the Chinese into Laos and Cambodia as a barrier to the Vietnamese." See Memorandum of Conversation, "Secretary's Meeting with Foreign Minister Chatchai of Thailand," 26 November 1975, State Department, in William Burr (ed.), *The National Security Archive Electronic Briefing Book* No. 192, Document 17 www.gwu.edu/~nsarchiv/NSAEBB/ NSAEBB193/index.htm.

4 A repertoire of resistance identities emerged out of the common imperial experience, ranging from essentialized constructs of Japaneseness or
Indianness, to visions of pan-Asian solidarity or universalistic socialist ideals.
For a particularly clear discussion of the question of national identity formation in Asia, see Narangoa and Cribb (2003).

5 See Paromita Biswas's unpublished PhD thesis for an interesting discussion
of the ambivalence of Indian radical nationalist intellectuals who looked to
Japanese empire as a means to protect Asia from European imperialism, but
at the same time sought to "gain American support for Indian independence even as they championed an Asian unity against western imperialism"
(Biswas, 2008: 43).

6 Nationalist leaders in Burma, Indonesia and Siam (Ne Win, Sukarno and
Suharto, Phibunsongkhram) worked with the Japanese during the Second
World War, as did Subhas Chandra Bose and the Indian National Army
(INA). They were acting for primarily instrumental reasons: using Japan to
get rid of European colonial rule, just as Japan was using them to accredit
the idea of Japancentric Pan-Asian solidarity. The instrumental character of
the relationship should not obscure the fact that there was significant convergence around the idea of an autonomous Asia. For an insightful examination
of the military cooperation between Southeast Asian nationalists and the
Japanese military, see Joyce C. Lebra (2010).

7 Mills's prescient analysis of the creation of a permanent military machine
at the outset of the Cold War remains relevant today. Mills astutely noted
that the reproduction of that machine would become an end in itself, a
perpetual-motion machine made possible by "an emergency without foreseeable end" in which "war or a high state of war preparedness is felt to
be the normal and seemingly permanent condition for the United States."
That state of being concentrated power in the hands of the "new warlords."
Given the expansion of American power that stretched after 1945 deep into
Europe and Asia, "domestic decisions . . . are increasingly justified by, if not
made with, close reference to the dangers and opportunities abroad" (Mills,
2000).

8 Ho Chi Minh cooperated with the precursor of the Central Intelligence
Agency, the Office of Strategic Services (OSS), in the late phases of the Second
World War and asked President Truman for assistance in ending French
colonial rule. The U.S. ignored the request. Ho had likewise vainly peti-
tioned President Wilson during the Versailles conference in 1919 to support
Vietnamese independence. The story of these tragically unfruitful efforts is
discussed by an OSS participant, Major Achimedes Patti in *Why Vietnam?*
(Patti, 1982).

9 Some senior State Department officials argued for a U.S. break with the
European colonial powers in Asia. See, for instance, "Memorandum by the
Chief of the Division of Near Eastern Affairs (Ailing) 79," *FRUS Diplomatic
Papers, 1943: The Near East and Africa*, Vol. IV (1943), p. 239. The
Memorandum of 1943 argued that the U.S. should not align their intelligence
operations with those of the British since this would lead to the identification
"[by] the Burmese and all of the colonial Asiatics with British imperialism."
On the colonial policies of the Roosevelt administration in Asia, see: Robert
J. McMahon (1999); Robert J. McMahon (1981); Frances Gouda and Thijs
B. Zaalberg (2002); Foster Rhea Dulles and Gerald E. Ridinger (1955); John

J. Sebrega (1986); Gary Hess (1972). For a careful reading of U.S. policy in Africa, see Ebere Nwaubani (2001).

10 The extent of Japan's wartime devastation is well described by John Dower (2000). In addition to 2.7 million civilian and military casualties, one-quarter to one-third of the country's wealth had been destroyed. The "entire economic structure of Japan's cities" had been wrecked: "Sixty-six major cities, including Hiroshima and Nagasaki, had been heavily bombed, destroying 40 percent of these urban areas overall and rendering around 30 percent of the population homeless. In Tokyo ... 65 percent of all residences were destroyed. In Osaka and Nagoya, the country's second and third largest cities, the figures were 57 and 89 percent.... Close to 9 million people were homeless when the emperor told them they had fought and sacrificed in vain" (pp. 44–48). In his ambiguously apologetic interview in the documentary film *The Fog of War*, former U.S. Defense Secretary Robert McNamara, who was one of the "architects" of the Vietnam War, raises but does not answer the important question of the nuclear bombing of Japan that followed the earlier bombing campaigns: "Why was it necessary to drop the nuclear bomb if LeMay was burning up Japan? And he went on from Tokyo to firebomb other cities. 58 percent of Yokohama. Yokohama is roughly the size of Cleveland. 58 percent of Cleveland destroyed. Tokyo is roughly the size of New York. 51 percent of New York destroyed. 99 percent of the equivalent of Chattanooga, which was Toyama. 40 percent of the equivalent of Los Angeles, which was Nagoya. This was all done before the dropping of the nuclear bomb." *The Fog of War: Eleven Lessons from the Life of Robert S. McNamara*, directed by Errol Morris, Sony Classics, 2003.

11 In the late forties the U.S. government sought to revive the Japanese economy by restoring trade linkages with its former colonies rather than focussing on exports, the quality of which were considered inferior and unfit for U.S. market needs, to the United States. South Korea signed a trade agreement with Tokyo in 1949 under U.S. pressure that "revived ... the classic pattern of unequal trade in which Korea would export to Japan rice, tungsten, ores, fish products, animal hair and the like, and import from Japan cement, sheet glass, radios, machinery and transportation equipment." But this did not go very far due to Korean resistance to being brought once again into a subaltern position in a Japan-centered production and trade system. Japan's revival came instead through the special procurements during the Korean War that also gave South Korea some leverage to assert its economic prefer- ences. As Jung-en Woo emphasizes in her study of South Korean postwar industrialization, Rhee "fought tooth and nail against the American concep- tion of the post-war East Asian order" with Japan at its apex and "hand- cuffed Americans in Korea" after the war by skillfully leveraging security issues into greater economic autonomy. Rhee's "favorite method of mana- cling Americans was constant threats to blitzkrieg into North Korea and frightening Americans into maintaining their troops in Korea as a force of stability and moderation." See Woo (1991: 42–72).

12 KMT military forces in Burma became involved in the opium trade in the early 1950s to finance their "secret war" with the People's Republic of China. According to Alfred McCoy, the Central Intelligence Agency (CIA) was an active participant in the KMT's operations and later used KMT assets and

other mercenaries financed by the trade during the Vietnam War. See McCoy (1972) and Lintner (1999).

13 During talks with Park in Washington in 1965, Lyndon Johnson requested the deployment of one South Korean division in Vietnam, a demand that Park acceded to quickly. The idea of sending troops into Vietnam had been raised years before, first by Syngman Rhee in the late 1950s, and by Park who offered to Kennedy to send troops in 1961. Their aim was to tether the United States to South Korea.

14 Following Park's coup d'état in 1961, the United States expressed some concern over the nationalism of the colonels, which they worried could lead to nonalignment. Their authoritarianism was another reason for qualms. But they soon came to appreciate both of these attributes. Ambassador Samuel Berger "found positive elements" such as "energy, earnestness, determination and imagination" in the coup leaders. See Byung-Kook Kim and Ezra F. Vogel (2011).

15 Havens notes that the war had significant effects in specific sectors such as repair and maintenance for U.S. aircraft, ships, and vehicles or the hotel and "entertainment" industries to service U.S. troops stationed in or rotating through Japan. It also more discreetly "helped to cement the close transpacific relations between Japanese and U.S. defence firms."

16 See Cynthia Enloe (2000).

17 On Southeast Asia, see Mark Berger (2008); Daniel Fineman (1997); Bradley R. Simson (2010). In Malaya and Singapore the windfall revenues of the early 1950s, created by the boom in commodity prices following the outbreak of the Korean War, allowed both governments to enlarge and train the military and police and expand the operations of the intelligence organizations to mount a successful counterinsurgency campaign against the Malayan Communist Party. On the general phenomenon of war and economic development, see Stubbs (1999).

4. DEVELOPMENTAL STATES AND FLYING GEESE

1 France's level of industrialization was significantly lower than the United States' and that of other major European countries prior to the Second World War. The country's share of world manufacturing in 1938 (4.4 percent) was seven times lower than that of the U.S., three times lower than Germany's, and less than half of Great Britain's. Aiming to restore France's position in international affairs, the deeply interventionist postwar state instituted planning and invested heavily and selectively in state-created or newly nationalized industrial sectors and infrastructure. This led to what Robert Boyer of the French Regulation School terms an "economic miracle." By the 1970s, France had become a significant industrial power. "The most decisive contribution to industrial dynamism derives from the determining role of the State in the reconstruction of infrastructures, the stimulation of mass production through nationalizations, the control of credit through the nationalized sector such as the Bank of France, and the construction of system of social coverage of unprecedented amplitude" (Boyer, 1998:10) On this subject, see also Loriaux (1999) and Chang (2003).

2 Historical sociological and historical political economy scholars made signifi-

cant contributions in the 1980s on the state and state–society relations. See Skocpol et al., 1985.

3 In the *Making of the English Working Class*, E. P. Thomson remarks: "It can be argued that Britain in the Industrial Revolution was encountering the problems of "take-off"; heavy long-term investment—canals, mills, railways, foundries, mines, utilities—was at the expense of current consumption; the generations of workers between 1790 and 1840 sacrificed some, or all, of their prospects of increased consumption to the future."

4 Precapitalist colonization in Latin America constructed an economic system based on plantation agriculture and mining worked by slave labor that persisted after Independence in the form of the latifundia (hacienda) system of extremely concentrated elite land ownership worked either by slaves or peons. Industrial capitalist development in some countries, such as Brazil or Mexico, in the nineteenth and twentieth centuries did not fundamentally alter ownership patterns. Rather, the hacienda system proved resilient, adapting itself to modern and late capitalism by inserting agricultural production into global flows, while maintaining the economic dominance of a very small elite that channelled parts of its surplus into other economic sectors. For an institutionalist analysis of the reproduction of inequality, see Sokoloff and Engerman (2000). For dependency perspectives see Furtado (1970) as well as Cardoso and Faletto (1979). The first five volumes of the *Cambridge History of Latin America*, edited by Leslie Bethell, provide detailed background on the colonial economic and social system (Bethell, 1985).

5 Concentration of land ownership in the Philippines (0.6 on the land Gini index) is midway between average Latin American levels and average Northeast Asian developers' levels. While the rate of tenancy dropped sharply in South Korea and Taiwan after 1950, it rose sharply in the Philippines, from 37 percent in the mid-1940s to 50 percent in the 1960s. Income inequality is likewise much greater than in the rest of East Asia, the ratio of the income share of the top 20 percent of the population to the bottom 40 percent being twice as large as in Korea. While GDP per capita and other aggregate measures were comparable in South Korea and the Philippines in the 1960s, subsequent divergence is correlated with the persistence of sharp initial differences in levels of inequality. See UNESCAP (2008).

6 Replacement of the U.S. dollar by Asian currencies or an Asian unit of account was a point of convergence among regional leaders. At the "Future of Asia" conference held in Tokyo in June 2003, Southeast Asian and Japanese officials were quite clear about their aims. According to partial transcripts provided by *Nikkei Weekly*, then Thai Prime Minister Thaksin Shinawatra told the gathering that East Asia should move gradually from a dollar-based fund to an Asian basket of currencies: "Funds held by Asian countries, which account for about half of the world's foreign currency reserves, used to be invested mainly in the U.S. and Europe. Now funds should head toward Asia thanks to the birth of an Asian Bond Market. . . . Although the Asia Bond Fund will start out in U.S. dollars, we hope to shift to Asian currencies in the future." Then Malaysia Prime Minister Mohamad Mahatir likewise said: "We will all benefit from the Asia Bond Market because it is Asian and is in our own interest, not a device for somebody else somewhere and imposed on us. Initially, the bonds should be denominated in the U.S. dollar but we should move away from the U.S. dollar in the future."

The former Japanese Prime Minister Ryutaro Hashimoto is reported to have declared: "The lessons learned from the Asian currency crisis are producing good results" (*Nikkei Weekly*, 2003).

7 "Further reciprocal cooperation to build a harmonious East Asia," Speech by Vice Minister of Commerce Yi Xiaozhun, 26 May 2008, reported by the *People's Daily* <www.english.peopledaily. com.cn/90002/93687/93689/6418402. html>.

5. CHINA'S STATE CAPITALIST MUTATION

1 Perroux (1994 [1973]) writes that a "unit is said to be active if through its own action and in its own interest it is capable of modifying its environment, that is the behaviour of the units with which it is in relation."

2 In April 2014 the Global Office of the International Comparison Program (ICP) of the World Bank announced new Purchasing Power Parity data for the world based on revised methodology that revisited GDP estimates for a number of global South economies. The revised calculations indicate that China would overtake the United States in 2014 as the world's largest economy in PPP terms. Though significant, this finding has to be nuanced: since PPP measures domestic rather than international purchasing power, China's new ranking does not mean that she has greater weight than the United States in the world economy. Measured at current exchange rates, the Chinese economy is still much smaller than that of the U.S. ($8.7 trillion in 2013 against $16.2 trillion according to IMF estimates), and per-capita GDP is very much lower, given respective population sizes ($11,000 against $43,808). Nonetheless, even when taking this corrective into account, the trend points unmistakably to China's increasingly central role in the global economy (World Bank, 2014).

3 The Net International Investment Position (NIIP) of a country is obtained by subtracting external liabilities from the total foreign assets owned by country residents. Japan has been the world's largest net creditor for the past quarter of a century, while China has been the world's second-largest net creditor for the past seven years. In 2013 the net external positions of Japan and China reached $2.98 and $1.9 trillion respectively. However, China has been the United States' first foreign creditor since 2008 and currently holds $1.26 trillion of Treasury securities. For statistical series on U.S. debt, see United States Treasury Department, "Major Foreign Holders of Treasury Securities," (www.treasury.gov).

4 In 1980 total Chinese emissions of CO_2 were about 1.4 billion tons while U.S. emissions were 4.6 billion tons. Chinese per capita emissions (1.4 tons) were 14.6 times less than U.S. per capita emissions (20.5 tons). By 2007, Chinese total emissions (6.071 billion tons) had surpassed the United States' (5.769 billion tons) and Chinese per capita emissions were one fourth of those of the U.S. For a detailed examination and discussion of the theoretical, practical, and ethical dimensions of the problem of burden-sharing to deal with global climate change, see Golub and Maréchal (2012). On China and global climate change, see Maréchal (2011).

5 See also Jean-François Huchet (2014), who argues that Chinese planners looked not only to the Japanese and Korean industrial systems but also to

French planning for guidance in setting up and implementing their industrial policies.

6 Nicolas Lardy argues that the "WTO-plus terms imposed on China . . . are so onerous that they violate fundamental WTO principles." The trade issues on which China made inordinate concessions at the demand of dominant states included market access issues (average statutory tariff on industrial products, sensitive agricultural products, and services) and rules-based commitments "going far beyond" those made by other countries that joined after 1995 (Lardy, 2002).

7 Jianyong Yue (2011) makes a forceful and systematic critique of the choices of the post-Mao leadership in his unpublished Ph.D. thesis. Jianyong argues that "the interaction of China's market 'socialism' and global capitalism generated a powerful self-reinforcing process that set China on a dependent path of development and locked in its dependency characterized by a technologyless industrialization in globalization." Reliance on FDI to stimulate growth for purposes of regime legitimation would have caused the decline of the state industrial sector (State Owned Enterprises) without generating technological spillovers: "The decline of the SOE's suggests that China's external integration is not a typical EOI approach in development terms . . . trade promotion in China's institutional context was not so much the symbol of mercantilism as part of the 'forced growth' regime that politically stressed export earnings rather than or even at the expense of the profitability of domestic firms. Technologyless industrialization highlighted the double effects of liberal globalization on the Chinese economy. On the one hand, it stimulated an export-oriented rapid economic growth based on China's comparative advantage in cheap labor; on the other hand, it blocked China's industrialization with the substitution of the SOE's by FDI" (p. 146).

8 The *xiagang* program was phased out in the 2000s by the State Council after it failed to produce appropriate results at firms and at local government levels, leaving former SOE workers in limbo, since no alternative system to deal with the unemployed had been put in place. For a detailed discussion, see Gold et al. (2009).

9 Urban-rural income differentials have been widening since the 1980s. According to a recent World Bank report, the urban–rural income ratio measured as the average income per capita of urban households divided by the average per capita income of rural households rose from 1.8 in 1985 to over 3 in the 2000s. "By 2002, per capita incomes for urban households were, on average, more than three times higher than those for rural households. Since that time, the urban–rural income ratio has remained well above 3.0." The author points out that the ratio is "very high by international standards" and reflects "the long-term consequences of past and current institutions and policies that have created unequal access between urban and rural residents to education, employment, assets and welfare benefits" (Sicular, 2013: 4).

10 Government health care expenditures dropped from 79 percent of the total spending on health care in China in 1980 to less than 48 percent in 2005. Total government welfare expenditures, health included, are a low 2 percent of GDP. For a systematic survey of social welfare in China, see Tony Saich (2008).

11 See Andrew Walder's and Gong Xiaoxia's discussion of the Beijing Workers' Autonomous Federation (gongzilian). "The organization," write the authors,

169

"played an increasingly pivotal role in the mobilization of street protests after the declaration of martial law; as the student presence in the square dwindled in the last days of May, the membership of gongzilian grew, its organization reached a high state of readiness, and it took a high profile in organizing the resistance to martial law. Moreover, while gongzilian lacked formally organized branches in places of work, it had a number of important informal ties to workers and work units throughout the city, from whom it enjoyed steady moral and material support until the rifle shots began to ring out. Unlike the student movement, the workers' movement had picked up momentum after martial law and appeared to gain confidence and strength as May turned into June" (Walder and Xiaoxia, 1993: 3).

12 Misleading Western reports at the time of the Tiananmen events depicted the struggle at the top as a divide between "reformists" and "conservatives," erroneously projecting Western categories onto China that had little to do with the actual leadership debates. The statists ruling China concurred on the need for firm state and Party ascendancy despite differing appreciations regarding the nature and pace of reform policy. In 1987 the Communist Party leadership stripped Hu Yaobang of his position as Secretary General of the Communist Party following mass student and worker protests that year. Deng Xiaoping sided with the decision despite the fact that Hu had been an important supporter of his economic liberalization agenda. Hu's death in 1989 sparked the Tiananmen events. Deng would similarly side with the majority of a divided Politburo, and retired but influential elements of the "old guard" in the Party, when forcing the resignation of CPC Secretary General Zhao Ziyang in 1989 for increasingly outspoken support given to the student and worker protests that were spreading throughout China. Deng's alliance with Chen Yun—the other pivotal figure in the late-1970s defeat of the Maoists and the political shift of the Third Plenum of the Eleventh Central Committee in 1978—and other critics of economic liberalization during the political repression of the 1989 movement briefly masked underlying tensions within the power structure over the course of capitalist "reform" that resurfaced in the early 1990s. While the faction associated with Chen Yun and Li Peng rejected the "radical reform policy" and advocated slowing liberalization, it would be wrong to paint it as stubbornly antireformist. Though they differed with Deng over the pace of change, and argued for more limited reforms embedded in the planning system, they concurred with him over the need for "economic construction" as an overriding national priority. In his insightful treatment of the leadership debates, Jianyong Yue makes the point that Deng as well as the leading market reformers on the "right" were just as much statists as their "left" critics. Zhao Ziyang was hardly a liberal: "Zhao Ziyang was no different [than Deng] in accentuating authoritarianism ... he got fascinated by the idea of neo-authoritarianism, a theory of political conservatism advocated by a small number of intellectuals who called for imitating the examples of South Korea and Taiwan" (Jianyong Yue, 2010: 115). For a contemporary assessment, see Zhao (1993).

13 In 2013 the Chinese *Legal Daily* published elements of an official report that broke down 2012 mass incidents into categories and percentages: social disputes/issues (24.4 percent), forced demolitions/removals (22.2 percent), conflicts between the police and the People (22.2 percent), conflicts between officials and the People (13.3 percent); defense of environmental

rights (8.9 percent), and ethnic conflicts (8.9 percent). The same report analyzed the demographics of protest: residents of cities and towns (51.1 percent), farmers/rural residents (46.7 percent). Incidents involving migrants accounted for 17.8 percent, students 11.1 percent and minorities 4.4 percent. Independent research on "large-scale mass incidents" between 2003 and 2008 involving more than 500 people showed that 108 out of 248 such incidents involved industrial workers from the state and non-state sectors, 26 stemmed from rural land requisition disputes, and 11 from environmental protests. Confrontations between people and local authorities accounted for 39 incidents (Yanqi Tong and Shaohua Lei, 2013).

14 A "socialist legal system with Chinese characteristics" came into being in the late 1970s, leading to the establishment of a large judiciary system and a growing body of law touching upon most aspects of socioeconomic life.

15 As Liu Kang notes: "Mao integrated Marxism with nationalism and radically reinvented 'national culture,' breaking away from Confucian and other traditional values. While this highly selective and contested 'new national culture' may have served Mao's revolutionary strategy of national autonomy and autarchy in the political, social, and economic realms, especially in the face of imperialist threats and containment, it did not succeed in laying the necessary cultural and ideological foundations for social reconstruction or modernization" (Liu Kang, 1996: 201).

6. Looking Forward

1 The United States intensively lobbied allied governments in Asia and Europe to keep them out of the AIIB, arguing that the Bank will not meet the strict standards of the IMF and the World Bank in terms of transparency, environmental and social responsibility, and democratic governance. The argument about standards elides the underlying political issue regarding rule-making in the world economy. As the *New York Times* notes: "The last-minute surge to join the bank was considered a major victory for China in a rare public showdown with the United States, which opposed the bank, as the two powers try to outmaneuver each other for influence in Asia" (Perlez, 2015). Due to Republican Party opposition in Congress to the reform of existing international institutions, the U.S., which has veto power at the IMF and WB, has consistently refused to give re-emerging countries a voice in the Bretton Woods institutions commensurate with their economic weight.

2 The Treaty of Wanghia signed on July 3, 1844, gave the United States the same extraterritorial rights as Britain was awarded in the Treaty of Nanking. Article XXI of the Treaty asserted: "Subjects of China who may be guilty of any criminal act towards citizens of the United States shall be arrested and punished by the Chinese authorities according to the laws of China, and citizens of the United States who may commit any crime in China shall be subject to be tried and punished only by the Consul or other public functionary of the United States thereto authorized according to the laws of the United States." American traders participated actively in the opium trade, the profits from which were invested, among other things, in the contemporary westward expansion in the United States. A new Treaty, negotiated under

Franklin D. Roosevelt in 1943, abrogated all of the provisions of previous treaties and agreements.

3 On China's voting record at the United Nations Security Council, see Holland (2012), and Shichor (2007).

4 The idea was formulated by then-vice-president Xi Jinping during a trip to Washington, D.C. in February 2012. He called for a "new type of relationship between major countries in the 21st century" based on "mutual understanding and strategic trust," "respecting each other's core interests," "mutually beneficial cooperation," and "enhancing cooperation and coordination in international affairs and on global issues." For a positive reading of the initiative and its reception in the United States, see Lampton (2013). For a negative reading, see Erickson and Liff (2014).

5 The report by *The Diplomat*, published 28 January 2014, is based on a talk given by Mearsheimer at the Center for the National Interest in Washington D.C. on 26 January.

6 Feis writes: "The habits and structure of British society . . . contributed to foster a natural harmony of action. In the small circles of power, financial power was united with political power and held mainly the same ideas . . . the main course of British foreign investment was in accord with the main national purposes. Partners of the important issue houses sat in the House of Commons or among the Lords, where they were in easy touch with the Ministry. In clubs, country week-ends, shooting parties, Sir Ernest Cassel, Lord Rothschild or Lord Revelstroke could learn the official mind and reveal their own; there was ample opportunity to discuss the wisdom or needs of the moment" (Feis, 1973: 87).

BIBLIOGRAPHY

Abu-Lughod, J. L. (1991) *Before European Hegemony: The World System A.D., 1250–1350*. New York: Oxford University Press.

Acharya, A. (2011) Can Asia lead? *International Affairs*, 87 (4): 851–69.

Agnew, J. (1998) *Re-visioning World Politics*. New York: Routledge.

Ahlers, A. L. and Schubert, G. (2009) Building a new socialist countryside: Only a political slogan? *Journal of Current Chinese Affairs*, 38 (4): 35–62.

Akamatsu, K. (1961) A theory of unbalanced growth in the world economy. *Weltwirtschaftliches Archiv*, 86 (2): 196–215.

Amin, S. (1997) *Capitalism in the Age of Globalization*. London: Zed Books.

Amsden, A. H. (2001) *The Rise of "The Rest": Challenges to the West from Late-Industrializing Economies*. New York: Oxford University Press.

———. (2007) *Escape from Empire: The Developing World's Journey Through Heaven and Hell*. Cambridge, Mass.: MIT Press.

Anghie, A. (2007) *Imperialism, Sovereignty and the Making of International Law*. Cambridge: Cambridge University Press.

Armstrong, C. K. (2010) The destruction and reconstruction of North Korea, 1950–1960. *Asia Pacific Journal*, 51 (2).

Arndt, H. W. (1987) *Economic Development: The History and an Idea*. Chicago: University of Chicago Press.

Arrighi, G. (1994) *The Long Twentieth Century: Money, Power and the Origins of Our Times*. London: Verso.

———. (1997) Capitalism and the modern world-system: Rethinking the non-debates of the 1970s. Paper presented at the American Sociological Association Meetings, New York, August 16–20, 1996. Binghampton, N.Y.: Fernand Braudel Center, Binghampton University.

———. (2003) The social and political economy of global turbulence. *New Left Review* 20 (March–April): 5–71.

———. (2005) Hegemony unravelling-1. *New Left Review* 32 (March–April): 23–82.

———. (2007) *Adam Smith in Beijing*. London: Verso.

Arrighi, G., Hamashita, T., and Selden, M. (eds.) (2003) *The Resurgence of East Asia: 500, 150 and 50 Year Perspectives*. London and New York: Routledge Curzon.

173

Asian Development Bank (ADB). *Asia Regional Integration Center.* http://aric. adb.org/integrationindicators.

Bair, J. (ed.) (2014) The political economy of commodity chains. *Journal of World-Systems Research,* 20 (1), Winter–Spring.

Bairoch, P. (1982) International industrialisation levels from 1750 to 1980. *The Journal of European Economic History,* 11 (1): 269–333.

———. (1997) *Victoires et déboires: histoire économique et sociale du monde du XVIème siècle jusqu'à nos jours.* 3 Vols. Paris: Folio Gallimard.

Bairoch, P., and Kozul-Wright, R. (1996) Globalization myths: Some historical reflections on integration, industrialization and growth in the world economy. *UNCTAD Discussion Papers* No. 113, Geneva: United Nations Conference on Trade and Development, 1–32.

Barrett, C. (2014) Chinese high speed rail leapfrog development. *China Brief,* 14 (13): 11–13, Washington, D.C.: The Jamestown Foundation.

Bayly, C. A. (2004) *The Birth of the Modern World, 1780–1914: Global Connections and Comparisons.* London: Blackwell.

Bayly, C., and Harper T. (2004) *Forgotten Armies: The Fall of British Asia, 1941–1945.* London: Penguin.

Beale, H. K. (1989 [1956]) *Theodore Roosevelt and the Rise of America to World Power.* Baltimore: Johns Hopkins University Press.

Beasley, W. G. (1987) *Japanese Imperialism, 1894–1945.* Oxford: Oxford University Press.

Beeson, M. (2004) The Rise and Fall (?) of the Developmental State: The Viscissitudes and Implications of East Asian Interventionism. In L. Low (ed.) *Developmental States: Relevancy, Redundancy or Reconfiguration?* Hauppauge, N.Y.: Nova Science Publishers, 29–40.

Bellah, R. (1985 [1957]) *Tokugawa Religion, the Cultural Roots of Modern Japan.* New York: Free Press.

Berger, M. (1994) The End of the Third World? *Third World Quarterly,* 15 (2): 257–75.

Berger, M. T. (1999) Bringing History Back In: The Making and Unmaking of the East Asian Miracle. *Internationale Politik und Gesellschaft,* 3 (July): 237–52.

———. (2008) The End of Empire and the Cold War. In M. Beeson (ed.) *Contemporary Southeast Asia.* New York: Palgrave Macmillan.

Bernard, M., and Ravenhill, J. (1995) Beyond Product Cycles and Flying Geese: Regionalism, Hierarchy, and the Industrialization of East Asia. *World Politics,* 47 (2): 171–209.

Bethell, L. (1985) *The Cambridge History of Latin America.* Cambridge: Cambridge University Press.

Bironneau, R. (ed.) (2012) *China Innovation Inc.* Paris: Presses de Sciences Po.

Biswas, P. (2008) *Colonial displacements: nationalist longing and identity among early Indian intellectuals in the United States.* Ph.D. Thesis, University of California Los Angeles.

Blussé, L. (2008) *Visible Cities: Canton, Nagasaki, and Batavia and the Coming of the Americans.* Cambridge, Mass.: Harvard University Press.

Bo, Fu (2003) China hides its intentions again. *Le Monde dipmlomatique – English Edition* (March).

Boianovsky, M. (2013) Friedrich List and the Economic Fate of Tropical Countries. *History of Political Economy,* 45 (4): 647–691.

Bose, S. (2006) *A Hundred Horizons: The Indian Ocean in the Age of Global Empire*. Cambridge: Harvard University Press.

Bouissou, J.-M. (2003) Quand les sumôs apprennent à danser : la fin du modèle japonais. Paris: Fayard.

Boyer, R. (1998) Heurs et malheurs de l'industrie française: 1945–1995: Essor et crise d'une variante étatique du modèle fordiste. Paris: CEPREMAP.

———. (2001) Comprendre un changement d'époque. In R. Boyer and P-F. Souryi (eds) *Mondialisation et regulations: Europe et Japon face à la singularité américaine*. Paris: La Découverte, 7–22.

Braudel, F. (1985) *La Dynamique du capitalisme*. Paris: Arthaud.

———. (1992 [1984]) *The Perspective of the World, Civilization and Capitalism 15th–18th Century*. Los Angeles: University of California Press.

Buckley, C. (2012) China top military paper warns U.S. aims to contain rise. *Reuters* (January, 10).

Burgi, N. (ed.) (2014a) *La Grande Régression. La Grèce et l'avenir de l'Europe*. Lormont: Le Bord de l'eau éditions.

———. (2014b) Grèce. Fractures transatlantiques et divisions européennes. *P@ ages Europe* (February).

Cabestan, J.-P. (2005) The Many Facets of Chinese Nationalism. *China Perspectives* 59 (May–June).

Cain, P. J., and Hopkins, A. G. (2000) *British Imperialism, 1688–2000*. London: Longman-Pearson.

Campbell, K., and Andrews, B. (2013) Explaining the US 'Pivot' to Asia. London: Chatham House.

Campos, J., and Root, H. (1996) *The Key to the Asian Miracle: Making Shared Growth Credible*. Washington, D.C.: The Brookings Institution.

Cardoso, F. H., and Faletto, E. (1979) *Dependency and Development in Latin America*. Berkeley: University of California Press.

Carr, E. H. (2001) *The Twenty Years' Crisis: 1919–1939: An Introduction to the Study of International Relations*. London: Palgrave Macmillan.

Castells, M. (2000) *The Rise of the Network Society*. Oxford: Blackwell.

Cerny, P. (1997) Paradoxes of the Competition State: The Dynamics of Political Globalization. *Government and Opposition*, 32 (2): 251–74.

Chan, K. W. (2010) The Household Registration System and Migrant Labor in China: Notes on a Debate. *Population and Development Review*, 36 (2) 357–64.

Chang, Ha-J. (2002) *Kicking Away the Ladder: Development Strategy in Historical Perspective*. New York-London: Anthem Press.

Chatterjee, P. (1993) *The Nation and its Fragments: Colonial and Post-Colonial Histories*. Princeton: Princeton University Press.

Chaudhuri, K. N. (1991) *Asia Before Europe: Economy and Civilization of the Indian Ocean From the Rise of Islam to 1750*. New York: Cambridge University Press.

Chen, J. (1980) *State Economic Policies of the Qing Government, 1840–1895*. New York: Garland.

Chida, T., and Davies, P. N. (2012) *The Japanese Shipping and Shipbuilding Industries: A History of Their Modern Growth*. New York: Bloomsbury Academic.

Chin, G. (2007) Between 'outside-in' and 'inside-out': the internationalization of the Chinese state. In D. Zweig and Z. Chen (eds.) *China's Reforms and International Political Economy*. New York: Routledge, 155–70.

Cho, H. (2013) South Korea's experience with global financial crisis. In A. Bhushan (ed.), *How to Prevent the Next Crisis: Lessons from Country Experiences of the Global Financial Crisis.* Ottawa, Ont.: The North–South Institute, 93–113.

Chu, G. (2005) *China and the Great War: China's pursuit of a new national identity and internationalization.* New York: Cambridge University Press.

Cohen, B. J. (2009) The Future of Reserve Currencies. *Finance and Development* (September): 26–29.

Cox, M. (2012) Power Shifts, Economic Change and the Decline of the West? *International Relations* 26 (4): 369–388.

Cox, R. (1979) Ideologies and the New International Economic Order: reflections on some recent literature. *International Organization*, 33 (2): 258–259.

Cox, R. W., with Schechter, M. G. (2002) *Plural World: Critical Reflections on Power, Morals and Civilization.* London: Routledge.

Crafts, N. (1985) *British Economic Growth during the Industrial Revolution.* Oxford: Clarendon Press.

———. (2014) Productivity Growth during the British Industrial Revolution: Revisionism Revisited. *Working Paper Series 204*, Warwick: University of Warwick.

Cui, L. (2007) China's growing external dependence. *Finance and Development*, 44 (3) (September). Washington, D.C.: International Monetary Fund.

Cullather, N. (1996) 'Fuel for the good dragon': The United States and industrial policy in Taiwan, 1950–1965. *Diplomatic History*, 20 (1): 1–25.

Cumings, B. (1981) *The Origins of the Korean War.* Princeton, N.J.: Princeton University Press.

———. (1984) The origins and development of the Northeast Asian political economy: Industrial sectors, product cycles, and political consequences. *International Organization*, (38) 1: 1–40.

———. (1992) The Wicked Witch of the West is dead. Long live the Wicked Witch of the East. In M. J. Hogan (ed.), *The End of the Cold War: Its Meaning and Implications.* Cambridge: Cambridge University Press, 87–102.

———. (1999) *Parallax Visions: Making Sense of American – East Asian Relations.* Durham, N. C.: Duke University Press.

———. (2009). *Dominion from Sea to Sea: Pacific Ascendancy and American Power.* New Haven: Yale University Press.

Davis, L. E., and Cull, R. J. (1994) *International Capital Markets and American Economic Growth (1820–1914).* New York: Cambridge University Press.

De Vries, J. (1994) The industrious revolution and the Industrial Revolution. *Journal of Economic History,* 54 (2): 249–70.

De Vries, J., and Van der Woude, A. (1997) *The First Modern Economy: Success, Failure, and Perseverance of the Dutch Economy, 1500–1815.* Cambridge: Cambridge University Press.

Deane, P. (1979) *The First Industrial Revolution.* Cambridge: Cambridge University Press.

Dieter, H., and Higgott, R. (2002) Exploring alternative theories of economic regionalism: From trade to finance in Asian co-operation. *CSG Working Paper* No 89/02, Center for the Study of Globalisation and Regionalisation, University of Warwick.

Dirlik, A. (1998). *What Is in a Rim?: Critical Perspectives on the Pacific Region Idea.* Boston: Rowan & Littlefield.

Dixon, C. (1991) *South East Asia in the World-Economy*. Cambridge: Cambridge University Press.

Dos Santos, T. (1970) The structure of dependence. *American Economic Review*, 60 (2): 231–36.

———. (1971) The structure of dependence. In K. T. Fann and D. C. Hodges (eds.), *Readings and U.S. Imperialism*. Boston: Porter Sargent.

Dower, J. (2000) *Embracing Defeat: Japan in the Wake of World War II*. New York: W. W. Norton.

Duara, P. (2009) *The Global and Regional in China's Nation-Formation*. London: Routledge.

Dulles, F. R., and Ridinger, G. E. (1955) The Anticolonial Policies of Franklin D. Roosevelt. *Political Science Quarterly*, 70 (1): 1–18.

Economist, The (2012) State-owned enterprises: The state advances. 19 October.

Eltis, D. (2000) *The Rise of African Slavery in the Americas*. Cambridge: Cambridge University Press.

Emmerson, D. K. (1998) Americanizing Asia. *Foreign Affairs* (May–June).

Enloe, C. (2000) *Bananas, Beaches and Bases: Making Feminist Sense of International Politics*. Los Angeles: University of California Press.

Erickson, A., and Liff, A. (2014) Not-so-empty talk: The danger of China's "new type of Great Power relations." *Foreign Affairs* (October 9).

Escobar, A. (2004) Beyond the Third World: imperial globality, global coloniality and anti-globalisation social movements. *Third World Quarterly*, 25 (1): 207–30.

———. (2010) Latin America at a crossroads. *Cultural Studies*, 24 (1): 1–65.

Evans, P. B. (1995) *Embedded Autonomy: States and Industrial Transformation*. Princeton: Princeton University Press.

Evans, P. B., Rueschemeyer, D., and Skocpol, T. (1985) *Bringing the State Back In*. Cambridge: Cambridge University Press.

Falk, R. A. (2004) *The Declining World Order: America's Imperial Geopolitics*. New York: Routledge.

Fan, S., and Kanbur, R. (2009) China's Regional Disparities: Experience and Policy. Paper prepared for the China Economic Research and Advisory Programme.

Fedorowich, K., and Thompson, A. S. (eds.) (2013) *Empire, Migration and Identity in the British World*. Manchester: Manchester University Press.

Feis, H. (1974 [1930]) *Europe: The World's Banker, 1870–1914*. Clifton, N.J.: Augustus M. Kelley Publishers.

Ferreira, F. et al. (2004) *Inequality in Latin America: Breaking with History?* Washington, D.C.: The World Bank.

Feuerwerker, A. (1992) Questions about China's early modern economic history that I wish I could answer. *The Journal of Asian Studies* 51 (4): 757–69.

Fineman, D. (1997) *A Special Relationship: The United States and Military Government in Thailand, 1947–1958*. Honolulu: University of Hawaii Press.

Flemes, D. (2013) Network powers: Strategies of change in the multipolar system. *Third World Quarterly*, 34 (6): 1016–36.

Forsberg, A. (2000) *America and the Japanese Miracle: The Cold War Context of Japan's Postwar Economic Revival, 1950–1960*. Chapel Hill, N. C.: University of North Carolina Press.

Frank, A. G. (1966) The development of underdevelopment. *Monthly Review*, 18 (4): 17–31.

———. (1969) *Capitalism and Underdevelopment in Latin America*. New York: Monthly Review Press.

———. (1998) *ReOrient: Global Economy in the Asian Age*. Berkeley: University of California Press.

Fröbel, F., Heinrichs, J., and Kreye, O. (1980) *The New International Division of Labour: Structural Unemployment in Industrialised Countries and Industrialisation in Developing Countries*. Cambridge: Cambridge University Press.

Furtado, C. (1970) *Economic Development of Latin America: Historical Background and Contemporary Problems*. Cambridge: Cambridge University Press.

Gallagher, J., and Robinson, R. (1953) The imperialism of free trade. *The Economic History Review*, New Series, 6 (1): 1–15.

Gereffi, G. (1989) Rethinking development theory: Insights from East Asia and Latin America. *Sociological Forum*, 4 (4): 505–33.

———. (2014) Global value chains in a post-Washington consensus world. *Review of International Political Economy*, 21 (1): 9–37.

Gerschenkron, A. (1962) *Economic Backwardness in Historical Perspective*. Cambridge, Mass.: Harvard University Press.

Gill, S. (1995) Globalization, market civilization and disciplinary neoliberalism. *Millennium*, 24 (3): 399–423.

Gilpin, R. (1981) *War and Change in World Politics*. New York: Cambridge University Press.

———. (1987) *The Political Economy of International Relations*. Princeton, N.J.: Princeton University Press.

———. (1995) APEC in a new international order. *National Bureau of Asian Research*, 6 (5).

Gindin, S., and Panitch, L. (2012) *The Making of Global Capitalism: The Political Economy of American Empire*. London: Verso.

Gold, T. B. et al. (eds.) (2009) *Laid-Off Workers in a Workers' State: Unemployment with Chinese Characteristics*. London: Palgrave Macmillan.

Golub P. (1997) Southeast Asia feels the chill. *Le Monde diplomatique, English edn.* (December).

———. (2010) *Power, Profit and Prestige: A History of American Imperial Expansion*. London: Pluto Press.

———. (2011) The Berlin Consensus: Europe's blind march forward to depression. *Le Monde diplomatique, English edn.* (December).

———. (2013) From the new international economic order to the G20: How the "global South" is restructuring world capitalism from within. *Third World Quarterly*, 34 (6): 1000–1015.

Golub, P., and Maréchal, J.-P. (2012) Overcoming the planetary prisoners' dilemma: Cosmopolitan ethos and pluralist cooperation. In P. G. Harris (ed.), *Ethics and Global Environmental Policy: Cosmopolitan Conceptions of Climate Change*. Cheltenham, U.K.: Edward Elgar, 150–74.

Goody, J. (1996) *The East in the West*. New York: Cambridge University Press.

———. (2006) *The Theft of History*. Cambridge: Cambridge University Press.

Gordon, D. M. (1988) The global economy: New edifice or crumbling foundations? *New Left Review* 1/168 (March–April).

178

Gouda, F., and Zaalberg, T. B. (2002) *American Visions of the Netherlands East Indies/Indonesia: U.S. Foreign Policy and Indonesian Nationalism, 1920–1949*. Amsterdam: Amsterdam University Press.

Graz, J.-C. (1999) *Aux sources de l'OMC. La Charte de la Havane, 1941–1950*. Geneva: Droz.

Greenspan, A. (1998) The Ascendance of Market Capitalism, Remarks by Chairman Alan Greenspan before the Annual Convention of the American Society of Newspaper Editors. Washington, D.C.: The Federal Reserve Board (April 2).

Habermas, J. (2001) *The Postnational Constellation: Political Essays*. Cambridge: Polity Press.

Halliday, F. (2002) For an international sociology. In S. Hobden and J. M. Hobson (eds.), *Historical Sociology of International Relations*. Cambridge: Cambridge University Press, 244–64.

Hamashita, T. (ed. M. Selden and L. Grove) (2008) *China, East Asia and the Global Economy: Regional and Historical Perspectives*. New York: Routledge.

Hardt, M., and Negri, A. (2000) *Empire*. Cambridge: Cambridge University Press.

Harootunian, H. (2000) *Overcome By Modernity: History, Culture and Community in Interwar Japan*. Oxford: Princeton University Press.

Harper, M., and Constantine, S. (2010) *Migration and Empire*. Oxford: Oxford University Press.

Havens, T. (1987) *Fire Across the Sea*. Princeton, N.J.: Princeton University Press.

Hegel, G. W. (1899) *The Philosophy of History*. New York: Colonial Press.

Heilmann, S., and Shih, L. (2013) The rise of industrial policy in China, 1978–2012. *Harvard-Yenching Institute Working Paper Series*.

Hein, L. (2008) The cultural career of the Japanese economy: Developmental and cultural nationalisms in historical perspective. *Third World Quarterly*, 29 (3): 447–65.

Held, D. and McGrew, A. (2000) *The Global Transformations Reader*. Cambridge: Polity Press.

Helleiner, E. (2009) Enduring top currency, fragile negotiated currency: Politics and the dollar's international role. In E. Helleiner and J. Kirshner (eds.), *The Future of the Dollar*. Ithaca: Cornell University Press.

———.(2014) *The Status Quo Crisis: Global Financial Governance After the 2008 Meltdown*. Oxford: Oxford University Press.

Hess, G. (1972) Franklin Roosevelt and Indochina. *The Journal of American History*, 59 (2): 353–68.

Higgott, R. (1998) The Asian economic crisis: A study in the politics of resentment. *New Political Economy*, 3 (3): 333–55.

Hirschman, A. O. (1980 [1945]) *National Power and the Structure of Foreign Trade* (expanded edn.). Berkeley: University of California Press.

Hobsbawm, E. (1990) *Industry and Empire: from 1970 to the Present Day*. London: Penguin.

Hobson, J. M. (2010) Back to the future of nineteenth-century Western international thought? In G. Lawson, C. Armbruster, and M. Cox (eds.), *The Global 1989: Continuity and Change in World Politics*. Cambridge: Cambridge University Press, 23–50.

Holland, C. (2012) Chinese Attitudes to International Law: China, The Security Council, Sovereignty, and Intervention. *Journal of International Law and Politics Online Forum* (July).

Hopkins, T. K., and Wallerstein, I. (1986) Commodity chains in the world-economy prior to 1800. *Review* (10)1 (Summer): 157–70.

Houben, V., and Lindblad, T. (1999). *Coolie Labour in Colonial Indonesia: A Study of Labour Relations in the Outer Island, c. 1900–1940.* Wiesbaden: Harrassowitz.

Howe, S. (2003) American empire: The history and future of an idea. *Open democracy.net*, (June 12).

Hsiao, F. S. T. and Hsiao M. (2000) Economic Liberalization and Development: The Case of Lifting Martial Law in Taiwan. University of Colorado, Department of Economics, Discussion Paper 99–29.

Hu, A. (2007) Five major scale effects of China's rise on the world. *Discussion Paper 19* (April), The University of Nottingham China Policy Institute, U.K.

———. (2012) *China in 2020: A New Type of Superpower.* Washington, D.C.: Brookings Institution Press.

Huang, Y. (2001) The Role of Foreign-Invested Enterprises in the Chinese Economy: An Institutional Foundation Approach. In S. Chen and C. Wolf (eds) *China, the United States and the Global Economy.* Santa Monica, CA: Rand Corporation, 147–191.

Huchet, J.-F. (2014) From dirigism to realism: Chinese industrial policy in the era of globalisation. In X. Richet, V. Deltei and P. Dieuaide (eds) *Strategies of Multinational Corporations and Social Regulations: European and Asian Perspectives.* Berlin: Springer, 57–76.

Hui, W. (2003) *China's New Order, Society, Politics, and Economy in Transition.* Cambridge, Mass.: Harvard University Press.

———. (2005) An Asia that isn't the East. *Le Monde diplomatique, English edn.* (February).

Hung, H-f. (ed.) (2009) *China and the Transformation of Global Capitalism.* Baltimore, Md.: Johns Hopkins University Press.

Huntington, S. (1991) America's changing strategic interests. *Survival* 33 (1): 3–17.

Ikenberry, J. (2008) The rise of China and the future of the West: Can the liberal system survive? *Foreign Affairs*, 87 (1): 23–37.

INED (2006) L'évolution de l'espérance de vie en France. *Graphique du mois*, 5, October.

Inikori, J. E. (2002) *Africans and the Industrial Revolution in England: A Study in International Trade and Economic Development.* New York: Cambridge University Press.

International Monetary Fund (2007) *Regional Economic Outlook: Asia Pacific.* Washington, D.C.: IMF (October).

———. (2013, 2014) *World Economic Outlook Database.* Washington, D.C.: IMF.

Iriye, A. (1972) *Pacific Estrangement: Japanese and American Expansion, 1897–1911.* Cambridge, Mass: Harvard University Press.

———. (1987) *The Origins of the Second World War in Asia and the Pacific.* New York: Routledge.

Irokawa, D. (1988) *The Culture of the Meiji Period.* Princeton: Princeton University Press.

Jaffrelot, C. (ed) (2007) *Hindu Nationalism: A Reader.* Princeton, N.J.: Princeton University Press.

Jansen, M. (1970 [1954]). *The Japanese and Sun Yat-sen.* Stanford: Stanford University Press.

Jevons, W. S. (1865) *The Coal Question: An Enquiry Concerning the Progress of the Nation, and the Probable Exhaustion of our Coal Mines.* London: Macmillan (Google Digital Book).

Johnson, C. (1982) *MITI and the Japanese Miracle.* Stanford: Stanford University Press.

———. (1999) The developmental state: Odyssey of a concept. In M. Woo-Cumings, *The Developmental State.* Ithaca: Cornell University Press, 32–60.

Kang, L. (1996) Is there an alternative to (capitalist) globalization? The debate about modernity in China. *boundary 2*, 23 (3): 193–218.

Kasahara, S. (2004) The Flying Geese Paradigm: A critical study of its application to East Asian regional development. *UNCTAD Discussion Papers* No. 169. Geneva: United Nations Conference on Trade and Development.

Kaskenniemi, M. (2004) *The Gentle Civilizer of Nation's: The Rise and Fall of International Law 1870–1960.* Cambridge: Cambridge University Press.

Katz, R. (1998) *Japan: The System that Soured: The Rise and Fall of the Japanese Economic Miracle.* Armonk, N.Y.: Sharpe.

Katzenstein P. J. (1993) A world of regions: America, Europe and East Asia. *Indiana Journal of Global Legal Studies*, 1 (1): 65–82.

———. (ed.) (1996) *The Culture of National Security: Norms and Identity in World Politics.* New York: Columbia University Press.

———. (1997) *Network Power: Japan and Asia.* Ithaca, N.Y.: Cornell University Press.

Katzenstein, P. J. and Rouse M. (1993) Japan as a Regional Power in Asia. In J. A. Frankel and M. Kahler (eds), *Regionalism and Rivalry: Japan and the United States in Pacific Asia.* Chicago: University of Chicago Press, 217–48.

Keck, Z. (2014) US–China rivalry more dangerous than Cold War? *The Diplomat* (January 28).

Kennedy, P. (2010) Asia's rise: Rise and fall. *The World Today*, 66 (8–9).

Keynes, J. M. (1920) *The Economic Consequences of the Peace.* New York: Harcourt Brace and Howe.

Kim, H.-A. (2004) *Korea's Development under Park Chung Hee: Rapid Industrialization, 1961–79.* London: Routledge.

Kim, P., and Vogel, E. F. (eds.) (2011) *The Park Chung Hee Era: The Transformation of South Korea.* Cambridge, Mass.: Harvard University Press.

Kim, S. J. (1970) South Korea's involvement in Vietnam and its economic and political impact. *Asian Survey*, 10 (6): 519–32

Kissinger, H. (1994) *Diplomacy.* New York: Simon and Schuster.

Kohli, A. (1999) Where do high-growth political economies come from? The Japanese lineage of Korea's "developmental state." In M. Woo-Cumings (ed.), *The Developmental State.* Ithaca and London: Cornell University Press, 93–136.

———. (2004) *State-Directed Development: Political Power and Industrialization in the Global Periphery.* Cambridge; Cambridge University Press.

———. (2009) Nationalist versus dependent capitalist development: Alternate pathways of Asia and Latin America in a globalized world. *Studies in Comparative International Development*, 44: 386–410.

Kojima, K. (2000) The "flying geese" model of Asian economic development: Origin, theoretical extensions, and regional policy implications. *Journal of Asian Economics*, 11: 375–401.

Koopman, R., Wang, Z., and Wei, S-J. (2012) Estimating domestic content in exports when processing trade is pervasive. *Journal of Development Economics*, 99: 178–89.

Krasner, S. (1985) *Structural Conflict: The Third World Against Global Liberalism*. Berkeley and Los Angeles: University of California Press.

Krugman, P. (1994) The myth of Asia's miracle. *Foreign Affairs*, 73 (6): 62–78.

Kuhn, P. (1999) *Les origins de l'État chinois moderne*. Paris: Éditions de l'École des hautes études en sciences sociales.

Kuznets, S. (1955) Economic growth and income inequality. *American Economic Review*, 45 (March): 1–28.

LaFeber, W. (1997) *The Clash: A History of U.S.–Japan Relations*. New York: W.W. Norton.

Lai, W. L. (2007) They came in ships: imperialism, migration and Asian diasporas in the 19th century. *Seventh Jagan Lecture*. Toronto: York University.

Lampton, D. (2013) A new type of major power relationship: Seeking a durable foundation for U.S.–China ties. *Asia Policy*, 16 (July): 51–68.

Landes, D. (1998) *The Wealth and Poverty of Nations: Why Some Are So Rich and Others So Poor*. New York: W.W. Norton.

Lardy, N. R. (2002) *Integrating China into the Global Economy*. Washington, D.C.: Brookings Institution.

Lebra, J. C. (2010 [1977]) *Japanese-Trained Armies in Southeast Asia*. Singapore: ISEAS Publishing.

Lee, C.-K. (2000) Pathways of labour insurgency. In E. J. Perry and M. Selden (eds.), *Chinese Society: Change, Conflict and Resistance*. London: Routledge.

———. (2007) *Against the Law: Labor Protests in China's Rustbelt and Sunbelt*. Los Angeles: University of California Press.

Lee, W., and Chang, I. (2014) US aid and Taiwan. *The Asian Review of World Histories*, 2 (1): 47–80.

Leffler, M. P. (1984) The American conception of national security and the beginning of the Cold War. *American Historical Review*, 89 (2): 346–81.

Leitenberg, M. (2006) Deaths in wars and conflicts in the 20th century. Cornell University Peace Studies Program, Occasional Paper No 29, 3rd edition.

Li, L. (2010) Rights consciousness and rules consciousness in contemporary China. *The China Journal*, 64 (July): 47–68.

Linden, G., Kraemer, K. L., and Dedrick, J. (2009) Who captures value in a global innovation network? The case of Apple's iPod. *Communications of the ACM*, 52 (3): 140–44.

Lintner, B. (1999) The secret war. In B. Lintner (ed.), *Burma in Revolt: Opium and Insurgency Since 1948*. Chiang Mai: Silkworm Books, 125–57.

Lipietz, A. (1984) Le fordisme périphérique étranglé par le monétarisme central. *L'Actualité économique*, 60 (1): 72–94.

Littlefield, W. (1905) After the war, what? Outlook in the Orient. *New York Times*, September 3.

Liu, Chang (2013) U.S. fiscal failure warrants a de-Americanized world. Beijing: Xinhua, October 13.

Liu, W., and Dicken, P. (2006) Transnational corporations and "obligated embeddedness": Foreign direct investment in China's automobile industry. *Environment and Planning A*, 38 (7): 1229–47.

Loriaux, M. (1999) The French developmental state as myth and moral ambition. In M. Woo-Cumings (ed.), *The Developmental State*. Ithaca: Cornell University Press, 235–75.

Louis, W. R. (2001b) The Dissolution of the British Empire. In J. M. Brown, *The Oxford History of the British Empire*. Vol. IV, The Twentieth Century. New York: Oxford University Press, 329–56.

———. (2001a) Introduction. In J. M. Brown, W. R. Louis, and A. M. Low (eds.), *The Oxford History of the British Empire*. Vol 9: The Twentieth Century. New York: Oxford University Press, 1–46.

Lyons, P. (2006) *American Pacificism: Oceania in the U.S. Imagination*. New York: Routledge.

Mann, M. (1984) The Autonomous Power of the State: Its Origins, Mechanisms and Results. *Archives européennes de sociologie*, 25: 185–213.

Maréchal, J.-P. (2011) *Chine / USA Le climat en jeu*. Paris, Choiseul éditions

———. (2012) À qui profite la mondialisation? *EspacesTemps.net*, Laboratoire, Sept. 25.

Marx, K. (1963) *Marx on Colonialism*. New York: International Publishers.

———. (1977) *Capital: A Critique of Political Economy*. Vol 1. New York: International Publishers.

Marx, K., and Engels, F. (2012) *The Communist Manifesto: A Modern Edition*. London: Verso.

Mazower, M. (2006) An international civilization? Empire, internationalism and the crisis of the mid-twentieth century. *International Affairs*, 82 (3): 553–66.

———. (2012) *Governing the World: The History of an Idea*. London: Allen Lane.

McCoy, A. (1972) *The Politics of Heroin in Southeast Asia*. New York: Harper & Row.

McMahon, R. J. (1981) *Colonialism and Cold War: The United States and the Struggle for Indonesian Independence, 1945–49*. Ithaca, N.Y.: Cornell University Press.

———. (1999) *The Limits of Empire: The United States and Southeast Asia since World War II*. New York: Columbia University Press.

Mead, W. R. (2014) The return of geopolitics: The revenge of the revisionist powers. *Foreign Affairs* (May/June).

Mearsheimer J. J. (2001) *The Tragedy of Great Power Politics*. New York: W.W. Norton & Co.

———. (2010) The Gathering Storm: China's Challenge to US Power in Asia. *The Chinese Journal of International Politics*, 3: 381–96.

Mertha, A. (2014) *Brothers in Arms: Chinese Aid to the Khmer Rouge, 1975–1979*. Cornell: Cornell University Press.

Mills, C. W. (2000) *The Power Elite*. New York: Oxford University Press.

Minns, J. (2001) The labour movement in South Korea. *Labour History*, 81 (November): 175–95.

Minns, J., and Tierney, R. (2003) The labour movement in Taiwan. *Labour History*, 85, (November): 103–28.

Mokyr, J. (1990) *The Lever of Riches: Technological Creativity and Economic Change*. New York: Oxford University Press.

Moore, B., Jr. (1966) *The Social Origins of Dictatorship and Democracy: Lord and Peasant in the Making of the Modern World.* Boston: Beacon Press.

Morgan, K. (2000) *Slavery, Atlantic Trade and the British Economy 1660–1800.* Cambridge: Cambridge University Press.

Morgenthau, H. (1965) We are deluding ourselves in Vietnam. *New York Times,* April 18.

Moriguchi, C., and Saez, E. (2008) The evolution of income concentration in Japan, 886–2005: Evidence from income tax statistics. *The Review of Economics and Statistics,* 90 (4): 713–34.

Morris-Suzuki, T. (1996) The frontiers of Japanese identity. In S. Tonnesson and H. Antlöv (eds.), *Asian Forms of the Nation.* Richmond Surrey: Curzon Press, 41–66.

Mukherjee, R., and Subramanian, L. (1998) *Politics and Trade in the Indian Ocean World: Essays in Honour of Ashin Das Gupta.* New Delhi: Oxford University Press.

Murray, M. J. (1980) *The Development of Capitalism in Colonial Indochina 1870–1940.* Berkeley: University of California Press.

Nakamura, I. (1981) Human capital accumulation in premodern rural Japan. *The Journal of Economic History* 41 (2): 263–81.

Nakamura, J., and Miyamoto, M. (1982) Social structure and population change: A comparative study of Tokugawa Japan and Ch'ing China. *Economic Development and Cultural Change,* 30 (2): 229–69.

Narangoa, L., and Cribb, R. B. (2003) *Imperial Japan and National Identities in Asia, 1895–1945.* New York: Routledge Curzon.

National Science Foundation (2007) *Asia's Rising Science and Technology Strength: Comparative Indicators for Asia, the European Union and the United States.* Arlington, Va.: NSF07–319.

Naughton, B. (1999) China: Domestic restructuring and a new role in Asia. In T. J. Pempel, *The Politics of the Asian Economic Crisis.* Ithaca: Cornell University Press, 203–23.

Nayyar, D. (2013) *CatchUp. Developing Countries in the World Economy.* New York: Oxford University Press.

Needham, J. (1954) *Science and Civilisation in China.* 1. Introductory orientations. Cambridge: Cambridge University Press.

Negroni, C. (2012) China market challenges plane makers. *New York Times:* May 14.

Nel, P., and Taylor, I. (2013) Bugger thy neighbour? IBSA and South–South solidarity. *Third World Quarterly,* 34 (6): 1091–1110.

Nolan, P. (1993) *State and Market in the Chinese Economy: Essays on Controversial Issues.* London: Palgrave Macmillan.

———. (2001) *China and the Global Business Revolution.* Basingstoke, U.K.: Palgrave.

———. (2002) China and the global business revolution. *Cambridge Journal of Economics,* 26 (1): 119–37.

Nwaubani, E. (2001) *The United States and Decolonization in West Africa, 1950–1960.* Rochester, N.Y.: University of Rochester Press.

Nye, J. (1993) *Harness the Rising Sun: An American Strategy for Managing Japan's Rise as a Global Power.* Lanham, Md.: University Press of America.

———. (2015) *Is the American Century Over?* Cambridge: Polity Press.

O'Sullivan, C. D. (2007) *Sumner Welles: Postwar Policy and the Quest for a New*

World Order. The Gutenberg-e program. New York: Columbia University Press.

Obama, B. (2015) Remarks by the President in State of the Union Address. (January 20). Washington, D.C.: The White House.

Organization of Economic Cooperation and Development and World Trade Organization (2013) Trade in value added (TIVA) indicators: China. Paris: OECD-WTO.

Ouyyanont, P. (2001) The Vietnam War and tourism in Bangkok's development, 1960–1970. *Southeast Asian Studies*, 39 (2): 157–87.

Ozawa, T. (2005) Asia's labor-driven economic development, flying-geese style: An unprecedented opportunity for the poor to rise? *Discussion Paper N° 40.* New York: APEC Study Center, Columbia University.

Park, C-h. (1963) *The Country, The Revolution and I.* Ann Arbor: University of Michigan.

Parthasarathi, P. (1998) Rethinking wages and competitiveness in the eighteenth century: Britain and South India. *Past and Present*, 158: 79–109.

———. (2001) *The Transition to a Colonial Economy: Weavers, Merchants and Kings in South India, 1720–1800.* New York: Cambridge University Press.

———. (2009) Historical issues of deindustrialization in nineteenth-century South India. In G. Riello and T. Roy (eds), *How India Clothed the World: The World of South Indian Textiles, 1500–1850.* Leiden-Boston: Brill, 415–36.

Patti, A. (1982) *Why Vietnam?* California: University of California Press.

Pearson, M. (2007) Governing the Chinese Economy: Regulatory Reform in the Service of the State. *Public Administration Review*, 67 (4): 718–30.

Pempel, T. J. (1999a) Regional ups, regional downs. In T. J. Pempel (ed.), *The Politics of the Asian Crisis.* Ithaca, N.Y.: Cornell University Press, 62–78.

———. (1999b) The developmental regime in a changing world economy. In M. Woo-Cumings (ed.), *The Developmental State.* Ithaca, N.Y.: Cornell University Press, 137–181.

Pentagon Papers, The (1971), Gravel Edition, Vol. I, Chapter 4, U.S. and France in Indochina, 1950–56. Boston: Beacon Press.

Perlez, J. (2015) Stampede to join China's development bank stuns even its founder. *New York Times* (April 2).

Perroux, F. (1994 [1973]) *Pouvoir et économie généralisée.* Grenoble: Presses Universitaires de Grenoble.

Perry, E., and Selden, M. (eds.) (2003) *Chinese Society: Change, Conflict and Resistance.* London: Routledge-Curzon.

Perry, S. (1998) *La politique chinoise des Etats-Unis: 1989–1997.* Ph.D. Thesis. Paris: EHESS.

Piketty, T. (2014) *Capital in the Twenty-First Century.* Cambridge, Mass.: Harvard University Press.

Pitts, J. (2006) *A Turn to Empire: The Rise of Imperial Liberalism in Britain and France.* Princeton, N.J.: Princeton University Press.

Polanyi, K. (1972 [1944]) *The Great Transformation: The Political and Economic Origins of Our Time.* Boston, Mass.: Beacon Press.

Pomeranz, K. (1993) *The Making of a Hinterland: State, Society and Economy in Inland North China, 1853–1937.* Berkeley: University of California Press.

———. (2000) *The Great Divergence: China, Europe, and the Making of the Modern World Economy.* Princeton, N.J.: Princeton University Press.

185

Pottier, C. (2003) *Les Multinationales et la mise en concurrence des salariés*. Paris: L'Harmattan.

Prakash, O. (2007) The transformation from a pre-colonial to a colonial order: The case of India. *The ICFAI Journal of History and Culture*, 1 (3).

———. (2009) From market-determined to coercion-based textile manufacturing in eighteenth-century Bengal. In G. Riello and T. Roy (eds.), *How India Clothed the World: the World of South Asian Textiles, 1500–1850*. Leiden-Boston: Brill, 217–53.

Rawksi, E. (1991) Research themes in Ming-Qing socioeconomic history: The state of the field. *The Journal of Asian Studies*, 50 (1): 84–111.

Richards, J. (2002) The opium industry in British India. *The Indian Economic and Social History Review*, 39 (2–3): 149–80.

Riello, G., and Roy, T. (2009) The world of South Asian textiles, 1500–1850. In G. Riello and T. Roy (eds.), *How India Clothed the World: the World of South Asian Textiles, 1500–1850*. Leiden-Boston: Brill, 1–30.

Risse-Kappen, T. (ed.). (1995) *Bringing Transnational Relations Back In*. Cambridge: Cambridge University Press.

Robertson, P. (2015) Mismeasuring China's military spending. VoxEU.org, 31 March. http://www.voxeu.org/article/mismeasuring-china-s-military-spending

Robinson, W. I. (2004) *A Theory of Global Capitalism*. Baltimore, Md.: Johns Hopkins University Press.

Roger Louis, W. (1999) Introduction. In J. Brown and W. Roger Louis (eds.), *The Oxford History of the British Empire: The Twentieth Century*. Oxford: Oxford University Press, 1–46.

Rosenau, J. N. (1989) Global changes and theoretical challenges: Toward a postinternational politics in the 1990s. In E.-O. Czempiel and J. N. Rosenau (eds.), *Global Changes and Theoretical Challenges: Approaches to World Politics for the 1990s*. Lanham, Md.: Lexington Books, 1–20.

Rosenberg, J. (2005) Globalization theory: A post mortem. *International Politics*, 42: 2_74.

Ruggie, J. G. (1982) International regimes, transactions, and change: Embedded liberalism in the postwar economic order. *International Organization*, 36 (2): 379–415.

Saich, T. (2008) *Providing Public Goods in Transitional China*. New York: Palgrave Macmillan.

Said, E. (2003 [1979]) *Orientalism*. New York: Vintage Books.

Saito, O. (2005) Pre-modern economic growth revisited: Japan and the West. *Working Paper No. 16/05*. Department of Economic History: London School of Economics.

Salisbury, L. E. (1944) The Pacific front, colonial Asia. *Far Eastern Review*, 1 (25): 235–7.

Schaller, M. (1982) Securing the great crescent: Occupied Japan and the origins of the Cold War in Asia. *Journal of American History*, 69 (2): 392–414.

Schwartz, H. (1989) *In the Dominions of Debt: Historical Perspectives on Dependent Development*. Ithaca, N.Y.: Cornell University Press.

———. (2009) Housing finance, growth, and the U.S. dollar's surprising durability. In E. Helleiner and J. Kirschner (eds.), *The Future of the Dollar*. Ithaca, N.Y.: Cornell University Press.

Sebrega, J. J. (1986) The Anticolonial Policies of Franklin D. Roosevelt: A Reappraisal. *Political Science Quarterly*, 101 (1): 65–84.

Seers, D. (1969) The meaning of development. *IDS Communication No. 44.* Sussex: Institute of Development Studies.

Sen, A. (1999) *Development as Freedom.* New York: Knopf.

Shapiro, J. (2012) *China's Environmental Challenges.* Cambridge: Polity Press.

Shichor, Y. (2007) China's voting behavior in the U.N. Security Council. *China Brief,* 6 (18), Washington D.C.: The Jamestown Foundation.

Shin, G-W. (1998) Agrarian conflict and the origins of Korean capitalism. *American Journal of Sociology,* 103 (5): 1309–51.

———. (2007) Introduction. In G-W. Shin and D. Schneider (eds.), *Cross Currents: Regionalism and Nationalism in Northeast Asia.* Washington, D.C.: Brookings Institution Press.

Sicular, T. (2013) The Challenge of High Inequality in China. *Inequality in Focus,* World Bank: Poverty Reduction and Equity Department 2 (2).

Simson, B. R. (2010) *Economists with Guns: Authoritarian Development and U.S.-Indonesia Relations, 1960–1968.* Stanford, Calif.: Stanford University Press.

Skinner, G. (1985) The Structure of Chinese History. *The Journal of Asian Studies.* 44 (2): 271–92.

Smith, A. (2005) *An Inquiry into the Nature and Causes of the Wealth of Nations.* Hazelton, Pa.: Electronic Classics Series, Jim Manis.

Smith, T. (1988) *Native Sources of Japanese Industrialization, 1750–1920.* Berkeley: University of California Press.

Soeya, Y., Tadokoro, M., and Welch, D. (2011) *Japan as a 'Normal Country': A Nation in Search of Its Place in the World.* Toronto: University of Toronto Press.

Sokoloff, K., and Engerman, S. (2000) History Lessons: Institutions, Factor Endowments, and Paths of Development in the New World. *Journal of Economic Perspectives,* 14 (3): 217–32.

Stallings, B. (1995) *Global Changes, Regional Response: The New International Context of Development.* Cambridge: Cambridge University Press.

Starrs, S. (2013) American economic power hasn't declined—it globalized! Summoning the data and taking globalization seriously. *International Studies Quarterly,* 57: 817–30.

Stern, N., et al. (2013) A New World's Development Bank. Project Syndicate. May 1.

Stiglitz, J. (1996) Some lessons from the East Asian miracle. *The World Bank Research Observer,* 11 (2): 151–77.

———. (2002) *Globalization and Its Discontents.* New York: W. W. Norton.

Stockholm International Peace Institute (2014) Trends in world military expenditure 2013. *Factsheet.* Stockholm: Sipri.

Stubbs R. (1999) War and Economic Development: Export Oriented Industrialization in East and Southeast Asia. *Comparative Politics,* 31 (April): 337–55.

Subramanian, A., and Kessler, M. (2012) The renminbi bloc is here: Asia down, rest of the world to go?, *Working Paper 12/19.* Washington, D.C.: The Peterson Institute for International Economics.

Subramanian, L. (ed.) (1988) *Politics and Trade in the Indian Ocean World: Essays in Honour of Ashin Das Gupta.* Delhi: Oxford University Press.

Sugihara, K. (1990) Japan as an engine of the Asian international economy, c. 1880–1936. *Japan Forum,* 2 (1): 127–45.

———. (2009) The resurgence of intra-Asian trade, 1800–1850. In G. Riello and T. Roy (eds.), *How India Clothed the World: The World of South Asian Textiles, 1500–1850*. Leiden and Boston: Brill, 139–72.

Summers, L. (2004) The United States and the global adjustment process. Speech at the Third Annual Stavros S. Niarchos Lecture, March 23, Washington D.C.: The Peterson Institute for International Economics.

———. (2015) It is time the US leadership woke up to a new economic era. *Financial Times*, April 6.

Teng, S-y., and Fairbank, J. K. (1979) *China's Response to the West: A Documentary Survey 1839–1923*. Cambridge, Mass.: Harvard University Press.

Thompson, E-P. (1966) *The Making of the English Working Class*. New York: Vintage.

Thorpe, M. (2004) Inward Foreign Investment and the Chinese Economy. In H. Kehal (ed) *Foreign Investment in Developing Countries*. London: Palgrave Macmillan, 50–77.

Tilly, C. (1985) War making and state making as organised crime. In P. Evans, D. Ruschemeier, and T. Skocpol (eds.), *Bringing the State Back In*. Cambridge: Cambridge University Press, 169–91.

Tong, Y., and Lei, S. (2013) *Social Protest in Contemporary China, 2003–2010: Transitional Pains and Regime Legitimacy*. London: Routledge.

Trocki, C. (1999) *Opium, Empire and the Global Political Economy: A Study of the Asian Opium Trade 1750–1950*. London: Routledge.

Tucker, R. (ed.) (1978) *The Marx-Engels Reader* (Second edn.). New York: Norton.

United Nations. (1970) International Development Strategy for the Second United Nations Development Decade, *UN Documents* A/res/25/2626. New York: United Nations.

———. (1974) Declaration on the Establishment of a New International Economic Order. UNGA, Sixth Special session, A.RES/5-6/3201.

United Nations Conference on Trade and Development. (2012) *South–South Trade Monitor No. 1*. Geneva: UNCTAD.

———. (2014) *World Investment Report 2014*. Geneva: UNCTAD.

United Nations Development Program. (2013) *Human Development Report: Rise of the South*. New York: UNDP.

United Nations Economic and Social Commission for the Asia and the Pacific. (2008) *Economic and Social Survey of Asia and the Pacific, 2008*. New York: United Nations.

United States International Trade Commission. (1998) *The Changing Structure of the Global Large Civil Aircraft Industry and Market: Implications for the Competitiveness of the U.S. Industry*. Publication 3143. Washington, DC: USITC.

United States National Security Strategy. (2015). Washington, D.C.: The White House (February).

Van Bijlest, V. A. (2003) The icon of Japan is nationalist revolutionary discourse in India 1890–1910. In L. Narangoa and R. B. Cribb (eds.), *Imperial Japan and National Identities in Asia, 1895–1945*. New York: Routledge Curzon, 23–42.

Van de Ven, H. (2014) *Breaking with the Past: The Maritime Customs Service and the Global Origins of Modernity in China*. New York: Columbia University Press.

Wade, R. (1990) *Governing the Market*. Princeton, N.J.: Princeton University Press.

Wade, R. (2002) The American empire and its limits. *Destin Working Papers Series*. No. 02–22. London: London School of Economics.

Walder, A. G., and Xiaoxia, G. (1993) Workers in the Tiananmen protests: The politics of the Beijing Workers' Autonomous Federation. *The China Journal*, 29 (January).

Wallerstein, I. (1980) *The Modern World-System*. Vol. 2: *Mercantilism and the Consolidation of the European World-Economy, 1600–1750*. New York: Academic Press.

———. (1989) *The Modern World-System*. Vol. 3: *The Second Era of Great Expansion of the Capitalist World-Economy, 1730–1840s*. New York: Academic Press.

———. (2000) The three instances of hegemony. In I. Wallerstein (ed.), *The Essential Wallerstein*. New York: The New Press.

———. (2003) *The Decline of American Power: The U.S. in a Chaotic World*. New York: W. W. Norton & Co.

Walt, S. M. (2006) *Taming American Power: The Global Response to U.S. Primacy*. New York: W.W. Norton.

Wang, E. (2008) Booming, China faults U.S. policy on the economy. *New York Times*, June 17.

Wasserstrom, J., and Perry, E. (eds.) (1994) *Popular Protest and Political Culture in Modern China*. Boulder, Colo.: Westview Press.

Weber, M. (2005) *The Protestant Ethic and the Spirit of Capitalism*. London: Routledge.

Wei, P. (2003) Toward a consultative rule of law regime in China. *Journal of Contemporary China*, 12 (34): 3–43.

Weisbrot, M. (2007) Ten years after: The lasting impact of the Asian financial crisis. In B. Muchhala (ed.), *Ten Years After: Revisiting the Asian Financial Crisis*. Washington, D.C.: Woodrow Wilson International Center for Scholars, 105–18.

Weiss, L. (2007) *The Myth of the Powerless State*. Hong Kong: UP Publications.

Wesseling, H. (1997) *Imperialism and Colonialism: Essays in the History of European Expansion*. New York: Praeger.

Westad, A. O. (2012) *Restless Empire: China and the World Since 1750*. New York: Basic Books.

Will, P.-E. (1994) Développement quantitatif et développement qualitative en Chine à la fin de l'époque impériale. *Annales* 49 (4): 863–902.

———. (1999) Entre passé et present. Introduction. In P. Kuhn, *Les origins de l'État chinois moderne*, Paris: EHESS, 12–68.

Williams, E. (1994) *Capitalism and Slavery*. Chapel Hill: University of North Carolina Press.

Wolf, M. (2010) *Fixing Global Finance*. Baltimore, Md.: Johns Hopkins University Press.

Wong, J. Y. (2002) *Deadly Dreams: Opium and the Arrow War (1856–1860) in China*. Cambridge: Cambridge University Press.

Wong, R. B. (1997) *China Transformed: Historical Change and the Limits of European Experience*. Ithaca, N.Y.: Cornell University Press.

Woo, J.-E. (1991) *Race to the Swift: State and Finance in Korean Industrialization*. New York: Columbia University Press.

Woo-Cumings, M. (1993) East Asia's America problem. In M. Woo-Cumings and M. Loriaux (eds.), *Past As Prelude: History in the Making of a New World Order*. Boulder, Colo.: Westview Press, 137–58.

———. (1998) Market dependency in US–East Asian relations. In A. Dirlik (ed.), *What Is in a Rim? Critical Perspectives on the Pacific Region Idea*. Boston: Rowan & Littlefield, 163–86.

———. (1999) *The Developmental State*. Ithaca, N.Y.: Cornell University Press.

Woo-Cumings, M., and Loriaux, M. (1993) (eds). *Past as Prelude: History in the Making of a New World Order*. Boulder, Colo.: Westview Press.

World Bank. (1993) *The East Asian miracle: economic growth and public policy*. Washington: World Bank.

———. (2011) *Global Development Horizons 2011: Multipolarity—The New Global Economy*. Washington, D.C.: The World Bank.

———. (2014) *The World Bank: Data*. data.worldbank.org.

World Trade Organization and Institute of Developing Economies–Japan External Trade Organization. (2013) *Trade Patterns and Global Value Chains in East Asia: From Trade in Goods to Trade in Tasks*. Geneva: WTO.

Xiang, L. (2014) China and the international "liberal" (Western) order. In T. Flockhart, C. A. Kupchan, C. Lin, et al. (eds), *Liberal Order in a Post-Western World*. Washington, D.C.: Transatlantic Academy, 107–20.

Xu, B., and Lu, J. (2009) Foreign direct investment, processing trade and the sophistication of China's exports. *China Economic Review*, 20: 425–39.

Yip, W., and Hsiao, W. (2014) Harnessing the privatisation of China's fragmented health-care delivery. *The Lancet*, 384: 805–18.

Yue, J. (2011) *Dilemma of national development in globalization: the politics behind China's accession to the WTO*. Ph.D. Thesis. London: London School of Economics.

Zhao, S. (1993) Deng Xiaoping's southern tour: Elite politics in post-Tiananmen China. *Asian Survey*, 33 (8): 739–56.

———. (1998) A state-led nationalism: The patriotic education campaign in post-Tiananmen China. *Communist and Post-Communist Studies*, 31 (3): 287–302.

———. (2003) Political Liberalization without Democratization: Pan Wei's proposal for political reform. *Journal of Contemporary China*, 12 (35): 333–55.

———. (2006) *Debating Political Reform in China: Rule of Law vs. Democratization*. London: M.E. Sharpe.

Zhu, A., and Kotz, D. (2011) The Dependence of China's Economic Growth on Exports and Investment. *Review of Radical Political Economics*, 43: 9–32.

INDEX

191

Gandhi Mohandas, 154, 157
General Agreement on Tariffs and Trade (GATT), 76
Gereffi, Gary, 9, 16–17, 21
Gini coefficient, 89, 90, 96, 108, 167n5
    See also income inequality
global value chains, 9, 16–17, 21, 91, 94, 101, 103, 108–9, 115
globalization
    contemporary 95, 104, 108, 110, 131, 169n7
    late modern vii–ix, 2, 16, 18–21, 29–30, 57
    theory, x, xi, 9, 16–21, 101, 107–9, 112–13, 131, 145.
        See also postnational hypothesis
Great Britain, ix, xi, 1, 12, 32, 61, 64, 123, 166n1
    See also United Kingdom
Great Depression, 48–51
great divergence, 2, 30

Ho Chi Minh, 61, 164n8
    See also Vietnam
Hobsbawm, Eric, 2, 40
Hong Kong, viii, 5–6, 75, 77, 82, 94–5, 109, 135, 138, 144
Hu Jintao, 117

ICT revolution, 18
imperialism
    European, 1–5, 22, 29, 31, 41–5, 62–4
    Japanese, 44–5, 48–53
    Marx, 3–4, 160n1
    U.S., 62–4, 73, 148–9, 151
    See also unequal treaties
income inequality, 87–90, 96, 108, 153, 156, 167n4
    See also Gini coefficient
indentured labor, 40, 42
India
    early modern development, 7, 30–3, 36
    in empire, 3–5, 39–42, 44, 160–1n1
    Indian National Army, 52
    in late modern Asian trade, 48
    nationalism, 58, 131, 153–4
    See also China, war: opium wars; textile(s)
Indian National Army, see India
Indian Ocean, 36–7

Indochina, 29, 40, 42, 55, 63
Indonesia: civil war, 56
industrial policy, 25, 107, 117
industrial revolution, ix, x, 1–4, 7, 10–11, 29–30, 32–4, 37, 39, 45, 57, 84, 124, 150, 157, 162n4, 167n3
    and unevenness, 3, 10–12
International Monetary Fund (IMF), vii, 8–9, 99, 101, 103, 105, 132, 149, 168, 171n1
intraregional trade, 9, 74, 100, 103

Japan
    1902 Anglo-Japanese agreement, 49
    foreign direct investment (FDI), 24, 70, 72, 93–4
    imperialism, 45, 52–3, 58, 62
    invasion of China (1937), 22, 50
    Meiji model, 44, 52–3, 56–8, 69, 78
    Meiji reformers, 22, 43, 46, 85
    Meiji state, 2, 21, 81, 121
    Ministry of International Trade and Industry (MITI), 76, 77, 82
    nationalism, 23–4, 29, 48–9
        See also developmental states; imperialism; nationalism
    Shinto, 52
    Shogunate, 35
    early Showa era, 50, 129
    Tokugawa era, 22, 31, 35, 38, 43, 46, 48
        See also flying geese theory
Java, 36
Johnson, Chalmers, 76–7, 79–83

Keynesian welfare state, 68, 76, 88
    See also industrialization
Khmer Rouge, 54, 56, 163n2

land reform (East Asia), 87–90
Latin America, 2, 6, 9, 14, 19, 24, 36, 66, 79–80, 89–90, 148, 156, 163n1, 167n4
    See also South America
League of Nations, 50, 62
legitimacy
    emerging countries, 153
    international institutions, 132
    state legitimacy, 78, 82–3, 86, 88, 106, 109, 110, 125, 127–9, 131
    See also China